Doomed to Repeat

Doomed to Repeat

The Lessons of History
We've Failed to Learn

BILL FAWCETT

WILLIAM MORROW
An Imprint of HarperCollins*Publishers*

To my editor, Will Hinton.
Your insights and suggestions
made this so much better. Thank you.

HarperCollins books may be purchased for educational, business, or sales promotional use. For information please write: Special Markets Department, HarperCollins Publishers, 10 East 53rd Street, New York, NY 10022.

FIRST EDITION

Designed by Diahann Sturge

Library of Congress Cataloging-in-Publication Data has been applied for.

ISBN 978-0-06-206906-1

13 14 15 16 17   OV/RRD   10 9 8 7 6 5 4 3 2 1

CONTENTS

INTRODUCTION

*Those who cannot remember the past are condemned to
repeat it.*

—GEORGE SANTAYANA (1863–1952),
THE LIFE OF REASON

The march of history is less a steady stride than a series
of stumbles and forward falls.

And the stumbles the United States, Europe, and the
rest of the world are taking at the beginning of the twenty-first
century are neither new nor unique.

Your great-great-great-grandparents and their leaders had
to overcome their own versions of the same problems that you
wake up worrying about. In many cases they found a way to
fix, or at least survive, all those various woes. That is what this
book is about.

Doomed to Repeat looks at many of the worst and most threatening problems society faces today—and that society faced throughout history. These pages are filled with "lessons of the past."

Each topic in this survey is worthy of an entire library of books. In many cases there are shelves devoted to a topic's problems and solutions. In fact, if you find a topic that is mentioned here to be of particular interest, go ahead and delve into more comprehensive works on it, or at least read further about it on the Internet.

Despite the title, this is not a book of doom and gloom. The title warns that we need to learn from the past to solve today's problems, not that they are impossible to overcome. For a tome about the worst disasters, collapses, and perplexing conundrums facing the world today, you might find it surprisingly upbeat. As the author, I make no excuse for the optimistic tone, since this is my own personal interpretation. I choose not only to see the glass as half full, but to have confidence that it can be filled to the rim. If nothing else, knowing that terrorism, depressions, speculation bubbles, arguments about official languages, and attempts to make a nation out of Afghanistan are not new should be reassuring. Our ancestors and forefathers not only survived almost identical challenges to the ones faced today, but many times they dealt with them successfully.

Doomed to Repeat might give you hope. It is a reminder that the current problems, which right now seem to threaten your entire well-being and prosperity, are not insoluble . . . if we can learn from history.

CHAPTER ONE

Afghanistan, Again?

When two armies approach each other it makes all the difference in the world which one owns only the ground it stands on and which owns all the rest. We saw this in the South African conflict, where we owned nothing beyond the light of our campfires, whereas the Boers rode where they pleased all over the country.

—WINSTON CHURCHILL (1874–1965),
THE SECOND WORLD WAR

Often Invaded, Almost Never Conquered

Perhaps the most pressing foreign policy and military problem facing the United States and its NATO (North Atlantic Treaty Organization) allies in 2013 is dealing with the Taliban and the

Islamic extremists in Afghanistan. More accurately, it is the attempt by the United States to create a situation in Afghanistan where that nation will not easily revert to being a breeding ground and refuge for fundamentalist Islamic terrorists. To permanently eliminate that threat, the United States and NATO are striving to assist Afghanistan in becoming a stable nation and, hopefully, a democracy. This is an exercise in what the U.S. State Department calls "nation building."

The theory behind the policy of nation building suggests that a strong central government will be able to prevent or control the terrorists. A further concern the United States is grappling with is ensuring that, regardless of the ultimate outcome in Afghanistan, the Islamic fundamentalist movement, called the Taliban, is unable to return to power. The group actively hosted and supported the al-Qaeda network and other terrorist groups when it was in control of Afghanistan.

On the day this chapter was written, the BBC World News headline read "Kabul Wakes Up to More Fighting." This headline could have been used hundreds of times during the last three millennia. There are many things about today's Afghanistan that make it one of the most difficult places in the world to turn into a unified and stable nation. Part of the problem is that the rural population is hard to reach. They are mostly illiterate (the literacy rate was 18.7 percent for males and 2.8 percent for females in 1978, and has improved only a little since) and often antagonistic, even to neighboring tribes. Another concern is the Afghan tribesmen's history of fanatical resistance to any foreign presence in their valleys. This tradition goes back nearly three millennia. Even today, there are few cities and very little infrastructure, such as roads or electrical grids.

In the past thirty years, both of the world's most powerful nations, the United States and Russia, have been deeply involved in that country. Both entered, at least partially, with the best of intentions. In the past two thousand years, a dozen nations have conquered Afghanistan only to find out that it was almost impossible to hold. The reason for this is the geography of the land, very little of which is flat. If you look at even a simple topographical map of Afghanistan, what you see is mountains and more mountains.

These mountains, and the valleys between them, both dominate and separate the region. This is reflected in the lives and allegiances of the people. There is not much national identity among the tribalized and locally loyal Afghan peoples. A look at the languages spoken inside Afghanistan shows half a dozen completely different tongues. Because of Afghanistan's mountainous landscape, even a language that is spoken by hundreds of thousands is broken up, with pockets of one tongue isolated inside an area dominated by another.

These are not local accents or dialects, but completely separate languages. Like languages, loyalties are local, because until very recently the connections between the main groups were limited by language, culture, and the difficulties presented by the mountain barriers. In many parts of the world this division into separate groups is referred to as "tribalism." Some of the Afghan tribes have millions of members, but many remain loyal to their own ethnic group rather than embracing any concept of a "nation" of Afghanistan. This lack of national identity leads to the real problem that faced first the USSR and now the United States. To turn Afghanistan into a democratic nation, it first has to become a nation. But both history and geography oppose this result.

There is one historical fact that has to be remembered as America attempts to build a lasting, democratic nation out of a land that holds half a dozen major, and numerous minor, ethnic groups that are geographically and culturally separate: that more complications occur because the wide range in views on Islam can divide those within a tribe. While most of the Taliban are Pashtun, only the more reactionary among that tribal group, a minority, support them. The government in Kabul, which the Taliban has sworn to destroy, is also heavily Pashtun. So Afghanistan is a "nation" whose boundaries were set not by tradition, not based on culture or trade, not even based upon history. The closest thing that there has been to an Afghan nation was the relatively short-lived Durrani Empire. It was much larger than the current country, and was itself dominated by only one of the ethnic groups. Afghanistan, as we know it on a modern map, was in no way based on an already existing country or even a shared culture or awareness. Britain decided and imposed where the borders would be to create what was considered "Afghanistan." This was simply an imperial administrative region created with no regard for the languages, cultures, loyalties, or antagonisms of the "natives" who lived there. It was designed not for the people but to make life easier for European bureaucrats. To simplify the administration, the British lumped a number of very different cultural and tribal areas into one unrelated mass with nothing in common but being controlled by the same British governor.

The fact that Afghanistan is an artificially joined land whose borders were imposed from the outside is the basis for many of this nation's modern problems. While some sense of national identity was developed by educated and urban Afghans as a result of the Soviet invasion, the rural population of Afghanistan, about 80 percent of its twenty-one million citizens, still has only a weak sense of national identity and a strong sense of tribal loyalty. For many, their national leaders don't even speak the same language.

When they think of someone who is an Afghan, most people picture one of the Pashtun, who live in the south of the country. They are the most numerous of the many tribes, comprising 42 percent of the population. But even at that size, they are not a majority of the population. The Tajik comprise 27 percent of the population, while six other distinct ethnic groups each make up between 2 percent and 9 percent of the Afghan peoples. The center of Afghanistan is split by the magnificent Hindu Kush mountain range. These mountains have divided the country linguistically and culturally, and encouraged the development of several different and often traditionally antagonistic tribes. The northern part of Afghanistan contains the Uzbeks, Turkmen, and Tajiks, whose culture is Turkic and more closely related to that of adjacent nations (including Turkmenistan, Uzbekistan, Tajikistan, Pakistan, and even Iran) than to that of the nationally dominant Pashtun. Between these groups are the Hazaras, who live in the mountains and valleys in the center of the nation. They have their own culture and generally join with the northern peoples to resist Pashtun control of the nation as a whole. There are also a number of smaller ethnic groups, including the Nuristanis of the Hindu Kush, who often have light, even blond hair and pale eyes. This diverse and physically separated population is another barrier to the residents of Afghanistan looking past their local needs and viewing their nation as a whole. This ethnic split is demonstrated today in everything that happens in this artificially joined land. The disparities were reflected by an AP news story, dated April 12, 2010, which stated:

Pakistan's northwest has also been in the headlines lately because of a proposal before Parliament to change the name of the North West Frontier Province to Khyber-Pakhtunkhwa. The name change was pushed by the

Awami National Party, a Pashtun nationalist group that
leads the provincial government in the northwest.

While internationally we see a border and parts of two nations,
many of the Pashtun peoples still see only their tribal lands,
regardless of which group of outsiders claims parts of it. The
article continued:

> Many non-Pashtun groups in the northwest have opposed
> the idea, and hundreds of protesters took to the streets in
> Abbottabad, some of whom were armed, according to the
> police.
>   Police fired tear gas and bullets into the crowd after
> they attacked two police stations and torched several ve-
> hicles, killing seven people and wounding more than 100
> others, said local police official Asif Gohar Khan.

So the geography has been both the protector and the di-
vider of this part of the world. Divided by mountains and joined
by narrow passes and long valleys, most of its people identify
with their area and ethnic group and not with Afghanistan as
a nation.

Afghanistan has always been inviting to conquerors. This
land of high mountains and natural warriors has long been
an easy country to invade, with its few natural borders and a
population concentrated in separate valleys. The area has also
proven time after time to be a nearly impossible land to hold. In
the sixth century BCE, Cyrus the Great added much of the area
to his Persian Empire. The tribes acknowledged him, but the
reality was that, outside of the trade cities, this meant virtually
nothing. It remained a part of the Persian Empire for almost 250
years until Darius III was defeated by Alexander of Macedon.

In 331 BCE, Alexander the Great won the battle of Gaugamela, and by doing so he ended the Persian Empire, taking control of all its land. After losing that battle, Darius fled across what is today Afghanistan—not because it was a place where he was welcomed, but because even then it was a hard land to travel through or pursue someone across. Alexander himself followed with parts of his army, sometimes leading as few as five hundred horsemen in the pursuit. This went on for weeks and gave the new emperor his first look at the rugged mountains and valleys of the Hindu Kush. Alexander never did catch up to the fallen Persian emperor. Eventually, Darius was betrayed and killed by his own generals and the few soldiers who remained. Alexander and his army returned to Babylon to enjoy the fruits of their victory.

Alexander returned to Afghanistan the next year to ensure the area's loyalty. During his pursuit of Darius, he had discovered that, with the Persians gone, the violent and divided tribes and cities considered themselves independent. And that independence complicated the Macedonian king's plans for a new conquest. Alexander could not leave with the threat those warlike tribes represented poised over the heart of the new empire. He had to win control, or at least subdue the region, before he could lead his army against India. The Macedonian leader found, as the United States is finding out today, that he had to conquer not a single country, but rather each valley and the numerous fortified mountaintops and cities. He spent almost a year of his short life doing this. All of widespread Persia fell to him after the one battle, but it took numerous battles and sieges for him to gain control of what is today's Afghanistan.

Once the country was conquered, or perhaps more accurate, reconquered, Alexander was able to easily dominate the satraps of southern Afghanistan. However, the areas in the north proved difficult, even to one of history's greatest military geniuses. Having conquered the entire Persian Empire in less than five years, Alexander the Great had to spend more than a year in near constant warfare to defeat each northern Afghan city or stronghold individually. While doing so he received some of his most serious injuries, including a chest wound he nearly died from. Yet by the end of 329 BCE, the northern Afghan areas were in revolt against Macedonian rule and had to be subdued once more.

Upon his death, Alexander's empire broke up, and each valley or ethnic group was again fairly independent during the chaos of the Successor Wars.

In one way, Alexander gained more from his conquest of northern Afghanistan than most invaders have since. It was there, in 328 BCE, that he met the daughter of Oxyartes, a local Bactrian chief. Rokhsana (her name has been anglicized to Roxanne) was said to have been a brilliant, beautiful, and alluring woman. Certainly Alexander was more than smitten with her, and in 327 BCE, they married. She was sixteen years old at the time. This was not Alexander's only marriage. The Macedonian conqueror had already adopted the Persian tradition of having several wives. This tradition of polygamy was really part symbolic political alliance and part hostage taking. Of course, the marriage to Roxanne did ensure the loyalty of the formerly rebellious Bactrian region and the support of her father's troops.

Alexander and Roxanne had a child, Alexander IV, born after Alexander had died. He was considered to be Alexander the Great's heir. But in the chaos of the Successor Wars that followed Alexander's death at the age of thirty-three, mother and child became pawns of Cassander, who controlled Macedonia and much of Greece. He claimed to rule as Alexander IV's guardian, but in 310 BCE, he ordered for both mother and son to be killed.

After Alexander the Great's death, there was no effort made to maintain a united Afghanistan. The four governors Alexander had appointed were virtually independent of one another, and the Empire was divided among the rival Macedonian commanders. They ruled from cities whose names are now familiar to Americans: Kabul, Sistan, Qandahar, and Baluchistan.

From the beginning, the mountainous geography dividing the lands known today as Afghanistan dictated the nature of the residents and of any war fought against them. The leaders of the two great early empires—the only two real empires of their age—had to conquer this land city by city and valley by valley. Even then, the land was divided among many ethnic groups. Some, like Bactria, became allies, while others never accepted foreign rule. Both empires found the conquest difficult, and their control quickly faded once they could not enforce their commands.

The Allied forces in Afghanistan today face many of the same problems as did Cyrus and Alexander: the very nature of the people and geography. There is no unified whole. Afghanistan may be a nation on the map, but not in the minds of its citizens. The land has always divided its people. The residents of each valley are more concerned with their own region than with the very abstract concept that it is part of a greater whole. The primitive conditions of most of the country mean that each valley or village is a self-contained entity. The dominant group, the Pashtun, is from the largest and richest valley.

Much more important to an Afghan is the success of his local area and his ethnic group. As it was when Alexander the Great had to conquer each individual city and fort, they still think of themselves as Pashtun or Tajik, not Afghan. They are more citizens of their villages, or at most provinces, than of their nation. This has meant that control of one part, or even many of its cities, does not mean the entire nation has been pacified. The Bactrian people, whose descendants still occupy parts of northern Afghanistan, were Macedonian allies only through the decision of their local leader and because Alexander had married that leader's daughter. When Alexander died that tie was lost and their loyalty ended. In their minds they had never been part of Alexander's empire; it was just Bactrians following their tribal chief. Nor has time diminished the ethnic rivalries every conqueror has had to overcome. Like the Bactrians more than two thousand years ago, many of the farmers in the Herat or Kunduz provinces do not think of themselves as being part of a whole and have no tradition of loyalty to those who rule in Kabul.

A look at the two more recent attempts to dominate Afghanistan, those of the British and then the Russians in the nineteenth century, can shed a good deal of light on the situation facing the Russian and American armies in the twenty-first century.

A Very British Disaster

In the late eighteenth century, the two superpowers of that day, Russia and England, both took an interest in Afghanistan. The British, having completed the conquest and domination of India, were likely more than a little overconfident. Afghanistan seemed weak, poor, and divided when compared to the much more populated and prosperous Raj they already controlled. This led them to believe that they could easily and quickly replicate their success in Afghanistan. The Russian Empire also was becoming a major military power as the czars first westernized their armies.

The story of the diplomatic competition for empire known as the "Great Game" and the subsequent British disaster really began earlier, when an impressive leader, Ahmad Shah (who reigned from 1747 to 1773), loosely united Afghanistan. His empire actually extended beyond Afghanistan's current boundaries, stopping only where it reached mountains or empty deserts. It was known as the Durrani Empire, after Ahmad Shah's clan, which, as is usual with Afghan leaders, was his power base. Ahmad Shah's empire was much poorer and more thinly populated than other nearby kingdoms. It thrived primarily due to the loot taken as it expanded and from raiding adjacent kingdoms. But the richest area they raided, India and modern-day Pakistan, was becoming part of the British Empire and was too strong to attack. This meant that when the expansion stopped, so did the income needed to maintain an army and administer Ahmad Shah's new empire.

When Ahmad Shah died, the empire was inherited by his son, Timur, but the feudal system that had worked for his father began to fail. Soon the Durrani Empire was in constant need of money and unable to improve the land or educate its people. When every family member is needed just to produce enough food for survival, there is not time or money left for education or the arts.

Timur was the opposite of Ahmad in almost every way. He was basically an inept wastrel. Still, the Durrani Empire was strong enough to survive twenty years of Timur's reign. When he died, he left behind an empire that was much smaller than his father's, along with twenty-three sons and no named heir.

The scramble among his sons for the throne further debilitated the impoverished empire. Different ethnic groups and tribes supported different sons. Each followed the allegiances of their local chief. Control was finally won by the fourth son,

Zemaun. His success was due mostly to the support and efforts of a powerful noble, Poyndah. But Zemaun soon proved no better than his father. He too was more interested in enjoying the position than in leading his kingdom. Worse yet, by the standards of the proud Afghan nobles, he was ungrateful and disloyal. Zemaun failed to reward, in any way, the man who helped place him on the throne, instead showering sycophantic court followers with wealth and titles.

It is rarely a good idea to both further impoverish your empire with high living and then alienate all of the most important soldiers and warriors. The divided and tribal nature of Afghanistan again determined what happened. The real power in the empire was the local chiefs, who were part of it only for the wealth and power it gained them, and only when it suited them—and they no longer gained any local advantage. Soon, virtually all of the various tribes and leaders ceased to be allies or under Durrani control. Zemaun needed to find a way to once more regain their loyalty. To accomplish this he needed wealth, which meant loot. So, the new emperor turned to the Afghans' traditional method of restoring wealth: invading India.

The attempted raid was a dismal failure. Zemaun was unable to raise and pay for more than a small force of twelve thousand disheartened and poorly armed soldiers that included less than five hundred cavalry. With his "army," Zemaun pranced along India's border, but was wisely afraid to actually enter any part of the country. The soldiers knew that they could not face highly trained sepoys and European Regulars in the British garrisons. And since Zemaun's soldiers had no sense of loyalty beyond their paychecks, he soon found that they were unwilling to fight at all.

But all of the posturing with thousands of potential invaders attracted the notice of the Honourable East India Company in Calcutta. India was becoming part of the British Empire, or at least in its area of control, and the quasi-governmental East India Company was the tool the British used to control it. The private company had its own army (commanded by Regular officers "on leave"), ambassadors, and forts, and was tied closely to the British government. The company also controlled the major ports and directly ruled many of the provinces and cities. It was, for all intents, a tool of Whitehall, but it maintained the fiction of being a private concern until it was simply dissolved by the government decades later when it lost its use as a cat's-paw. The company was responsible for both maintaining order within India and protecting much of the frontiers.

The warlike tribes of Afghanistan had been raiding into India for centuries. Not understanding just how inept and powerless the grandson of Ahmad Shah really was, the British had to take the threat seriously. From their side of the border the danger of an invasion by thousands of fierce Afghan raiders seemed ominous. So, in 1797, when the new governor-general arrived from London to take over control of the subcontinent while Zemaun was putting on his show, everyone was expecting the Afghans to sweep south as they always had. After all, Ahmad Shah had himself cut a swath of pillage and conquest that led the Afghan tribal warriors deep into India only forty years earlier. The British did not know just how hollow the Durrani threat had become, and felt they had to react.

There was also a very real fear that an Afghan invasion would set off a revolt inside India. The British had just consolidated much of their control, and many Indians were very restive. Most of the remaining Indian nobles could see the threat and conspired to drive out the British. There were millions of Indians being dominated and exploited by just tens of thousands of British. The East India Company had to show the people that they could protect India from Zemaun or any other invaders. So they took the threat seriously and prepared to respond with force.

The East India Company had to react, or at the very least appear to send a force to protect India from the potential threat in order to quell internal unrest. The Indian tradition was that the ruler had to defend the land and, in particular, stop the Afghan raiders. If the English were seen to be unable to do this they would lose legitimacy in the eyes of the entire population. Revolt by the millions of Indians against the thousands of British would follow. The Company began to prepare their local forces to resist what appeared to be a real threat. But neither the Company officials nor the very concerned Indian peoples—who had heard from their parents about the fierce Afghan warriors— understood that this threat was hollow.

By the time the British had amassed a real defense army, the threat was gone. All of the delays and useless marching probably helped undermine what little credibility the third Durrani emperor had. After weeks of posturing at the border, he lost control of his empire completely. Zemaun really only controlled the men he paid. All other Afghan warriors were loyal to their tribal chiefs. Revolts by the larger tribes had forced Zemaun to turn his army around and fight, unsuccessfully, to retain his throne. The tribal chiefs then placed a series of other "emperors" on the Imperial throne, but kept the real power themselves. During the next few years, first Zemaun's cousin, Mahmaoud, then his cousin's brother, Soojah, became emperor. By the end of Soojah's reign, what little power the central government of the Durrani Empire once had simply faded.

Beyond the worry about a Durrani attack destabilizing India, the British were concerned with a European threat that spurred them to deal with the last of the Durrani emperors. For almost a decade, England had been at war with Napoleon's France. Napoleon had made it clear that he understood much of England's wealth and power came from her colonies, particularly India. British diplomacy's main goal was to make sure that it would be nearly impossible for Napoleon to invade India. To ensure that Afghanistan would not become a French ally, a British delegation arrived in the Durrani capital of Kabul in 1809. By the time they had established themselves, new messages were delivered from Calcutta: The mission was no longer important. Any chance of France invading India was gone, blocked by Wellington's string of victories against Napoleon's forces in Spain. The British delegates were ordered to not negotiate anything substantial. So both Soojah Shah and the Company men professed their friendship and signed a meaningless agreement. When it became apparent Soojah's hold on the throne was weakening, the delegation took his advice and returned to British-controlled Hindostan, which was, incidentally, the area Zemaun had planned to invade and pillage to save his treasury. Within six months, Soojah, having lost the support of the tribal leaders, fled to British India, where he was granted a comfortable stipend and a villa. The British kept him for the simple reason that someday he might be of political value as a figurehead or to justify Company intervention in Afghan affairs. In fact, a few years later the British did use Soojah to justify their invasion of Afghanistan. This was during the era when diplomats and spies fought hidden battles in exotic places. It was the embodiment of why the Prussian general and author Carl von Clausewitz had defined war as being "an extension of politics." At this point, it will not surprise anyone to learn that diplomacy during this time period was often referred to as the "Great Game." The control of the wealth of the Orient was the primary diplomatic, and occasionally military, goal for Russia, England, and France.

Once Napoleon was defeated, the Great Game featured the British working hard to contain an expansionist Russia. By 1838 the Russian Empire was expanding both west and south and was soon occupying or controlling many weaker nations such as Uzbek, Turkmenistan, and Tajik (tribal lands to the north of Afghanistan). Seeing this, the British became concerned that the czar was getting too close to India. Russia's need to control or occupy the nations along its southern border, including the many new republics there, and the West's desire to separate these same new nations from Moscow, can be seen as a continuation of the Great Game.

Russia had already made a pawn of Persia, modern-day Iran, and Persian forces were already chewing away parts of what remained of the hollow Durrani Empire. The British felt they had to act before Russia gained control of Afghanistan. So on the pretext of returning an aging Soojah to his "rightful throne," the British Army of the Indus, several thousand strong, marched into Afghanistan. What resistance the British met was quickly defeated. Even fortified cities that many felt were impregnable by Afghan attack fell quickly to the Irish Lieutenant General John Keane's modern army. Again Afghanistan proved easy to conquer initially.

By August 1839, the British had placed Soojah on the throne in Kabul. Some of the British units were recalled to India. But the Europeans were acting as if Afghanistan were a European nation, ruled from its capital by a central authority. They soon found out that this was not the way the Durrani Empire really worked. It quickly became apparent that Soojah had no real popular support, even among his former tribesmen, and only British arms maintained his position. Their treaty with Soojah meant nothing, but not understanding the tribal and divided nature of the country, the British thought that controlling the

Durrani capital was the same as controlling the entire land. They soon and painfully found that the tribal leaders, not their paid-for emperor, had the loyalty of their people. After easily conquering most of Afghanistan, what remained of the Army of the Indus was unable to hold it.

By 1841, tribesmen from all over the region had joined a rebel army led by Mohammed Akbar, the son of the Afghan ruler the British had deposed to put Soojah back on the throne. With a large portion of the army sent back to India, it was apparent by 1841 that the remaining British garrison in Kabul was too small to control the country or even keep open the road to India. The situation was made worse by indecisive leadership. It soon became obvious that they could not even hold Kabul, where all of the surviving English civilians had gathered under the protection of their army.

Kabul had little food and was indefensible. Before the city was even hard-pressed, an agreement was reached between Mohammed Akbar and the British governor to allow for the safe withdrawal of all British forces and dependents. But the Afghan tribesmen had no intention of letting the English just walk away. The long column of 4,500 soldiers and 12,000 dependents and civilians was attacked almost from the time it left Kabul. The slaughter was constant and relentless. Badly outnumbered and strung out along the road, the Europeans had no chance. Exactly one soldier, himself wounded, survived to tell what happened. It was the greatest loss of soldiers in one battle in British colonial history, and with hundreds of women and children killed it also was the worst single loss of life the British suffered during the entire colonial era.

England responded with a series of punitive raids, but never again tried to occupy Afghanistan. The country remained tribal with the Durrani "emperor" careful to not challenge the tribal chiefs. Ironically, in 1857 the current Durrani ruler, Dost Mohammad, actually invited a British army back into Kabul in hopes of using it to counter an invasion threat by the Persians. The only time Afghanistan was unified in the past thousand years was under Ahmad Shah, and that was a charismatic construct based on one man being followed by the tribal leaders, rather than having any power in his own right. Once he died, the empire quickly degenerated into a shadow with no real intrinsic authority.

The full Army of the Indus was undefeatable, but the portion they left behind after completing the "conquest" was unable to hold Afghanistan. From 1837 to 1841, the British acted as if the Durrani Empire was a national state in the European model. In reality, Afghanistan was then still as tribal and divided as when Alexander had to subdue the land city by city and valley by valley two thousand years earlier. The English thought having their pawn as the emperor would give them control of all of Afghanistan. Instead, it gave them exactly nothing. Eventually, almost twenty thousand men, women, and children paid a terrible price for the mistake.

The Game Continues

The British impetus for invading Afghanistan had been to do so before the Russians did. Seeing the fate of the British, the Russians learned and did not themselves invade at that time . . . so in an ironic way that British goal was achieved. But almost a century and a half later, the Soviet Union, under the Communists, tried again to dominate Afghanistan. The big opportunity came in 1979. The Republic of Afghanistan, a democracy, had been established in 1973, but the attempt at democracy had failed. The two traditional problems of ethnic strife and corruption had immediately weakened the central government. This was the result of the same problem every central authority has had from Alexander's successors to the later Durrani emperors: when your loyalty is to your ethnic group and not the central government, there's the temptation to exploit any position in the central government for the benefit of yourself or your own tribe, even at the expense of that government. During the six-year experiment with democracy, few resisted the temptation. By 1979, the Afghan republic's officials had become so universally corrupt and ineffective that they alienated most of the different ethnic groups, including many Pashtun, whose fellows controlled much of the new government. The result was that the Communist Party, under the moderate Nur Muhammad Taraki, was voted in as the best alternative to fix the mess. Taraki was a practical politician and a friend of Soviet leader Leonid Brezhnev.

Taraki attempted to balance the concerns of the two major Afghan ethnic groups: the Khalqis (his own group) and the Pashtun. He even split the seats on his cabinet equally between them, but this led only to more infighting. There was also a constant challenge to Taraki's leadership by another member of the Khalqis faction, Hafizullah Amin. When Amin finally achieved power, most reports agree that he had Taraki killed in his sleep. Securely in control after Taraki's death, Amin, a hard-line Communist, pushed the party line by consolidating private farms into collectives and demanding women's rights. This antagonized the farmers and was contrary to the traditional Islamic role for women. In a matter of days he had alienated many of the most influential men and all of those who were devout Muslims. Opposition in all forms began to organize. It was not long before Amin clamped down on both his ethnic and political opponents. Within a few weeks, *Time* magazine's headline read: "30,000 Imprisoned and 2,000 Executed." Not surprisingly, Amin's attempts to radically remake Afghanistan, right after taking power, resulted in massive unrest. The more numerous Pashtun were united in their opposition.

The Soviets had been touting Afghanistan as an example of how being a Communist nation could help a country develop. They continued to bring in doctors, engineers, and teachers, and build schools, hospitals, and public buildings. But within months, Amin's hard-line and ethnocentric approach undid the feeling of goodwill that the Soviets' efforts had established over many years. In 1979, the KGB assassinated Amin with the hope that much of the resistance was to him as an individual. It wasn't. Amin was replaced by Babrak Karmal. This put the future leaders of Afghanistan on notice as to their fate should they be more loyal to their ethnic group, in this case the Khalqis, than to Moscow.

The Soviets were anxious to support what they still perceived as a major Communist showcase and success. They also feared that the overthrow of the Communist government in Afghanistan would inspire unrest among the Islamic populations in the neighboring Soviet republics. In reaction, Moscow greatly increased the number of military advisers assisting Karmal. They poured in aid and took a more direct interest in assisting the government in Kabul to suppress unrest. But even the larger number of Soviets—including special forces—was unable to stop a growing popular revolt. The limited number of elite units simply could not be in enough places to make a difference or hold enough ground to protect their puppet government. Virtually every leader beyond a few of the Khalqis and hard-line Communists felt that the government in Kabul was controlled by the USSR. In addition, the hard-line Communist antagonism to religion drove the most religious in every tribe to resist.

Soon it became clear that, like the British in 1841, the government in Kabul no longer controlled more than a few cities. On December 25, 1979, Soviet army forces poured across the border and began securing the country, ostensibly at the request of Mohammed Habibullah, the next man they had handpicked to be president. Within weeks there were eighty-five thousand Soviet combat soldiers and airmen in Afghanistan. The intention was to overwhelm the growing opposition with both the number of troops and technology.

It should be noted that 1979 was barely four years after the Americans pulled out from the extended disaster that was Vietnam. If any lesson was learned by the Red Army from the American loss, it must have been the wrong one. Surprisingly, many of the officers who helped to extend and orchestrate that American failure in Vietnam were the same ones who were in command in Afghanistan. The Russians had supported and advised the guerrilla war fought by the Vietcong and North Vietnamese. They armed, trained, supervised construction, built SAM missile sites, and even provided satellite and other intelligence to the North Vietnamese. Eventually, they faced irregular troops armed in the same way by the Americans. It is hard not to say that they should have known better, having recently been on the other side of the equation.

The revisionist reason for invading that is now popular in Russia is that they were in Afghanistan trying to control the drug fields and trade. The real reason is much murkier. To begin, Brezhnev was upset over the murder of Taraki, whom he held in high regard. He blamed Amin and was anxious to take real control of the nation. The Politburo, the leaders of the

Communist Party in Moscow, saw Afghanistan not only as a chance to keep a Communist government in power, but also as a way to expand their control in a vital border area. Afghanistan is central to the Middle East, bordered not only by three parts of the Soviet Union, but also by Iran and Pakistan. It even has a small connection to China. Controlling this central Asian location had been the goal of the Russian governments—first under the czar and then under the Communists—for more than two centuries. The Soviet leaders also felt that controlling Afghanistan would be a visible crack in the much-too-successful American diplomatic program of "containing the expansion of Communism" begun while Harry Truman was president. And in contrast to how America fared in Vietnam, those in control in Moscow were convinced that by treating the diverse peoples of Afghanistan well they would be successful in winning them over. The country was poor and illiterate, and the USSR's wealth and teachers could change that. They believed that the Red Army would be welcomed for the benefits it could bring and the stability it offered. This was true in that the Soviet troops initially met little resistance as columns led by tanks swarmed into Afghanistan. Like the British in 1837, the Soviets had no trouble deploying troops around the countryside and occupying the cities. Also like the British, they quickly found that once the warlords and tribal leaders had decided to oppose them, there was nothing they could do to completely suppress the revolt.

The British were driven out of Afghanistan after four years and over twenty thousand deaths. The Red Army spent a decade in Afghanistan, with an estimated seventy-five thousand fatalities and many times that number wounded or maimed. Gradually, the attitude and missions changed from nation building to occupation and punitive actions. More than a million Afghans were killed—basically one out of ten in a population of thirteen million. The Soviets failed to win over the different tribes. They failed to curtail the drug trade. They failed to effectively occupy anything but a few cities. They failed in every way, and that has left a scar on the Russian military as deep and pervasive as the one Vietnam left on the United States. By spring of 1989, there were no Soviet soldiers in Afghanistan. Without Soviet support, only a few cities were controlled by the Communist government . . . and not for long.

Even a superpower could not, in a decade, subdue or control the diverse peoples of Afghanistan. The only success the Red Army achieved had been shared by all of the past invaders of the mountainous nation: the normally violently opposed ethnic groups united, but only against them. This time, the United States supported the insurrection in a reversal of roles from Vietnam, but with the same effect. They provided advisers, training, and medical supplies, and worked with the Pakistanis to create military bases from which the Russians could be challenged. Eventually the CIA supplied high-profile weapons, such as Stinger missiles, to the Afghans. These nullified the powerful helicopter-borne Soviet forces and took away the USSR's edge on mobility in the mountainous country. Ten years after invading an impoverished and backward nation, the modern, incredibly powerful Red Army, having virtually unlimited support and resources, retreated from Afghanistan. By February of 1989 the last soldier of the Red Army was gone and the most radical of the resistance groups, the Taliban, had begun to take control.

America's Turn

On October 7, 2001, Operation Enduring Freedom was launched in Afghanistan by the United States and its allies. It consisted primarily of arming and coordinating a number of "friendly" warlords in a push to take control of the country from the Taliban. This strategy worked, but it also had the effect of reinforcing the local power of the tribal and ethnic leaders. With each valley independent and self-supporting, there was no strong need for what a centralized government could provide. This holds true even if that government weren't one of the most corrupt in the world. This lack of national identity is why working through the local warlords was so effective and why doing this reinforced their power, which may have actually slowed the process of the American effort to turn Afghanistan into a single, democratic nation.

Cyrus, Alexander, the East India Company, the Red Army, and now the American army have all entered Afghanistan with little resistance, but none have easily occupied the country. There are many parallels in the problems and actions of all four world powers spread over three millennia. The first three invaders failed to maintain control of what they had conquered. The last is still awaiting history's judgment. The Americans are different in one way: from the beginning, they have stated that they have no intention of remaining in Afghanistan. Having demonstrated in Iraq that the United States lives up to that promise, the question remaining is this: Will this stated intention remove enough opposition so that the nation-building effort can finally succeed?

A lot of questions have been answered by history, and the challenges faced by NATO in Afghanistan have been clarified. But many remain unanswered. Perhaps technology will overcome the factors of navigating terrain that have stymied so many armies in the past. While other armies have been called in to settle what is effectively, again, a civil war, does the religious fanaticism of the Taliban mean the more moderate Afghan fighters will at least remain neutral? Or perhaps that won't matter, and the Afghan people will react traditionally, with dogged resistance, to the new invader. After three thousand years of regular invasions, Afghans' antipathy toward any foreign power's soldiers being anywhere on their land runs deep in the culture. That alone may explain the strange belligerence shown by the soldiers and officials of the "friendly" Afghan government toward the American troops assisting them. When uniformed Afghan soldiers fire at American troops or support rioters, they are doing what has been the norm for generations: joining ranks against any and all outsiders. It is simply part of a tradition ten times older than the United States itself.

Even when Afghanistan is technically united, stability is hardly common. A list of recent Afghan governments strains both credulity and grammar. Since World War I, Afghanistan was first ruled by monarchs, from 1919 until 1964; then there was a constitutional monarchy for another decade; and finally there was a republic that lasted only six years, followed by a Communist state. But the Communists were unable to rule or even maintain order over the many warlords and tribes. Finally, they had to call in the Soviet army in 1979. This was followed by ten years of Soviet occupation, a civil war from 1990 to 1996, and then the Taliban theocracy. In 2001, having perhaps learned from history, NATO worked with the warlords and drove the Taliban out of most of the country. Since then the Taliban has been replaced by a NATO-supported central government whose effectiveness varies greatly among provinces.

The good news might be that such a long list of very different governments over such a short time shows that Afghanistan certainly can and has changed . . . which is not the same thing as achieving stability. The bad news is that establishing a long-lasting, democratic nation capable of sustaining itself involves changing three millennia of attitudes, ethnic animosities, and tradition. In some ways, the NATO approach, with a set departure date and efforts to actually improve the quality of the government in Kabul, offers a chance to succeed where many others have failed. It does take into account the basis of most resistance to outside influences. Pushed by the West, the current Afghan government is even gingerly attempting to root out some of the corruption that both results from and reinforces the national identity problem. NATO leaders have acknowledged all of these problems, but it remains to be decided whether they will succeed in overcoming the ethnic and religious strife that has kept Afghanistan divided.

CHAPTER TWO

Terrorism, Still

I was called a terrorist yesterday, but when I came out of jail, many people embraced me, including my enemies, and that is what I normally tell other people who say those who are struggling for liberation in their country are terrorists. I tell them that I was also a terrorist yesterday, but, today, I am admired by the very people who said I was one.

— NELSON MANDELA (1918–)
ON *LARRY KING LIVE*, MAY 16, 2000

The Roots of Terrorism

A terrorist is someone who engages in actions that create terror for political purposes. The U.S. government's official legal defi-

nition of terrorism (U.S. Code Title 22, Ch. 38, Para. 2656f[d])
is "premeditated, politically motivated violence perpetrated
against noncombatant targets by subnational groups or clandes-
tine agents." Here, we are going to look at the classic roots of
terrorism, its modern evolution, and how we may or may not
be applying many of the lessons of the past in today's struggle.
But to do that in less than several hundred volumes, we need to
limit the definition of a terrorist.

To count as a true terrorist attack, the violence must be
personal. Civilians are hurt, not "nations." When thousands
of people, acting together, instill terror and ruin on another
nation, it is called a war. So the term here is meant to describe
the actions of individuals and small groups only. These groups
may be part of a larger faction, but they number, at most, a few
dozen people for any one action.

This definition of terrorism includes literally hundreds of
groups over the past two millennia. Certainly during the American Revolution, the loyal Tories, who were often beaten and
burned out or driven from their homes by the Committees of
Correspondence or rebel militia, would call what happened to
them terrorism. So have the Arab Palestinians, who suffered a
similar fate two hundred years later. Since terrorism is intended
to inspire fear among those opposing the perpetrators, and such
acts certainly did, a number of American and Zionist patriots
who later became national leaders have to be included on any
historically accurate list, despite the cause's eventual success.
This makes the point that terrorism can work to drive away
others, while at the same time destabilizing a nation. There is
no question that today's weapons give even a few fanatics the
ability to put hundreds or even millions of lives at risk. C-4,
dirty bombs, and anthrax increase their threat, but the nature
of the terrorist has not changed. Today, terrorism might feel

like a modern problem. It isn't. Whether you picture a terrorist as a Bolshevik throwing a Molotov cocktail into a crowd or a member of al-Qaeda flying a plane into a building, they are part of a tradition that likely goes back as far as there have been governments and rulers.

Daggerman

The poorly dressed man tried to look casual as he moved through the temple. The air beneath the high, brightly painted ceiling was filled with the smells of incense and sweat. As usual, there was a crowd. Some gathered around the rabbis as they spoke, others bartered with the merchants lined up along the polished walls. The carvings and wall hangings depicted scenes from the Book. The man recognized the well-known image of Abraham about to sacrifice his son. The dagger depicted looked very much like the one he had hidden in his sleeve. Perhaps this was a sign, the man thought. Well, no angel was going to save the traitor.

For the slightest moment he wondered if what he was about to do was sacrilege. He was in a most holy place. His steps faltered, then continued. The real sacrilege here was what the evil men from the West had done to all of this holy land and to all of those around him who had been seduced from the true faith by the comfort and wealth of the West.

He had been told that this man's death would be a sacred act, one worth sacrificing his own life for. That had been five days ago, just before he had left the village. Now the time had come to show he was a true patriot.

He repeated to himself that what he would soon do was right and just. The oppressors of his people were the godless, the ones who had no true faith. He would be hailed as a martyr and guaranteed eternal happiness.

Tightening his shoulders, the man pushed through the crowd toward his target. To the men he walked past he looked like just another worshipper, a young man from a small town who was a bit overwhelmed by Jerusalem, nervous and not too well dressed.

The patriot was relieved to see that the fat merchant he had been sent to kill had set up his table in the expected place. It was a cleverly carved table now unfolded near a door in the far-left corner of the outer temple.

The door was bolted on the other side. He had tried it the day before. It would not provide any means of escape, but the open area in front of it would allow him to actually step behind the table and the man whom he was to make a deadly example of.

A few steps farther and the beginnings of doubt appeared. The young man feared failure more than the consequences of success. He had practiced the killing stroke for weeks, but only on straw men and one bleating sheep. One swift blow and the deed should be done. He had to succeed. He had sworn so before his family and the elders, promised before the Creator that he would strike even if he had to die to do it. They had praised him as a martyr fighting to regain the land of his people. If he failed there was no going back. The disgrace would be worse than dying. He would be known as a coward and an apostate. Neither he nor his family would ever be forgiven, ever be welcome.

For too long his people had been controlled by the evil empire and its lackeys. They had stolen his people's land so that they could build roads and sinfully rich homes. And his people were forced to do the invader's bidding. Once his family had owned a farm not far from this very temple, but now it was covered with the homes of unbelievers and foreigners. The thought of dying no longer made him hesitate; it just summoned an anger that hastened his steps.

The man recalled how his father had died a martyr years before. His family, now residing in Galilee, the home of the resistance, had been sworn enemies of the occupiers for three generations. There had never been any question as to what his future held. He had spent the previous months learning to use weapons and studying the words of the prophets. There was no question in his heart that dying a martyr would earn him a special welcome and comfort. Failure would be blasphemy.

He approached the target. Being noticed by the heavily armed soldiers would make his a purposeless sacrifice. This man became rich by selling goods to the evil empire, and for that he was to be made an example of.

The merchant did not notice the young man as he approached.

The man's long robe chafed his skin and felt damp. With an intake of breath he stepped to the side and then behind the traitor's table.

The doomed merchant turned and then must have known. His eyes went wide and he opened his mouth to yell.

The dagger that was fastened under the loose sleeve of the young believer's left arm came free, and with a graceful sweep he brought the long knife up and plunged it into the traitor's heart. Blood poured down the iron blade as it slid between the merchant's ribs, soaking the front of his robe. It felt warm and smelled different from that of the sheep the young man had killed.

The only sound that came out of the traitor's open mouth was a sighing gurgle.

For a long moment the killer heard nothing. He was overwhelmed with relief that he had proved worthy. Then the screams of those nearby swelled. Soon it seemed everyone was yelling and pointing at him.

This he had not rehearsed. For a moment he froze. Then he saw the soldiers; in that instant he decided to go down fighting. Taking a half-step back, the killer raised the long blade and then thrust it forward.

He never completed the blow. The weapons of half a dozen soldiers tore into him. There was a moment of terrible pain as the killer fell backward to land on top of his victim. He had not expected that becoming a martyr would hurt so much. Then the soldier's weapons struck again, better aimed this time, and the pain ended.

Beginnings

There is an irony to that story of terrorism and assassination. It could be a fairly reasonable representation of a resident of today's Palestine making an attack on a Jewish merchant. It is a scene similar to those that actually occurred for more than a century in Jerusalem and the other cities of Judea. But although it takes place in Israel, it is not today's Israel. Both the victim and the terrorist were Jews living more than two thousand years ago. The evil empire was Rome and the terrorist was a member of the Sicarii.

Israel, known then as Judea, had been free since driving out the Seleucid Empire, and it was restored as an independent nation in 160 BCE. But part of the price of freedom had been making an agreement with the Roman Empire. By 40 BCE, Rome controlled Israel in almost every way that mattered except its name, as it remained an "allied nation" rather than a province. When an outright revolt against this domination, led by Judas of Galilee (not to be confused with Judas Iscariot), in the year 6 CE was crushed, the Sicarii was formed. Their goal wasn't to attack the Romans—this they generally left to the Zealots, armed Jewish rebels who traveled in large numbers and attacked Roman soldiers and civilians in what we would today call a guerrilla war. Rather than use open, small-scale warfare, the assassins targeted those whom they felt were too close or too supportive of the Roman occupation. To do this they would hide daggers, called *sicae* in Latin, up the sleeves of their loose robes, and once near their targets, they would stab them. There was no way to distinguish a Sicarius from the general population. Anyone could be a Sicarius, and this added to the terror they invoked. The purpose was simply to terrorize anyone and everyone who considered cooperating with the Romans. This is the same technique used by the Vietcong on village elders, as well as in Iraq when the insurgency targeted those assisting the American occupation, such as interpreters or friendly government officials. The Sicarii's targets were almost always other Jews. Yes, one of the first detailed historical records of terrorists is one of Jews terrorizing other Jews, and it takes place in the same real estate that is today Israel and Palestine.

We know of the Sicarii from a somewhat biased source. They are described in some detail by a man who first was known as Joseph ben Mattathias. He was originally a Zealot who helped lead the revolt against Rome in 70 CE. As a Zealot leader, he once tried to broker peace between the Zealots and Rome. When that failed, he changed sides and became a historian who eventually moved to Rome and took the name Flavius Josephus, Flavian being the family name of the current emperor. (Yep, he sold out big-time, and for him personally, it worked.) Josephus was, in fact, the very model of the men the Sicarii targeted. This may partially explain why he moved to Rome and stayed there. His account of the Jewish War, written in 78 CE, is history's main, and almost only, source of information on the terrorists he called the Sicarii. It is likely that the actual terrorist group did not use a Latin name and that during their sixty years of assassinations, there were actually several small groups, each with its own name. *Sicarii* is the linguistic equivalent of "anarchists" or "terrorists."

So what happened to the Sicarii? Certainly, the Romans, the kings, and their appointed governors actively sought out and suppressed these terrorists with varying degrees of success. Rome had good intelligence services and ruthless inquisitors. But what finally ended the Sicarii's campaign of terror was a success followed by a terrible failure. While the Sicarii were terrorizing the locals, the Zealots (in Hebrew, *kana'im*) focused on driving out the Romans. They organized themselves as a military force, and at their height controlled virtually all of the cities of Judea. They gained popular support when Florus, the Roman governor of Judea, stole a large amount of silver from the Temple in Jerusalem, in 66 CE. When the Syrian governor, Cestius Gallus, took the Zealots too lightly and sent south a small, poorly trained force of legionnaires (who were more accustomed to garrison duty than fighting a Zealot army), the Zealots actually defeated the Roman legion. That success was also their undoing.

Rome ruled by intimidation. Even more important than not allowing anyone to revolt, Rome could not tolerate or forgive being handed a military defeat. The illusion of being undefeatable was what allowed an empire that never fielded more than fifty legions (at most, three hundred thousand soldiers) to thrive, and at this time they had fewer than forty to dominate the Mediterranean world.

The revolt started when Florus broke a basic Roman rule. Rome dominated its known world not only with force but also by knowing better than to unnecessarily antagonize those it ruled.

But the governor, who shared a general Roman contempt for the Jewish peoples, stole a large amount of silver from Temple treasure. This outraged the Jews. They rose up and wiped out the relatively small Roman garrison in Jerusalem. The revolt spread until all of Judea had thrown out the Romans and pillaged the homes and warehouses of many formerly favored Gentiles. Hundreds of Romans were killed or had to flee. This is when the governor of Syria sent his legionary force. However, the legion's commanders were arrogant and assumed that the Jews were a disorganized mob who would flee at the sight of a real soldier. Instead it was the Syrian troops who were defeated and routed.

Since the defeat of a legion was an example Rome could not afford to let stand, they reacted strongly. Judea was a poor backwater area, but what if somewhere important, like Egypt or Greece, got ideas? The response was to send in sixty thousand crack legionnaires, led by their best general, Titus, who would later become the Roman emperor. The three legions (V Macedonica, XV Apollinaris, and XII Fulminata) landed on the Galilean coast and spread through the area that was the heart of the revolt: Galilee. The Romans were plainly making an example of the Jews as they killed or enslaved more than one hundred thousand in Galilee alone. Those Jews who survived this attack fled to Jerusalem, where the moderate leaders knew they could not defeat the new legions and tried to make peace with Rome. Those moderates soon died at the hands of the Sicarii or the mobs urged on by the more radical revolutionaries.

By 68 CE, no leader in Jerusalem was left alive who would even suggest moderation or peace. The Zealots themselves were split and ill prepared. The different parts of Jerusalem were jealously controlled by the leaders of the various factions. Few were good military leaders and some were simply irrational.

One group of fanatics even destroyed most of the food stored in the city just as the siege began. This was done with the foolish assumption that the people would fight harder and inspire divine intervention sooner. Before long, the countryside around Jerusalem was controlled by the Romans. When they finally put Jerusalem under siege, the result was inevitable and tragic. This is the point in time when Flavius Josephus went to Titus and tried to negotiate peace. When it failed, he chose to stay with the Romans.

Jerusalem fell in a series of bloody attacks, and the last of the Zealots retreated to an upper fortress and held out until the Romans built siege towers. Not only did Judea lose all independence and become a province, but the Second Temple was destroyed, and Flavius maintained that hundreds of thousands more Jews died or were sold into slavery. The elimination of the Jewish moderates by their own people doomed Jerusalem and the Second Temple. This destruction then spelled the end of the Sicarii. The last of the Zealots—almost a thousand men, women, and even children—died in the mountain fortress of Masada after a three-year siege.

The Paradox

We must spread our principles, not with words but with deeds, for this is the most popular, the most potent, and the most irresistible form of propaganda.
—MIKHAIL BAKUNIN (1814–1876), RUSSIAN ANARCHIST

After World War I, the nations of the world, encouraged by President Woodrow Wilson, formed an organization whose purpose was to settle future national disputes without warfare.

This was the League of Nations. In 1937, the League's official definition of terrorism was "all criminal acts directed against a State and intended or calculated to create a state of terror in the minds of particular persons or a group of persons or the general public."

One of the goals of a terrorist is to get a reaction, preferably an overreaction. In French, this is known as *propagande par le fait*, which translates as "propaganda by the deed." The colorful French term for a terrorist is *agent provocateur*, because the response provoked is more important than the action itself. Terrorists don't just bomb buildings to disrupt the work going on in the offices inside. The intention is to force an official response that negatively affects the general population. This also demonstrates that the government cannot keep civilians safe. By forcing the TSA ruling to have passengers remove their shoes to be X-rayed by airport security, the Shoe Bomber, Richard Reid, succeeded even as he failed. Even though he was such a blundering incompetent that he could not even light his own fuse, billions of shoes have been removed in airports because of his attempt to blow up a plane. That is the irony for a free nation combating terrorism. Even a reasonable response can encourage the terrorists to act again, hoping for an unreasonable response that will divide the people from their government.

To encourage political or social change, the terrorist needs to force the majority opinion to go from moderation to revolution. If things are even just "okay" in their lives, most people would prefer the status quo. Terrorists have to create a situation where the response of the government is such that it radicalizes the majority. But to do this they often attack and kill those in the very group they claim to be working for . . . because it is, in their minds, necessary for the greater good. The military version of this same attitude is "collateral damage." Even attacks on government officials or "collaborators" are as much for the response they can generate as they are for the physical damage that they cause. That is why terrorists' targets are those with symbolism—ones that will get a strong emotional or political reaction—such as a financial center, like the Twin Towers on 9/11. By this standard, strangely, that attack was incredibly successful. It got a powerful response, probably just not the one that al-Qaeda, the Taliban, or Osama bin Laden expected. Ten years later, that response has continued and cost Bin Laden and most of his commanders their lives. The Arab terrorists stated in their communications to each other that the morally weak and self-indulgent Americans would be intimidated by the attack, but instead the reaction resulted in continuing resolution.

The Real Assassins

The word "assassin" conjures up images of sinister Arabs with silly beards that they constantly stroke while threatening innocent maidens. In truth, the real and original mercenary murderers who were called by that name were the Hashishiyya, a group founded in Persia during the eleventh century. The Assassins—a European term derived from the name Hashishiyya— were a highly organized terrorist organization dedicated to returning control of the Islamic world to the Shiite sect. They operated all through the Arab world and on rare occasions in the newly formed Crusader states for almost two centuries. Their targets were mainly other Muslims. They even made two attempts on the life of the famous Muslim general Saladin, on one occasion wounding the warrior and on another killing one of his advisors, the Amir Khumartakin, when he recognized them in Saladin's camp.

The name given to them by others, Hashishiyya, refers to the myths involving them and the potent drug hashish. Yet in all the contemporary accounts from the eleventh to thirteenth centuries, there is no mention of the Assassins actually using any drugs before an attack or in their fortresses. Also, the Assassins were not the nemesis of the Crusaders. They were based primarily in Syria and what is now called Iran. There they bedeviled the Sunni rulers. The Assassins were also not above taking pay for a murder. It is very possible that they worked more often under hire of the Christian Crusaders than against them. Members of the Assassins often lived, with permission, on Christian lands and paid taxes to Christian lords. There was even a brief discussion of having all of the Assassins convert to Christianity.

The true twelfth-century Assassin would be sent after a target. Usually, just one was sent, or occasionally teams of two to four. They would spend several days studying the habits of their target and then strike when the victim was most vulnerable. The Assassins were the bogeymen of the European nobility. If they ever really did assassinate anyone in Europe, no one could prove it. There has been a persistent belief that Assassins were responsible for stabbing Conrad I of Outremer (King of Holy Lands) two days before he was crowned. Because the killing occurred in Jerusalem, this may be true. But there are no real examples of assassinations anywhere in Europe itself. Since the Assassins were dedicated to restoring Shiite rule, not conquering the Christians, there was little appeal for the religious terrorists to widen the scope.

Christian knights who protected pilgrims going to Jerusalem returned home with tales of Hasan-i-Sabbah, the Old Man of the Mountain, and his band of drug-crazed murderers. His Assassins were said to be unrelenting fanatics and cunning killers. They claimed that if an Assassin died before killing a target, another was sent to finish the job, and if needed, another and then another. Templars would regale a party they were guarding with stories of Assassins, armed with swords, dropping from dark ceilings or hiding under the desert sands. Like most war stories, the reality appears to be much less dramatic than the telling. These false stories also likely encouraged the pilgrims to appreciate, with donations, the knights who were protecting them. But to the many Sunni nobles and officials the Hashishiyya did kill, they were very real and very deadly terrorists. By the 1300s, the word "*assassino*" was already in common use in Italy, whose city-states like Venice continued to trade with the Arab nations, and was used to describe anyone who killed someone of note or wealth.

Based in a Shiite kingdom in what is now northern Iran, the Assassins carried out their murders for more than two centuries. The Sunni response was the execution of anyone suspected to be connected to the Assassins. Likely their actions also brought about increased alienation and distrust for those Shiites living in the Sunni cities. Since alienating their base from their target is a terrorist's goal, in this they were a success (the gulf between Sunni and Shiite remains wide and occasionally violent, even now). For all of their notoriety, the Shiite Assassins never did succeed in destabilizing the Muslim lands. Assassinations never brought down any of the Sunni rulers. The Sunni dynasty, so hated by the Assassins, fell not to them, but later to the Mongols, who swept over Baghdad in 1258 and Syria in 1260. Even then, that was cold comfort to these early terrorists, since a year earlier, in 1257, their fortress and base in Alamut had been destroyed and the organization broken by the advancing Mongols.

Along with these insights into the nature of what was the most powerful and well-organized terrorist cult in historical times, there is another lesson: The use of terror for political and religious purposes has been a major factor throughout Islamic history. And the most fanatic assassins were not just religious zealots; they were determined to undermine the Persian and Syrian governments.

Modern Terrorism

Terror is nothing other than justice, prompt, severe, inflexible.

— MAXIMILIEN DE ROBESPIERRE (1758–1794)

The terrorist as we know him today is often state-sanctioned, though of course not officially approved of. State-sanctioned terrorism is considered a weapon used by weak nations against the more powerful ones. There is little the government in Iran can publicly do to the United States, and few direct actions can be taken by the Palestinian leadership against Israel, so those states encourage and supply terrorists to attack the stronger nations. Where nations are not directly vulnerable, their citizens are. This is why terrorists mostly target jets and not army bases, and why Palestinians send rockets into Israeli towns and not at border posts—because civilian targets are more open to attack, and only through the disabling or destruction of such targets are powerful nations harmed not just physically, but much more greatly emotionally and in morale.

Whether homegrown or shipped in, terrorists have been a serious concern for over two millennia. Terrorist acts have started wars, ended negotiations, and affected the everyday lives of almost everyone in the world. If you want a good demonstration of how much terrorism affects everyone, just fly anywhere commercially. Looking at the many forms terrorism has taken in the past two centuries can give some insight into how to deal with the terrorists of today.

Luddites

The Luddites were a group of fanatics who were convinced that the Industrial Revolution would cause almost all workers to be replaced by machines. In the nineteenth century, this was a very serious and possibly fatal concern for anyone who was suddenly jobless. In England, the penalty for being a vagrant could range from imprisonment in a workhouse to execution. The Luddites' terrorist technique was to break into factories and destroy the machinery and attack anyone protecting it. The looms and mills of England were their most common target. Many of them were handweavers who had been displaced by the powered loom, which could produce as much cloth as a dozen weavers or more. After 1811, when the looms were introduced in the mills, a large group of once-skilled weavers were left unemployed.

The term *Luddite* began to be used generically, covering a range of similar groups. They were named after Ned Ludd, often called "King Ludd," who in the late eighteenth century destroyed two loom frames in "a fit of rage," as reported in the *Nottingham Review*. The article was widely read and repeated, and soon any damage to a frame or other machinery was attributed to Ned Ludd. When the unemployed issued proclamations, they began signing them either "Ned" or "King Ludd." For a few years the Luddites rallied the urban poor, and clashes could be violent. Small Luddite cells would incite riots and attacks on factories, often promoting them for several days in advance. Then the discontented and otherwise voiceless poor would provide the mob. Eventually, in the worst cases, the militia was called in. At their peak around 1813 there were Luddite cells in most cities and industrial towns. They all rationalized destruction and murder as being good for the workingman and believed that they were saving the countryside. It seems ecoterrorism is not a new idea.

The prosperity that industrialization brought lowered the number of unemployed and created a new class of well-paid workers. As the standard of living grew along with the general wealth of Britain, the Luddites lost their popular support and their ability to rouse mass protests. The Pentrich Rising, in 1817, was the last real Luddite success. The improved economy, combined with ruthless actions by private guards and police, eventually eliminated most Luddite terrorist cells. So the solution to these terrorists was a loss of support, as the target of their terror actually improved the workingman's life. Even today we refer to someone who does not approve of some new technology as being a "Luddite."

The Luddites, like some members of today's Occupy movement, ecoterrorists, and supporters of PETA, justified violence as being for the greater good. Once the economy improved, they lost their appeal and succumbed to the constant pressure of the factory owners and the government. It was the combination of the two that ended what was once a very vicious and highly destructive terrorist movement. Decades later, the few remaining members were generally referred to as anarchists.

Anarchists

The Greek word *anarchos* means "having no ruler." At the end of the 1800s a surprising number of intellectuals came to the conclusion that the only way to change anything was to tear down what was already in place. Unwilling to wait for the masses and voters to arrive at that realization, these intellectuals instead chose violence and destruction. The main belief of these thinkers was that man would be better off without any government. The reason they were terrorists was that they also believed that anything they did—assassinations, bombings, poisoning cities, etcetera—was acceptable because eventually those actions would lead the masses (or those who survived them, anyhow) to abolish government entirely.

Among those who saw no government as the best option were Karl Marx and Friedrich Engels, the philosophers of Communism. One of their tenets was that Communism was just a stage where men would learn to do without any government. Marx states clearly in his writings that at some point the Communist government would simply declare its job done and dissolve. Then all men would be totally free and there would be no more governments. He also advocated the anarchist philosophy that since the end was an ideal world, any means that got you to that end was acceptable. So no matter how evil or vicious a Communist was, he was doing the "right thing" since it worked toward the goal of true freedom . . . eventually. It is a very convenient rationalization.

The early search for a way to go beyond government quickly evolved into a movement that intended to disrupt society so that the working class could have more of a voice. Some saw this as a lofty ideal. Others saw it as a reason for terrorism. The reality was that each group had its own name and identity, but the press and politicians preferred to use the generic term "anarchist"—a convenient label the government could put on anyone they wanted to take action against—just as, today, there are hundreds of groups on the United States' "terrorist organization" list. But there is no question that most of those labeled anarchists one hundred years ago would easily qualify today as terrorists and make every TSA list. They were violent, uncaring of the immediate consequences of their actions, and true believers that they were doing the right thing.

A reflection of just how active and deadly some anarchist groups were can be shown by a look at their "successes." In the last two decades of the nineteenth century and first two of the twentieth, anarchists from several groups assassinated:

- Russian Czar Alexander II, blown up in 1881
- French President Sadi Carnot, stabbed in 1894
- Empress Elisabeth of Austria, stabbed in 1898
- President William McKinley, shot in 1901
- Finnish Governor-General Nikolai Ivanovich Bobrikov, shot in 1904
- Franz Ferdinand, Archduke and heir of Austria, shot in 1914

All of the anarchists liked bombs. They used them so regularly that even today, in cartoons, a terrorist is often shown holding a round bomb with a fuse burning. In reality, that type of "bomb" was a midcentury shrapnel artillery shell. The anarchist bomb of choice was dynamite, Alfred Nobel's invention. Most anarchists were young men, often more concerned with political change than ending government. They were found in most countries and looked just like everyone else, and nothing like the wild characters shown in the illustrations of the time. Depending on the group, the bombing of police stations, banks, headquarters buildings, or rallies of competing groups were all popular choices. From 1886 until 1920, anarchists bombed literally hundreds of places. Most attacks were on the local authorities, but noteworthy among their many attacks are the following:

- In 1886, a bomb was thrown into a crowd of protesters in Chicago, starting the Haymarket Affair.
- In 1894, a hidden bomb went off in the French Parliament, killing twenty representatives.
- Also in 1894, a bomb went off while still in the hands of its thrower, damaging the Greenwich Observatory in London.
- In 1910, dynamite was used to destroy a wall of the *Los Angeles Times* building during a metalworkers strike.
- In 1920, a cart packed with explosives was detonated on Wall Street.

Yes, less than a century ago, someone exploded 100 pounds of gunpowder combined with 500 pounds of scrap metal on the street outside the J.P. Morgan bank. Thirty died and hundreds were injured. The response to all the bombings and shootings was a rapid ramping up of the internal security forces all over Europe and the United States, followed by repression. Since the bombers claimed to be on the side of the unions and workers, the honest workers' organizations were soon facing government repression because of their attacks.

By 1900, in some countries literally thousands of police and military did nothing but hunt down anarchists. There was a saying in czarist Russia that when three men met to plot a revolution, two were fools and the third was a government spy. Even so, success was limited; until the anarchists acted, it was hard to pick them out among the masses of workers who were in the not-always-peaceful process of unionizing. And once they did act, it was too late.

The western European response was widespread police infiltration of all worker organizations. Laws were changed, which resulted in a loss of civilian rights and restrictions on public gatherings. The restrictions were aimed mostly at the working class, among whom the anarchist hid. The tightening then was not different in scope from those rights lost by Americans after 9/11.

By 1900, anyone whom the government wished to discredit was labeled an "anarchist." Anarchy was not organized, but the anarchists' thinking was international in scope. But by 1918 and the end of World War I, the rise of ethnic nationalism meant the threat of anarchy was replaced by politically and religiously motivated terrorists. In fact, a terrorist and a driving error started the "War to End All Wars."

The Most Successful Terrorist in History

If the measure of a terrorist's success is how much his act changes the world, then the most successful terrorist throughout history was a not-very-bright Serb named Gavrilo Princip. He was a member of a small group known among themselves and the Austrian secret police as the Black Hand. Almost by mistake, and mostly because of a missed turn, this terrorist, on June 28, 1914, had a much more dramatic effect on the world than al-Qaeda had on 9/11.

It all began when the heir to the Austrian throne decided to pay a state visit to one of the most restive of the many small nations in his father's empire: Bosnia and Herzegovina. Archduke Franz Ferdinand had been invited there to observe army maneuvers. The Bosnians were ethnic Slavs and resented being ruled by a distant European emperor. They wished strongly to instead join with their Slavic neighbor, Serbia. Serbia, in turn, encouraged this attitude and supported all forms of unrest in Bosnia.

The heir to the Austrian throne was the not-so-young and, as rumor would have it, more-brave-than-bright Archduke Franz Ferdinand. His wife, Sophie, accompanied him as usual. Even when advised of the risk of assassination, he insisted on going to Sarajevo in Bosnia as planned.

Security in 1914 was not as sophisticated as it is today. For example, even though Sarajevo was a center for anti-empire sentiment and full of anarchist groups, the visit was announced far in advance. Then, to ensure that the adoring crowds (or assassins) could properly welcome the Austrian heir, the exact route his auto convoy would take from the train station to Sarajevo City Hall was published in every newspaper. Finally, to give disaster every chance, the archduke and duchess rode in an open-top car.

The Black Hand was not the most competent organization. The entire group planted itself along the established route, armed with two bombs (probably grenades), a pistol, and a vial of cyanide. From the beginning, things did not go well. Despite the published maps of the route and the crowds lining the streets, Gavrilo Princip, who had the pistol, waited in the wrong place and missed the convoy completely. One of the other members did manage to throw a grenade, which bounced off Ferdinand's auto and exploded near the vehicle behind him.

The archduke and duchess reached City Hall with no more problems and there they graciously thanked everyone for their loyalty. It was decided that Ferdinand should return directly to his private train and Austria. Ferdinand disagreed and expressed an interest in thanking the two men who were wounded in the follow car. It was agreed then that he and Sophie would visit the hospital on the way back to the train. The mayor's driver offered to lead the royal couple's car to the hospital.

No one knows how the local driver got confused, but he did, missing a turn, and tried to double back. This required both the mayor's car and the archduke's car to turn around. To do this, the Austrian heir's driver pulled into an alley so he could back out and face the other direction. Standing in the alley was Gavrilo Princip of the Black Hand. He had missed the entire caravan when it was going to the city hall, and, feeling ill, was slowly walking home. Suddenly, the Serbian terrorist found himself a few feet from the open and stopped car containing the archduke and his wife. Princip still had his pistol and fired at both.

At the time the archduke and his wife were shot, Count Franz von Harrach had been riding on the running board of their Gräf & Stift Double Phaeton automobile. He gave an account of what followed in his memoirs:

As the car quickly reversed, a thin stream of blood spurted from His Highness's mouth onto my right cheek. As I was pulling out my handkerchief to wipe the blood away from his mouth, the Duchess cried out to him, "For God's sake! What has happened to you?"

At that she slid off the seat and lay on the floor of the car, with her face between his knees.

I had no idea that she too was hit and thought she had simply fainted with fright. Then I heard His Imperial Highness say, "Sophie, Sophie, don't die. Stay alive for the children!"

At that, I seized the Archduke by the collar of his uniform, to stop his head dropping forward and asked him if he was in great pain. He answered me quite distinctly, "It is nothing!"

His face began to twist somewhat but he went on repeating, six or seven times, ever more faintly as he gradually lost consciousness, "It's nothing!"

Then came a brief pause followed by a convulsive rattle in his throat, caused by a loss of blood. This ceased on arrival at the governor's residence.

Both Archduke Ferdinand and Duchess Sophie soon died. As a result, the Austrian army began to descend on Serbia. The small nation called for assistance from Russia, which meant that the Austrians invoked their treaty with Germany to balance Russia out. But Russia had a treaty with France, and a network of secret treaties soon dragged all of Europe into World War I. The real cause of the war was the Austrians invading Serbia because of the assassination of the archduke and the mutual defense agreements that resulted in the nations of Europe being dragged unwillingly into the fray. But the trigger that set it off was coincidence and the actions of one Serbian terrorist. Ill—possibly with tuberculosis—not very competent, and in the wrong place at the right time, Gavrilo Princip lit the fuse that changed the world forever. It is this possibility of having such an out-of-proportion effect that inspires today's terrorists and continues to frighten governments. Hopefully, between the advent of modern communications and the memory of a reluctant Europe dragged into war, one terrorist act in the future will not plunge a large part of the world into a new war. But it has happened, and it can never be forgotten lest it happen again.

Russia

Russia's regressive and repressive czarist government always had problems with restive intellectuals. In 1878, the People's Will became the leading anarchist group, using violence and intimidation. They were the first terrorists to develop many of today's techniques such as targeting government officials, bombing gatherings and buildings, and assassinating members of the royal family. They had the advantage of being able to use Alfred Nobel's new invention, dynamite. (It helps when figuring out who gets picked for the honor to remember that the Nobel Peace Prize is an exercise in Swedish guilt.) The People's Will developed the use of thrown and planted dynamite bombs into a science. They were able to use the explosive, which was both more powerful and easier to handle than the old black powder bombs, in dozens of fatal attacks all over Russia. They were also able to make larger bombs and to hide and transport them more easily, and the lightweight explosive was easy to throw. A few anarchists or terrorists were able to do much more extensive damage when armed with dynamite. In 1880, a large dynamite bomb was hidden by the People's Will under the czar's Winter Palace dining room. Alexander II was unharmed because, apparently, he was late for dinner. Seventy others, both guests and staff, were injured.

The anarchists' own success caused the doom of the group. In March of 1881, one of their members succeeded in killing the czar. He simply threw a few sticks of dynamite, already lit, under Alexander's horse as he rode past in a parade. Even though the terrorist also died, the reaction was far from what the People's Will leaders expected. They were convinced Alexander's death would spark a popular revolt. But instead it appalled most of the population. The Russian state concentrated its full resources on the destruction of this one anarchist group, and within months the People's Will ceased to exist.

Terrorists' expectations also seem to be their greatest vulnerability. They do not see the world in the same way that most people do, or they would not be terrorists. Whether it was killing the czar with dynamite or crashing jets into the World Trade Center, the reaction terrorists get is often far from what they expect. So it was in 1881 when the People's Will was hunted down and broken, and so it was again the day after the World Trade Center attack, September 12, 2001. This seems to be a lesson that the terrorists do not learn. The price of success is to invoke the often overwhelming wrath of your target.

Armenia

Another example of terrorist acts having the opposite effect as that intended can be found in the revolt of the Armenian people, who were unhappy as a part of the Ottoman Empire. The Ottomans were in obvious decline, and the nations they controlled suffered from stagnation and social repression. Terrorism was the response, with the intention of triggering a revolution.

By 1890, a "federation" of Armenian anarchists and revolutionary groups had formed. Buildings were blown up or occupied. Turkish officials were murdered by bombs and bullets. Small revolts shocked all parts of Armenia as villages declared themselves free of the empire and tried to enforce their independence. Each of these revolts was put down by the Ottoman army.

The activities of the members of the federation were not the only reason for the eventual Armenian revolt and the massacres that followed, but they certainly contributed in the most classic terrorist ways. Turkey's eventual response to all of this was so devastating that even today Armenia condemns the Turks for their grandfathers' genocide. In 1915, goaded by terrorist attacks within Turkey as well as Armenia, the Ottoman government virtually declared war on its own province of Armenia. All Armenians were treated as if they were hostile, and massacres of entire villages or even cities became common. The worst incident was in Monastir, Tunisia, and resulted in twenty-seven thousand Armenians being killed during the revolt or later executed. The terrorists reacted with more attacks, and by the time the uneven battle had ended the terrorists and revolutionaries were dead and a million and a half Armenians had been killed. Armenia was not freed for decades; when the Ottoman Empire collapsed after World War I, the country was incorporated into the equally repressive Soviet Union. Only in 1990, after the fall of the USSR, did Armenia become an independent nation.

Successful Terrorists

There are two groups of terrorists, by definition, that have succeeded in gaining independence for their nations in recent history. This is not to excuse their use of terrorist methods, but both of them had one factor in common that made the difference. These two groups were the Irish Republican Army (IRA), which was important in the establishment of the Republic of Ireland, and the Jewish terrorist organizations fighting for a Jewish Israel after World War II.

There is no question that the IRA waged a campaign of terror. Very often its targets were not the British soldiers, but fellow

Irishmen. Like the Sicarii, the IRA used violence to isolate the occupiers. The result of this was that after Irish independence was gained in 1937, with the British recognition of Irish sovereignty, there were a number of men all over Ireland who were comfortable with violence. Many set it aside, but a number of them simply became criminals. Others wanted to go further and formed the more vicious Provisional IRA.

Another ethnic group also had success using terrorist techniques to form their nation. Three years into World War I, the British army was in desperate straits and fighting Turkey with limited success. France was too hard-pressed to free up large forces to defend their Middle Eastern holdings. Both nations cut what deals they could with those who could give them support. To ensure the support of Europe's Jews, England signed the Balfour Declaration in November of 1917, granting them a homeland after the war was won.

> His Majesty's government view with favour the estab-lishment in Palestine of a national home for the Jewish people, and will use their best endeavours to facilitate the achievement of this object, it being clearly understood that nothing shall be done which may prejudice the civil and religious rights of existing non-Jewish communities in Palestine, or the rights and political status enjoyed by Jews in any other country.

The declaration was later incorporated into other documents and the mandate from the League of Nations gave control of Palestine to the British. Unfortunately, in October of 1915, Sir Henry McMahon, the first British high commissioner in Egypt, had promised to the restive Arabs an area to rule as the guardians of the Islamic holy places—including "the Arabian Peninsula (except Aden) and the Fertile Crescent of Palestine, Lebanon, Syria, and Iraq." Yes, they promised Palestine to both sides.

After World War II, the time came for Britain, still occupying the Palestinian mandate, to pay up. The Jews, after the horrors of the concentration camps, demanded their own land. Before WWII started, many Western nations refused to accept German Jewish immigrants. Almost all of those who did not get out of Germany died in Hitler's "Final Solution." The surviving Jews were determined to create a Jewish nation—Israel—so that never again would there be no place for Jews under threat to flee to.

World sympathy was on the Jewish side, but many understood that the Palestinians already living there also had rights. Trying to keep a lid on all of the volatility, the British hung on and antagonized both sides, but especially the Jews. The reaction was the rise of terrorist groups such as the Irgun and Lehi. These groups took a much more aggressive pose than the larger Zionist organization, the Haganah, which had enforced a policy of just defense and no reprisals. The new, more radical groups used bombs and assassinations not only to drive out the British, but also to intimidate the Palestinians. They bombed the King David Hotel in Jerusalem, killing almost four hundred English officers, and forced the abandonment of entire Palestinian villages by surrounding them with armed men and threatening to attack.

So here again is a situation where terrorism seems to have helped nation building. But that same terrorism planted the seeds that brought to Palestine the PLO and Hamas.

That both the Jewish groups and the Irish used terrorist tactics cannot be denied, but what they also had in common was a cause that allowed them to rally public opinion in the democratic nations. Their victories came from worldwide support, not as a direct result of their violence. (It is important to note that Gandhi proved in India that success can also be achieved without violence.) Once their goals were in sight, both groups also willingly stopped using terrorist tactics. This allowed world opinion to support their cause without appearing to support their terrorist actions.

The lesson is, strangely, that if your cause is just in the eyes of the people of Europe and the Americas, you may not only advance your cause but be forgiven for your terrorism . . . but only if you know when to stop being a terrorist. You also have to know when to stop acting like a terrorist and join the mainstream of world politics. In cases where terrorists have a goal that is clearly defined and specific, rather than just acting out of hatred, a degree of success can end their terrorism. Even when successful, often the individual terrorists are still not forgiven, but their people or nation are.

There is a darker lesson as well. Both Israel and the Republic of Ireland continue to suffer from terrorist concerns and attacks even decades after their success in using the same tools to free or form their nation. Legitimizing terror also legitimizes its use against you and even encourages it. The cost of success is the radicalization of a culture or a nation, an often irreversible change.

Counting the Cost

There is a calculation that most groups don't seem to make when they resort to terrorism; as seen in Israel and Ireland, by their very success, terrorists radicalize large numbers of individuals. Also, as the anarchists of the People's Will and, more recently, Osama bin Laden have personally seen, too dramatic a terrorist act can unite their victims. It can bring retribution against your group or allies rather than cause a revolution. History has shown that the resources of even a small nation, if concentrated on a single terrorist group, can and will grind it apart. And history has many examples, such as Judea, Armenia, Iraq, and Afghanistan, of how a major power can and will crush nations who harbor or support the terrorists that threaten them. Furthermore, even if the terrorist's larger cause succeeds, it does so at a price. The lesson is that there is a cost to anyone who supports and espouses terrorism.

History's Answer

Throughout history, many things have worked to prevent terrorism. The most effective results are seen when social and political situations change. This can be as relatively benign as the founding of the Irish Republic or as catastrophic as the Armenian massacres and the third Jewish revolt in 70 CE. Take away the population base or destroy the society, and the terrorists do go away. However, that is a rather drastic solution, since the cure is often worse than the disease. Genocide will stop terrorists, at least at first, but at far too great a cost.

The machine-smashing and anti-industrialization Luddites were basically disarmed because the workers they claimed to protect turned on them in self-interest. The situation of the workingmen improved, and they had a stake in keeping things going. So another, much more acceptable solution that history says works in the long run is to improve the lot of the discontented, so the small radical minority will find no support for their violence.

Has the United States learned from this solution? It seems that it has, and although the jury is still out on the nation building, what America is doing in Iraq and Afghanistan seems to be helping. The people in Iraq appear to have almost all rejected al-Qaeda. Just a few years ago, terrorists could hide among the population, but now they are regularly turned in. The same has proven true in such locations as the Helmand Province in Afghanistan. Helmand was the heart of the Taliban two years ago, but the combination of schools, medical care, and stability has again turned the general population against the Muslim extremists. In Afghanistan a lot of rebuilding is still needed and America's patience may fail, but the process is working. The greatest remaining concerns are that much of the nation's infrastructure remains primitive, its local government is universally corrupt, and much of its economy remains dependent on the cultivation of opium poppies.

The next lesson from history is that there will always be terrorists. You cannot eliminate every violent malcontent. But we have learned that if you concentrate on one major group, you can eventually crush it. This may be simply because a developed nation has so many more resources than any terrorist group or those rogue nations that support it. This was the case when the czar's secret police went after the People's Will when they assassinated Alexander II. This same approach has again been successfully applied to al-Qaeda in modern times.

Yes, again the intelligence establishment of the United States has followed a pattern tested by history. An intense and extended focus has again proven successful when employed against al-Qaeda. It has not been quick, but what was once a powerful, well-funded, and highly organized terrorist organization has been not only crippled but, in many locations, shattered. Even more important, the U.S. government's success in doing this has given it credibility in combating other unrelated groups such as domestic terrorists and drug cartels. Anyone who challenges the American government can have no doubt that the United States has the will and the ability to react.

Perhaps it is necessary to remember another lesson. The history of terrorism begins before Rome, and even Suleiman the Magnificent could not completely defeat the Assassins. Whether with a dagger or a bomb, some individuals see terrorism as a valid way to change the world. Even if one group is destroyed, another appears. The real success is in preventing them from gaining the kind of propaganda victory that comes from killing an archduke or smashing into the World Trade Center. And again here you have to say that the Western world's efforts have been surprisingly effective. It has been a decade since there was a successful attack on the United States anywhere near that level, and few in an even more vulnerable Europe. The combination of elimination of the terrorists' allies and bases with active suppression has shown success, albeit at a high financial cost. The surprisingly optimistic conclusion is that it appears, so far, that those combating terrorism have learned from history and have found success doing it.

CHAPTER THREE

North of the Sahara

> There is no longer a way out of our present situation
> except by forging a road toward our objective, violently
> and by force, over a sea of blood and under a horizon
> blazing with fire.
>
> —GAMAL ABDEL NASSER (1918–1970),
> PRESIDENT OF EGYPT

Or, simply said, "The very nasty means I am about to order are justified by their ends." Such words, uttered by a beleaguered North African leader, might sound vaguely familiar. These are the kinds of words used by ruthless dictators and their apologists, by terrorists demanding change, and the kind we hear when irrational violence poses as legitimate foreign policy. They are the kinds of words we have heard from the mouth of Muammar Gaddafi or Nasser's successor, Hosni Mubarak. Similar to Gaddafi's current situation, Nasser faced a coalition that included powerful Western nations like Great Britain and France. While the global landscape has changed significantly since the Cold War, Africa remains geopolitically important.

Egypt is unique in Africa as part of the Arab Spring movement that is still taking form long after those first revolts, but Egypt is also typical in the sense that it has been a battleground for outsiders. Since this has been the pattern for the last two thousand years, aversion to any Western interference as the new democracy forms is understandable. The negative response by the bulk of the Egyptians to European nonprofit groups "assisting" them in developing a democracy is not based on what those Western workers are doing. Instead, this sentiment has formed because these groups are trying to help in a place that has been battered and shifted by outsiders, and yet still retains the pride of being the greatest and nearly the first true civilization.

When you landed at Cairo Airport in the year 2000, you were greeted by a banner that read: "Welcome to Egypt, Now in Our Seventh Millennium." Egypt is rather unique in the historical breadth of its interactions with the West. While many African nations were not exposed to Europe until a few centuries ago, Egypt has been interacting with Europe for millennia. Egyptian culture is also very different from much of Africa, with a strong sense of identification as a nation and people, and an understandable shared pride in the nation's long history.

For most of its seven-thousand-year history Egypt has been independent. There were brief occupations in 671 BCE by the Assyrians and 525 BCE by the Persians, but neither lasted long enough to change the identity of those living along the Nile. In 332 BCE, Alexander the Great seized Egypt, which was again controlled by the Persians. By showing respect for Egyptian customs, in the same way he honored the other territories he conquered, he earned their respect. He founded Alexandria, a major port that became the capital until the rise of Islam in 641 CE. After Alexander's death, Perdiccas (who was serving as regent) appointed one of his generals, Ptolemy, as governor of Egypt. In 323 BCE, as Alexander's empire crumbled, Ptolemy retained control of Egypt by declaring himself pharaoh. He had the only army in Egypt, so no one was in a position to disagree. In the warfare between the generals who followed Alexander, Ptolemy repelled an invasion led by Perdiccas. Like all of the "successors" of Alexander, Perdiccas, from his own base in Macedonia, was trying to reunite the whole empire. They all failed, and Egypt remained independent. The Ptolemaic dynasty continued to rule Egypt for three centuries, becoming more "Egyptian" in their attitudes with each generation.

The last ruler of the dynasty was Cleopatra, Egypt's last pharaoh. Incidentally, the Ptolemys were Greek by descent and Cleopatra looked it ("Cleopatra" is a Greek, not an Egyptian, name). In 52 BCE, Cleopatra was a coruler with her younger brother, Ptolemy XIII. She was not keen on sharing power with him. Being a male, Ptolemy was declared pharaoh and through him his advisors had the real power. Cleopatra could look forward to a life of being honored, but powerless. She was caught conspiring against him, which prompted her exile to a distant corner of the kingdom. Ptolemy, pharaoh of Egypt at merely thirteen years old, then made a grievous tactical error. His father had borrowed a very large sum of money from Rome. This had been used to solidify his dynasty's hold on the country and improve his army. The loan had not been paid back. The young Ptolemy sought to mitigate the debt by delivering the head of a political rival to Julius Caesar.

Pompey the Great had been a powerful Roman leader and at first was a supporter and mentor to Caesar. But once Caesar began to consolidate power after returning from Gaul, Pompey sided with the Senate and opposed Caesar in the civil war that followed. His army's defeat by Caesar ended the war and Pompey fled to Egypt.

When Caesar and part of his army followed Pompey to Egypt, they were greeted on the dock by officials of the young pharaoh's court. Egypt was a close ally of Rome and a source for much of the empire's grain, yet it still maintained its independence. But what happened when Caesar arrived soured that relationship. When the Roman general and first consul landed on the dock in Alexandria, the leaders of the pharaoh's court presented Julius Caesar with his rival's head. It was recorded that Caesar both grew angry and wept. Pompey had been a Roman consul and was the widower of Caesar's daughter. Though they had been bitter political rivals, it seems likely Caesar had hoped to reconcile with Pompey. He could have greatly benefited from the older man's support in healing the split and gaining the support of those who had opposed him. Theirs was also a close personal relationship. The elder general had been Caesar's friend and earlier political ally. Since Caesar had already gained control of the empire, there was no longer a reason for him to fear Pompey and every reason for the older general to reconcile with Caesar.

It was the counselors of the young Egyptian pharaoh who seemed to believe they would curry favor with Julius Caesar by killing Pompey. There is no question that this angered Caesar instead. He was a proud Roman and probably disliked the fact that they had felt it was acceptable to murder a Roman patrician for their own gain. A short time later, when he learned of the dispute between the brother and sister, he appointed himself as a mediator between Cleopatra and Ptolemy XIII.

This was right after Caesar had been angry at being presented with Pompey's head, so it is likely the Roman leader already distrusted and disliked the male Ptolemy. To ensure the Roman would take her side, Cleopatra became Caesar's lover, giving him a daughter in 47 BCE. When Julius Caesar supported Cleopatra's claim, her brother's supporters gathered an army. Caesar and his legion backed Cleopatra in this Egyptian civil war, which ended only with her young brother's death. Cleopatra was established as the ruler of Egypt and a close ally of Rome. For several years the relationship was mutually beneficial, with Cleopatra even becoming a celebrity in Rome. She later returned to Egypt and gave birth to Caesar's only natural son, Caesarian.

After Caesar's assassination, Cleopatra threw her lot in with Mark Antony and Caesar's adopted son and heir, Octavian. After they won the civil war, Antony eventually came to live in Egypt with Cleopatra, where they wed. He was soon accused, probably accurately, of advancing Egypt's interests, as well as his own, instead of Rome's.

Antony was the effective ruler of the rich eastern half of the Roman Empire, with Octavian controlling the western half, including Rome itself. Fairly quickly, it became apparent that Antony saw himself as an independent ruler and not just a representative of the Roman Empire. He even went so far as to leave in his will the kingships of some of the Roman provinces in his area, as if they were his personal possessions and not those of Rome. He openly left the eastern nations of the empire to Cleopatra's children, separate from Rome.

When Octavian released a copy of Antony's will to the Roman public, they were outraged. Relations between Antony and Octavian quickly deteriorated, with the bulk of the Romans feeling betrayed by Mark Antony and so siding with Octavian. It was at this point that Octavian declared war on Antony and in effect on Egypt. After a series of military defeats, the last pharaoh and her lover became Octavian's captives in Alexandria. It was soon announced that they had killed themselves. Cleopatra and Antony's three children were taken in by Octavian's wife and raised in Rome. With the last of the Ptolemy heirs dead or out of the way and Roman legions in their cities, no one protested when Egypt became a Roman province. It remained a Roman, and later Eastern Roman (Byzantine), province until Rome lost it to the Arabs in 641 CE.

That was the first time, but hardly the last, that the diplomats or armies of Europe meddled with Egypt. For Rome, Egypt was a prize, a rich and fertile gem of a province. After five thousand years of mostly self-rule, Egypt was not again free for another twelve hundred years. Control from Byzantium was exchanged for control by the Ottoman Empire in 662. The Ottoman Turks technically still ruled the land of the Nile at the end of the eighteenth century, when Napoleon Bonaparte led a French invasion into Egypt.

Bonaparte was not yet the ruler of France but was an esteemed general. England was first Revolutionary France's and then Napoleonic France's archenemy. France sought to seize Egypt in an attempt to undermine Britain's access to India and the East Indies. It was the wealth of these regions that made Britain rich and powerful. Egypt was located along almost all of the numerous significant trade routes that still went to those regions. If France occupied Egypt, it would not only harm Britain's economy but also put the French within striking distance of India and the Far East. So once more, Egypt became a battleground between European powers.

Napoleon fancied himself a modern Alexander the Great. So when he conquered Egypt for a short time in 1798, the French general took a page out of Alexander's playbook, instructing his soldiers to treat the Muslims of Egypt with respect. He even portrayed himself as a Muslim convert in a bold but generally unsuccessful attempt at securing the support of the Egyptian public. They liked his respect for their beliefs, but not the taxes that followed.

France had early victories in the war, taking Alexandria and defeating the Mamelukes, the Turkish garrison comprised of mostly sword-armed cavalry, at the Battle of the Pyramids. The land campaign was rather successful; it was on the seas that Napoleon was defeated. Britain tracked down French warships and demolished them, seriously weakening France's position in the Mediterranean. Stranded on land, Napoleon consolidated his rule in Egypt, quelling several rebellions. But cut off from reinforcements, his efforts were doomed.

Napoleon actually departed after a decisive French victory against the last stronghold in Egypt held by the Ottomans at Abukir, a coastal fortress about fourteen miles north of Alexandria. However, after the costly victory, with his army diminishing and supplies running low, Napoleon recognized that defeat was inevitable. He also observed a tumultuous political situation in France. The leadership had lost the support of the people, and the chaos and violence of the Committees frightened those in power as well as the middle class of Paris. Too many heads had been sliced off without a good reason for any Frenchman to feel secure. The French people were ready for someone who would make them feel safe again. In the French capital anyone might prevail—particularly an ambitious and successful general returning from yet another conquest.

There was no French fleet left that could carry the entire army home. The British controlled the Mediterranean and would sink any transports sent. So Bonaparte abandoned his loyal soldiers and left secretly at night. He was accompanied by only a small number of trusted officers. Before leaving, he transferred control to a disillusioned General Jean Baptiste Kléber, who then was assassinated by the Egyptians. Kléber's successor soon saw surrender to the British as preferable to remaining in a hostile Egypt, and so the country was now directly controlled by the British Empire. Britain's hold gradually decreased after the fall of Napoleon in 1815, but the British Empire reserved for itself the special right to assist the Egyptians and protect their own interests there.

Rich, producing a surplus of grain, and strategically located, Egypt remained alluring for Europe's imperial competitors in the first half of the nineteenth century. The country's strategic importance increased markedly in 1869 with the completion of the Suez Canal. Egypt built the canal in a partnership with France. England, still the greatest sea power, benefited greatly from it. The canal was referred to by some as the "Highway to India," since it enabled ships to travel to India without taking the onerous journey around the southern tip of Africa. But Egyptian pride soon faded when it became apparent that to finance the canal the nation had spent beyond its means. The completion of the canal left Egypt heavily indebted to European banks, and the tolls did not bring in enough of a surplus to cover the interest due. To pay off this debt, Egypt sold its share in the canal to Britain. Britain and France used their leverage to secure important cabinet positions in Egypt, essentially forming a puppet government. By 1875, Egypt was effectively ruled from Paris and London.

Britain and France intervened in 1882 to protect their interests, quashing an uprising. The government remained a puppet and the Egyptian people knew it. A generation later the British were less oppressive, but they were still involved and intervened when they desired. Cooperation with the British probably peaked when Egypt proved helpful in countering the Ottomans during World War I. There was no question of mutual interest. The Ottoman Turk sultan had aligned with the Central powers and made no secret of his desire to add Egypt to his empire. After the war, nationalist movements compelled Britain to unilaterally declare Egypt's independence in 1922. Even so, the British retained garrisons and special interests. The last British troops did not leave Egypt until 1954. By this time, Egypt had gained a good deal of true self-rule.

After a coup in 1952, the Republic of Egypt was formed, with its first president General Muhammad Naguib. He lost a power struggle among the officers who controlled the government and was forced to resign in 1954. He was replaced by Gamal Abdel Nasser. Nasser took control in 1956 on the strength of not wanting too quick an implementation of democracy, since that would make it likely the Muslim Brotherhood would take power. (Sixty years later, his prediction seems to be coming true. In the first congressional elections in 2012, the Muslim Brotherhood won the most seats. Since the justification for military government in 1956 was preventing that exact thing from happening, the tension between the military and the Muslim Brotherhood becomes understandable.)

By 1956, the military in Egypt had begun to play the two sides of the Cold War against each other. Within a year, Britain and the United States withdrew financial support for building the Aswan Dam due to Egyptian support of the USSR. Nasser responded by nationalizing the Suez Canal. In response, Israel,

Britain, and France combined their forces and attacked Egypt. The goal was to topple Nasser's regime and to regain Western control of the canal. Though Israel, Britain, and France succeeded in their military objectives, they earned condemnation from both the USSR and the United States for their belligerence. The almost unique agreement by the two superpowers ensured that Nasser remained president and that Britain and France failed in seizing control of the canal. Russia loudly took the credit in Egypt. The result was an embarrassment for the West and solidified Egyptian support of the USSR (at least until Nasser was replaced by Anwar Sadat).

Recently, Egypt has again garnered headlines for its almost bloodless 2011 revolution. After decades of rule, President Hosni Mubarak was ousted. The rebellion presented a dilemma for the United States. The movement was pro-democracy, and President Barack Obama could scarcely condemn democracy in the Middle East. Conversely, Mubarak was a pro-West politician. He moved the nation away from the Soviets, encouraged investment by American companies, accepted massive aid from the United States, and even began using American military equipment. In his more than twenty years of ruling Egypt, Mubarak opposed those with fundamentalist religious influence and made peace with Israel, but also allowed the common Egyptian little say in how he governed. Many political observers in the United States and Israel were concerned that Mubarak would be replaced by an Islamic fundamentalist. They pointed to the organized presence of the Muslim Brotherhood in Egypt as evidence for this. It led to a mixed reaction when the protests first began. The United States government was torn between a more than half-century-old concern about the rise of the Muslim Brotherhood and its desire to support those striving to create a representative democracy.

With conflicting concerns, an unsettled President Obama delayed in formulating an official response, but eventually he came out in support of the movement. As is often the case for world leaders, he was faced with the delicate act of balancing ideology and strategic interests. His support for the self-determination of the Egyptian people stands in stark contrast to previous Western interactions with Egypt. In the past, strategic interests were paramount, and there was no hesitation about trampling the Egyptian people to secure those interests.

This is a new beginning, and Egypt is a very significant player in the Middle East, so the United States would benefit by maintaining a cordial relationship with it. However, it could suffer from the dangers of Islamic fundamentalists hijacking the country, which has been the fear of the Egyptian military and the dictators it has supported since 1923. Egypt is one of only a few Middle Eastern countries not aggressive toward Israel. If President Obama's decision pays off, his verbal support for the revolution may earn America some esteem in the Middle Eastern world. Or the needed reaction to the Egyptian government taking a hostile turn could cause massive damage throughout the region. Egypt's path to democracy will have been molded by seven thousand years of national pride and five invasions by Europe in the past two hundred years. After two thousand years of outsiders meddling and frequent occupation, the still-proud nation of Egypt is finding its own way.

CHAPTER FOUR

Sub-Saharan Africa

Africa is a continent in flames. And deep down, if we really accepted that Africans were equal to us, we would all do more to put the fire out. We're standing around with watering cans, when what we really need is the fire brigade.

—Paul David "Bono" Hewson (1960–),
lead singer for U2

Many Western observers are concerned about the growing Chinese presence in Africa. Chinese companies have aggressively forged partnerships there, distressing those who view China's influence as zero-sum with that of the West. The United States spars with China and occasionally with Russia today in the same region where Britain,

France, and Germany once vied for dominance. After World War II, American companies expanded into Africa, building infrastructure and exploiting that continent's mineral wealth. With America's foreign aid, engineers in the middle of the last century began building schools, hospitals, dams, and roads in sub-Saharan Africa, but as the Cold War faded the number of projects diminished.

Now the Chinese have used the same combination of state and corporate action to supplant the Americans. This is certainly recent history repeating itself. In the 1940s and 1950s, the United States' manufacturing growth was explosive and the limiting factor was resources. Now, China is the nation whose infrastructure and factories are growing in surges, and the Chinese are concerned with the same lack of raw materials that America once also turned to Africa to overcome. Today, the United States is in the position of Europe just after World War II. Areas it had once dominated now have closer relationships with China. But there is one significant difference: both China and the United States are spending billions trying to improve the lot of the people in the many African nations. They are also finding that the culture and tribalism in many countries, in both upper and sub-Saharan Africa, often frustrate their best efforts.

Still, temptation abounds in all of Africa. For the realist, Africa represents a strategic location where the United States should ingratiate itself so it can again secure political allies and natural resources. For the humanitarian, Africa is the natural starting point for combating injustice, famine, and disease. For any compassionate person, the genocides of Rwanda, Darfur, Somalia, the Democratic Republic of the Congo, and elsewhere tear at the heart. Even those who abhor war and militarism might think military intervention is justifiable in such instances. Again, the long history of intervention in African affairs shows that these opportunities are balanced by danger and the cost of many Africans' deep-seated resistance. Many of Africa's problems have persisted for centuries. Examining African interactions with the West over the last few centuries is useful for discerning the best course of action today.

The word *sahara* means "desert." Africa is really two worlds, divided by the Sahara. Where there is an Arab Spring and a political change in North Africa, the picture in sub-Saharan Africa is very different. There are two themes to address when you write about the modern history of sub-Saharan Africa. One is tribalism and the other is slavery, and both have long cultural roots. When the Europeans came, tribalism encouraged members of one tribe to see those in others simply as items to be captured and sold. Because of this the number of slaves sold increased massively. The tribal antipathy and sheer destruction wrought by the capture and sale of slaves to the Europeans profoundly changed much of Africa.

Africa's Most Precious Commodity: People

Slavery has had a profound effect on even today's sub-Saharan Africa. The transatlantic slave trade began around the middle of the fifteenth century. The Portuguese, then a major player in Europe, possessed unrivaled influence in Africa at the time. It was they who first began purchasing slaves for resale from the African kings living along the coasts. Portugal monopolized the slave trade from about 1440 to 1640 and was responsible for transporting six and a half million Africans—about 40 percent of the slaves taken from the continent. Though Portugal dwindled as a dominant power, the slave trade persisted. North America needed cheap labor to produce cash crops like cotton and tobacco. Native

Americans were generally considered poor laborers because of their susceptibility to European diseases. Having had no contact with Europe, the Native Americans had no immunity to any of the illnesses endemic throughout Europe and where Europeans had settled. Their vulnerability was used against them by the Spanish, who gave out blankets contaminated with smallpox and other diseases. There were European-induced epidemics in Florida, the Carolinas, and Virginia between 1519 and 1750, including outbreaks of smallpox, bubonic plague, typhus, mumps, influenza, yellow fever, and measles. These intentional plagues destroyed as many as two-thirds of the native populations, leaving some villages and areas uninhabited. Africans had been exposed to European diseases long ago; moreover, they were used to tropical conditions, making them ideal for work on the sugar plantations of the Caribbean. The slave trade became part of the infamous "Triangular Trade" between Africa, Europe, and North America. This trade entailed raw materials (molasses, lumber, rum, sugar, spices, cotton, tobacco, and minerals) making their way to Europe from North America; manufactured goods traveling from Europe to Africa; and slaves being carted off from Africa to North America. Human beings were being exchanged for trade beads (mostly colored glass), muskets, and ammunition.

Slavery was not a new institution in Africa. Islamic slavers had roamed parts of the continent for centuries. Europe merely perfected the trade. It was a traditional part of African society in many regions; moreover, many slaves had trickled into Europe over various trans-Saharan trade routes. As dominance of the seas was taken from the Portuguese and Spanish by the English and Dutch, their merchants took over the lucrative trade. At the height of the slave trade, Great Britain was the worst transgressor, carrying slaves to both the Americas and the Caribbean. Britain transported almost half of the six million

Africans seized during the eighteenth century. In total, around twelve million Africans were taken during the transatlantic slave trade, peaking around the end of the eighteenth century. Soon after that, most European nations banned both slavery and the slave trade.

By today's standards, slavery is a deplorable institution. The impact of the slave trade extended far beyond the personal liberty of the slaves. Families and tribes disintegrated as huge chunks of their population were stolen. However, we must not view Africa as a continent of hapless victims whose modern problems must rest solely on the conscience the West. Slaves were often initially taken by rival tribes, not Europeans. Even African governments were willing to allow some of their own people to be enslaved in exchange for guns and ammunition, since the alternative was to be attacked and overwhelmed by neighbors who did have modern weapons. But we do need to remember that part of the reason central Africa remains trapped in tribalism and poverty is the damage done by centuries of exploitation. Nor can Europeans forget the continuing resentment for this and for the colonialism that remains an undertone to discussions and negotiations. Not having been part of this slave trade may even help explain China's rapid success today, though Chinese money is probably more important.

Africa was depleted of many of its most able-bodied denizens between the fifteenth and eighteenth centuries. Some areas in central Africa lost half or more of their population, disproportionately young men and women (they were worth more). This had the effect of stifling development. It also discouraged farming, as the farmer was too easy a target. Today many scholars speculate that without the losses to slavery, several sub-Saharan nations would have double their current population and might well have developed their own industrial base.

Though the immorality of slavery seems clear to the modern observer, it was a more contentious issue a few centuries ago. Many prominent thinkers regarded it as acceptable and natural. Racial superiority was a given to Europeans. Though it was a perversion of Darwin's actual theory, scientific racism became popular as a justification for slavery and imperialism. Black Africans were viewed as inferior. Pseudoscientists would point to the shape of the skull or the dexterity of the toes to demonstrate the racial superiority of Caucasians. Others attempted to justify slavery by arguing for its morality. Some believed that "savage" races needed to be civilized by any means necessary. Others pointed out that slaves were almost invariably forced to at least follow the forms of Christianity, so they benefited from being slaves because their souls were "saved." Slavery was almost universally rationalized for three centuries as a way of extricating Africans from an inferior culture and exposing them to the virtues of civilized society.

Though Britain was one of the worst perpetrators of slavery, it partially redeemed itself by its role in ending the slave trade. Britain banned the slave trade in 1807. After the ban, British warships went from facilitating the slave trade to actively opposing it by using the Royal Navy to seize slave ships and banning it throughout the empire. This took away most of the Caribbean market for slaves, leaving only the southern U.S. states. While the United States and some other nations persisted in retaining slavery even as the British navy worked to shut such trade down, it was the American Civil War that finally ended the bulk of the slave trade. Still, the need for cheap labor continued after 1865. It was not long before the gaps left by the slave trade were filled by a subtler form of repression: colonialism.

Slavery in Africa did not begin with the sale of captives to the Portuguese and did not end when those sales stopped. It would be nice if it were possible to see African slavery as just a dark period in the continent's history. Unfortunately, in many Islamic and African cultures, various forms of slavery continue even today. In Sudan, the ownership of bound servants or concubines as property is still considered normal. The United Nations' Human Rights Committee has said that children are sold every day to become carpet slaves in India, Pakistan, and Nepal. There are hundreds of thousands of children who continue to work for just food, and legally they're completely without rights. At this moment in time, there are children and adults who remain legally enslaved as cane-cutters in Haiti and farm workers in southern Pakistan in a manner that has not changed since the plantations started. Finally, the modern variant of sex slavery involves tens of thousands of women and children and can be found in almost all nations, regardless of their laws. So slavery remains a problem everywhere and remains effectively legal in some parts of Africa even today, bringing with it all the ills and damage to society that come with such an institution.

Scrambling for Africa

There were several reasons the Scramble for Africa began in the early nineteenth century. For some, such as esteemed British explorer Dr. David Livingstone, there was a moral element to the undertaking. Livingstone and others believed themselves to be on a civilizing mission to spread the true faith. Other nations and explorers wanted to move into Africa for less idealistic reasons, namely, to improve their own fortunes. Many European nations were experiencing a deficit due to a slowing of trade with the Americas and saturation of the Oriental market. For example, the British could produce more cloth than they could use or sell. Africa provided a new destination for their exports. These nations were also seen as a source for numerous natural resources. Beyond hardwoods and crops there were deposits of almost every mineral, including gold. From copper and iron to manganese and silver, these minerals were needed by the modern factories of Europe. So with the righteousness of missionaries and the greed of robber barons, Europeans overwhelmed and took control of southern Africa.

One of the most valued resources was the diamond. The De Beers diamond company was founded by English-born businessman Cecil Rhodes. Today, Rhodes's name is associated with the Rhodes Scholarship, a prestigious award given to talented college students. Long revered in Britain as a national hero, he is now regarded as more of an embarrassment. Though Rhodes's commercial acumen is unquestioned—under his watch, De Beers came to control 90 percent of the world's diamonds—his moral compass is scrutinized more often. Racial disdain inspired his harsh treatment of the native populations. In 1888, Rhodes tricked the Ndebele king, Lobengula, into granting him mining concessions in Matabeleland. When Lobengula and his people resisted British encroachment, they were butchered by Britain's powerful Maxim machine guns. This was not only the approved way to handle any disputes between local leaders and the Europeans; it was also immensely popular with the press and the masses. In honor of Rhodes's deception and slaughter, the territory was named Rhodesia. Northern Rhodesia is now Zambia; Southern Rhodesia is now Zimbabwe. Today, with the nations controlled by the native population, Rhodes is held in disrepute in these countries. They have not forgotten his murderous campaign against their ancestors. It was a pattern that took place all over southern Africa, leaving changes and resentment one must understand in order to comprehend the situation today.

Rhodes was certainly not the only violent imperial agent. Henry Morton Stanley, a Welsh journalist and explorer who fancied himself Livingstone's heir, was commissioned by the Belgian king Leopold II to explore the Congo and secure territory for Belgium from 1874 to 1877. In those days, because of the wealth involved, most explorers were more mercenary than patriot, with such men as Stanley often working for the paycheck and fame, not for their own nation. This self-centered attitude was reflected in many of the actions of the men who claimed Africa for Europe. Contemporaries like Sir Richard Burton stated that "Stanley shoots negroes as if they are monkeys." He also regulated the behavior of his subordinates laxly; for instance, one of them purchased an eleven-year-old girl and offered her to cannibals so that he might study the way in which they cooked and ate her. Subjection to and internal acceptance of such dehumanization over centuries have contributed to the slow pace of development across the subcontinent.

It Has Been a Very Long Spring

Perhaps the African nation that still suffers the most from colonialism is the Democratic Republic of the Congo. The mercenary explorer Stanley spent over two years mapping the course of the Congo River. Based upon this, Leopold of Belgium began claiming the entire river basin. In 1884, the Congo Basin was "granted" to Leopold at a conference in Berlin attended by the leading European nations. (No one, at any point, asked anyone living there for an opinion.) In 1885, Leopold announced the Congo Free State, which was not free at all. In 1891, Belgium-led forces conquered the independent kingdom of Katanga and annexed it to the Congo. Then in 1892, the Free State took over the eastern Congo from the Arab-speaking traders who had ruled its cities for generations. Neither of the new additions shared culture or even language with the original Free State. This is part of the problem faced by Congo today: disparate people without even a common language struggling for, or against in many cases, national unity.

What they all had in common was that the region was immensely wealthy in resources and people. Belgium secured a very profitable rubber industry from the Congo. The profits were made possible via brutal subjugation of the indigenous people, who were treated like slaves, often with the approval of a well-bribed chieftain. Violence, starvation, disease, and a diminishing population were widespread. Mines that made Europeans wealthy were hellholes into which unwilling young men disappeared regularly.

In June of 1960, under pressure as the rest of post-WWII Europe released its colonies, Belgium granted the Republic of the Congo independence. Patrice Lumumba was prime minister and Joseph Kasavubu became the president. It was a large nation with tremendous potential and even greater problems. The Belgians had not really prepared the colony for independence in the manner that the British had successfully employed over the same period. Rather, they simply pulled out, expecting that there were enough soldiers to protect the still-European-owned corporate interests. By July of 1960, there had been a mutiny of the Congolese army and the culturally separate Katanga Province had declared its independence and created its own army. Belgian and then UN troops were sent in to occupy the mines and factories and see that they kept producing. By December 1960, Patrice Lumumba had been dismissed as prime minister, and in January 1961 he was assassinated. The UN suppressed the Katanga rebellion, and by August of 1961, it disarmed the Katangan soldiers. In 1965, the Congo's president, Kasavubu, formed an alliance with the Katangan leader, Moise Tshombe. But that same year, they were both thrown out in a bloody coup and Joseph Mobutu took power. By this time, the national government had little control of the countryside. In 1971, Mobutu named the Congo "Zaire," and by 1974 most of the European companies and mines were nationalized. In 1977 Zaire's economy collapsed. Mobutu tried to invite foreign investors back, but there was little trust. By 1989 Zaire was a classic dictatorship, and numerous rebel and ethnic factions were active throughout the country, the only thing they shared being a dislike for Mobutu.

What followed was typical of the pattern found in the history of many southern African nations. Realizing he was losing power, Mobutu bowed to foreign pressure and allowed the first almost-free elections, after which he retained control of the army, key ministries, and security forces, leading to increased resistance and further economic collapse. When Mobutu was unable to pay the army, it too revolted and he was forced to create a true coalition government, but retained command of the security forces and police. Note that during this time there were several independent armies (read: warlords) exploiting the chaos by taking control of Zaire's gold and diamond mines. They took the wealth from these mines by using forced labor under brutal conditions. This was the source of the "blood diamonds" banned today in most of the world.

By 1997 anti-Mobutu rebels had taken over much of Zaire. Then in 1998 rebels backed by Rwanda and Uganda rose up. Zimbabwe and Namibia sent in their own armies to meet these rebels, and proceeded to retain control of parts of the nation as well. The parts they tended to hold were, of course, those in which the valuable mines were located. By the middle of 1999, there were armies from six African nations in Congo, basically fighting over the corpse of the nation. Finally, in 2000 the UN sent in 5,500 peacekeepers to monitor a cease-fire it had brokered. By then an estimated two and a half million Congolese had died in the rebellions and invasions. Still the killing continued as various tribes vied for power and control. Not to mention that many warlords and their private armies still continued to occupy parts of Congo as well.

There were free elections in 2006 and an elected democratic government was formed. By then most of the adjacent nations had also withdrawn their troops. Though some held the gold and diamond mines until the very last minute, the UN demanded they leave and they complied. But the problems of tribal rivalries, a few remaining warlords, and regional rivalries led to more battles between the Tutsi-supported government and Hutu militias supported by Rwanda, and the violence had escalated again by 2008. More UN forces were sent in, and they began to report mass rapes and destroyed villages, and the fighting became even more brutal. So it continued. There is no happy ending to this story. The current Congolese president, Joseph Kabila, retained power by fixing the last election. Rebel armies remain in western Congo, and Hutu tribesmen continue to resist any government led by the rival Tutsi tribe—though their open warfare in Congo pales next to what happened in nearby Rwanda.

The lessons of history are there. They include the dangers of tribalism and remind us of the destruction that wanton exploitation of a population can have even decades after it has ended. There is less indication that these lessons have been learned by many of those in power in Africa. The Democratic Republic of the Congo, and unfortunately other nations such as the Ivory Coast, continue the cycle of ethnic conflict, coup, and rebellion.

Tutsis and Hutus

European involvement in Africa has had harmful consequences that deeply affected the future of former colonies. The tale of modern Rwanda shows that there is another even more damaging effect that keeps much of Africa unstable and impoverished. As in Afghanistan, discussed earlier, the first loyalty of many Africans is to their tribe. This can result in vicious and brutal conflicts that turn neighbor against neighbor. During the 1994 conflict in Rwanda, the cause and results were all very much African. On several occasions, hundreds of thousands died, but most of the Western world watched, doing little.

As usual, the violence in Rwanda can be traced to tribalism and the tribal conflicts that were made worse by European influence. In 1890, during the Scramble for Africa, Germany gained control of Rwanda. The Germans exacerbated existing ethnic tensions by privileging lighter-skinned Tutsis as the ruling class despite the Hutus' majority status. After World War I, Germany lost most of its colonial possessions as a result of the Treaty of Versailles. Belgium took control of Rwanda. Belgium was as inept a colonial ruler in Rwanda as it had been in the Congo. Its agricultural policies resulted in a famine that killed one-third of the population. It also maintained Tutsi dominance. Belgium officially recognized the Tutsi people as the "superior" race. It issued mandatory cards identifying the bearer as Tutsi, Hutu, or Twa (the third major ethnic group of Rwanda).

During the 1950s the two largest ethnic groups began to call for independence. The Tutsi desired to maintain the current social hierarchy whereas the Hutus wanted to end Tutsi minority rule. Belgium arbitrarily switched its support from the Tutsis to the Hutus. The result was the 1959 Rwandan Revolution, during which many Tutsis were slain or forced to find refuge in a neighboring country. In 1962 the colony gained independence and split into Rwanda and Burundi. Exiled Tutsi rebels attacked at the Rwandan borders, resulting in a Hutu crackdown on Tutsis within the country. In 1972 the Tutsi-controlled government responded to a Hutu rebellion by systematically killing two hundred thousand Hutus. A 1973 coup, led by Hutu Juvenal Habyarimana, resulted in a more moderate government, paving the way for economic and political stability. Despite this relative stability, institutionalized inequality was a remnant of the colonial era. Tutsis still owned most of the land while many Hutus were forced into becoming laborers.

In 1990 the Rwandan Patriotic Front (RPF), a group comprised mostly of Tutsi refugees, invaded northern Rwanda from Uganda. Despite initial setbacks, the RPF remained resilient. Habyarimana was forced to conciliate with the RPF and a cease-fire was agreed upon in 1993. The peace was a fragile one that shattered when Habyarimana and the president of Burundi, Cyprien Ntaryamira, were killed after Habyarimana's plane was shot down in April 1994. It is unclear to this day who orchestrated the assassination; each side blamed the other in the immediate aftermath, though later reviews suggested the act was performed by Hutu extremists in the military.

In Burundi, the death of Ntaryamira aggravated an ongoing civil war. In October of 1993, Burundi's first democratically elected Hutu president, Melchior Ndadaye, was assassinated by Tutsi extremists. Violence broke out between the two groups, killing between fifty thousand and a hundred thousand people within a year. When Ntaryamira, Ndadaye's successor, was assassinated in the aforementioned incident, tensions escalated. The border between Rwanda and Burundi became a land of butchery, as refugees from both conflicts met with violence.

The civil war persisted even after the end of the Rwandan conflict, not ending until 2005.

In Rwanda, the response to Habyarimana's death was even more heinous. The government distributed guns and machetes to Hutu militias to aid in the slaughter of Tutsis. It also used radio broadcasts to implore the Hutus to participate in the killing of all Tutsis and politically moderate Hutus. The government manipulated family ties and relationships to create "killing groups" called Interahamwe. The Interahamwe exists today as a terrorist organization based in Congo. During the Rwandan civil war, they perpetrated the bulk of the violence, particularly in rural areas.

During this period, the international community's response was paltry. The UN was certainly aware of the violence: it witnessed children being massacred at places like Gikondo, it knew some peacekeepers had been slain in the fray, and it knew Tutsis were being raped and killed in large numbers. Yet little was done to stop the violence. The UN, as a rule, does not intervene unless genocide is being perpetrated. Though there was no word more appropriate for what was occurring in Rwanda, no concerted attempt at peacekeeping was ever made. Requests by UN commanders on the ground to scale up the peacekeeping were consistently refused, mitigating the ability to intervene.

The total Rwandan death toll ranged between 800,000 and one million. The majority of these individuals were Tutsi, though some Hutus and many Twas were also slain. Countless others were displaced from their homes. Between 250,000 and 500,000 Rwandan women were raped during the genocide, with 70 percent of the surviving sexual-assault victims contracting HIV.

The conflict ended when the Rwandan Patriotic Front seized the capital of Kigali after several months of fighting. Millions of Hutus feared retaliation and fled into neighboring countries; thousands died in unsanitary refugee camps. The RPF established a coalition government that banned ethnic discrimination. Though there have been hiccups in Rwanda's attempt at rebuilding its fragile social order and crippled economy, it has been relatively stable since the genocide.

It is unfair to blame the genocide completely on colonialism, but the social hierarchy created by Germany and Belgium bred hatred and discontent. Arbitrary and inconsistent racial differences were emphasized by colonial administrators. These persisted after decolonization, causing many Hutus and Tutsis to regard each other with disgust. The West created a monster; when the monster reared its head, the West cowered, declaring the situation to be "too risky" to warrant involvement. As aid worker Carl Wilkens noted, "If the people in Rwanda ever needed help, now was the time. And everyone was leaving."

President Bill Clinton stated that inaction in the face of the genocide was his biggest regret, and President George W. Bush declared that such an event would never occur on his watch. Yet genocide has occurred for years in the Darfur region of Sudan while the world has done little. Sudanese president Omar al-Bashir has used oil revenue to sponsor a brutal campaign against "rebels"—defined as those who are not his Arab and Muslim supporters. The Arab Janjaweed, a state-sponsored militia group, has raped and murdered numerous black African farmers. While it is difficult to know how many in total have died during the conflict, estimates suggest the death toll is as high as 450,000. During this time, the West has offered little in response, only sanctions that have been rendered toothless by Sudan's dealings with nations like China.

To avoid a second genocide—and indeed end the one in Sudan—such paltry responses are unacceptable. A tentative peace has been brokered based on a Southern Sudan independence, but questions about who controls mines and oil deposits have resulted in new military action. The situation may yet improve in Sudan with the nation now split, but the ethnic and religious differences, added to the deep resentment caused by the civil war, could still result in a crisis similar to Rwanda's genocide. Such conflicts are becoming all too common with modern weaponry and communications. The next ethnic cleansing might evolve from the crisis in Sudan; it might emerge out of the civil war in Libya or Syria; it might occur in some unexpected region of the world far from Africa. But it will occur, and the West must not hesitate to act when it does. To avoid another humanitarian catastrophe, the Western nations and China must be willing to identify genocide and agree to stop it.

Britain's Take on Genocide: The Mau Mau Rebellion

After World War II, the British Empire was crumbling. The coffers had been drained by war debts, nationalism was mounting in many colonies, and the United States was actively lobbying its former allies to end colonialism. In some regions, Britain simply left—in India, for instance, Britain departed rather swiftly, which had a destabilizing effect. The colony split on religious grounds into two nations, Pakistan and India (and later Pakistan split again, forming Bangladesh). Since then India and Pakistan have fought several wars and continue to dispute their borders, but both nations have thrived by most standards. Many of the British colonies in Africa did not do as well.

In the 1950s in Kenya, tensions between the indigenous population and the white population were at an all-time high. Kenyan society was heavily segregated. More than half of the land was owned by thirty thousand white colonists, while nearly six million native Kenyans survived on the rest. When the colony was forming, white settlers had deprived blacks of land, forcing them onto reservations. Colonists also had forced indigenous people into providing labor for them. This created rifts between the European colonists and the Kikuyu, Kenya's largest ethnic group. The tension manifested in an anticolonial uprising known as the Mau Mau rebellion, led by Jomo Kenyatta.

The Mau Mau rebels frightened the colonists for several reasons. First, the rebels were viewed as barbarians. To join the cause required pledging an oath during a ritualistic ceremony. Colonists became anxious not knowing who had declared allegiance to the Mau Mau. Second, the Mau Mau committed several acts of violence against settlers and black loyalists. The assassinations and the pillaging were harrowing to the colonists. Not well armed but aggressive, the Mau Mau managed to also antagonize a large part of the indigenous Kenyan population, losing the vital local support any guerrilla movement needs. But in the short run they were a real threat to the relatively small white population and anyone working for them.

The British response to the Mau Mau was two-pronged. First, they brought in the British army. The soldiers went into Kenyan forests against a resilient insurgency. There were losses on both sides, and the Mau Mau were prevented from creating permanent bases. Despite not having any financial or military support, the rebels endured for several years. About twenty thousand insurgents faced an equal number of British troops supported by the Royal Air Force. Eventually, without local support or access to supplies or reinforcements, the Mau Mau became crippled.

The second response to the Mau Mau was far more insidious. Captured insurgents as well as countless civilians were rounded up and placed in internment camps. Many of the Mau

Mau rebels were from the Kikuyu tribe. Of the one and a half million Kikuyu in Kenya, most experienced detention at some point. Jomo Kenyatta was given a rigged trial and sent to live in isolation during the early stages of the conflict. This was a grave mistake; Kenyatta was rather levelheaded and had a moderating influence on the Mau Mau's tactics. He had prevented the worst atrocities and discouraged attacks on those Kenyans who worked on the farms and in the factories of the whites. His detention allowed younger, hotheaded minds to take over.

Whether a Mau Mau rebel or a villager caught up in a sweep, for the average detainee, life in the camps was miserable. If accused of affiliation with the Mau Mau, a suspect had to experience a brutal process called "screening." During screening, the suspect would frequently be tortured and humiliated until a confession was extracted. Guilt was less important than the confession. If the suspect remained reticent, he would often be killed. After giving what was frequently a false confession, the suspect was placed in a detention facility. He was subjected to malnutrition, abuse by the guards, and the constant specter of instant death. Guards suffered few consequences for their actions and often killed Kikuyu for sport, hunting them or forcing them to attempt an escape and shooting them down.

This is not to say the rebels were not guilty of some atrocities. They performed some heinous crimes and killed many of their loyalist countrymen in horrific fashions. Yet the British response was systematic in its brutality. Britain eventually granted certain concessions to the Kikuyu when people at home began investigating the British response. Kenyatta was freed and elections were held. Settlers were initially anxious about Kenyatta's release, though he alleviated their fears when he declared that Kenya's citizenry should put the bloodshed of the rebellion behind them and look toward Kenya's future.

In all, the Mau Mau slew about 250 British troops and civilians and about 1,800 black loyalists. By comparison, more than 50,000 Kenyans were killed. The numbers are subject to some controversy due to British attempts at concealing the actual numbers for detention and death. While these statistics are sobering, they fail to capture the suffering experienced by the Kikuyu people.

After the Mau Mau, former insurgents became neighbors of former informants. These informants had benefited greatly by betraying their brethren, receiving lavish salaries and perks. Comparatively, former members of the Mau Mau endured torture and detention. People rarely speak of the Mau Mau today. They live on in memories, but soon those too will be gone. History has been far kinder to the British than it has been to other perpetrators of genocide.

What can we learn from the Mau Mau rebellion? First, we must not forget that genocide is not just for the "uncivilized." It can be remembered by those living today as having been practiced by France in Algeria; Britain in Rhodesia, Kenya, and South Africa; and even the Chinese in Tibet. Not to mention, of course, the Nazis. People abandon their humanity from fear of loss of safety, in religious or political disagreement, due to a leader's or group's paranoia, or sometimes simply because of racism. The reaction to the oppression and white exploitation in Africa is shown in the taking of the white-owned farms in Zimbabwe and an almost reflexive antagonism toward and resentment of America and NATO nations by young men all over Africa. That even enlightened nations can so often and have so recently used such inhumane methods is a sobering lesson, and it's these events that continue to color the response of many African nations to the former colonial powers.

The heritage of antagonism tells the other lesson this history should teach. Today, the United States has experienced sizable criticism for its use of forceful interrogation tactics during the War on Terror. Waterboarding is a procedure that has particularly disturbed the international community. During the Mau Mau rebellion, torture created false confessions, bred resentment, and energized resistance. The imprisonment of whole ethnic groups in Kenya spawned antagonism that remains two generations later. What long-lasting enemies were made by even limited torture and military sweeps recently conducted in Iraq and Afghanistan? The United States or any other modern nation should proceed with caution when using such tactics, as appealing as they may be as short-term solutions; they often produce few benefits while incurring massive costs.

Liberia: Land of the Free, Home of the (Former) Slaves

There is one nation in Africa that began with at least a background and history of democracy. In this Liberia is rather unique. Founded and protected by the United States, it is one of only two African countries that weren't carved up by European powers near the end of the nineteenth century. The once-rich kingdom of Ethiopia is the other country. Ethiopia fought the British in 1868 and defeated the Italians twice, once in 1895 and again in 1935.

The history of Liberia is both exceptional and typical for sub-Saharan African nations. At the start of the nineteenth century, the fledgling abolitionist movement in the United States needed to garner more support. Slavery was a contentious issue, and racism was common even in northern "free" states. To placate those uncomfortable with the thought of freed slaves running rampant throughout the north, a "compromise" position was taken by many: to repatriate freed slaves to Liberia. Many in the United States—including prominent politicians like Henry Clay and James Monroe—believed that it would be difficult to incorporate freed slaves into American society. The fifth president of the United States is the namesake of Liberia's capital, Monrovia, due to his role in its formation.

The Society for the Colonization of Free People of Color in America was founded in 1816 by mostly freed African Americans, Quakers, and evangelical Christians. Its goal was to both assist those African Americans who wished to return to Africa and fight for abolition. Of course, slaves in the southern United States did not have this option. At first the Society assisted those who wished to "return" and hoped to find in Sierra Leone a society in which they would not be second-class citizens.

But life in Sierra Leone did not go as planned for the so-called Americos. Generations of living in the antebellum South had altered the culture of these former slaves. They had different values and goals from the native population of Sierra Leone. The Americos had more in common with the European colonists in other African nations than with their own population. So the Americos established Liberia in 1822, and those who chose to move there became known as Americo-Liberians. Culturally different, many Americo-Liberians viewed the "natives" as savages incapable of understanding democracy. As a minority controlling the government and most of Liberia's wealth, the Americos worked to dominate the nation both politically and economically. Mutual mistrust formed between the two groups, and has lasted through most of the new country's history.

Liberia has always enjoyed the unofficial support of the United States. This has ranged from economic support to outright military intervention complete with the U.S. Marines landing in the country. Liberia modeled its government after America's. Even the political parties modeled themselves after the United States; for instance, the True Whig Party, Liberia's primary political party from 1877 to 1980, was named after the United States' Whig Party. Liberia also enjoyed privileges such as strong economic ties with the United States. Liberia's economy was modernized in large part due to its involvement with the America-owned Firestone Plantations Company, as well as the technical and economic assistance it received from the United States during World War II.

There were hiccups in the relationship; for instance, the United States stopped all assistance to Liberia because of the True Whig Party's support of forced labor in the 1920s. Parts of the Liberian army were involved in controlling de facto slave laborers on a Spanish-controlled island, and this fact became known during a presidential election. However, Liberia appeared to reform itself afterward and relations returned to being cordial.

Though Liberia had been founded quite literally in the name of liberty, democratic problems emerged. Americo-Liberians were often oppressive toward those who didn't share their lineage. Only black American colonists and their descendants were permitted to vote. Foreign trade existed merely to benefit the elite; there were also few laws protecting indigenous Liberians from exorbitant taxation or forced labor. The tension culminated in a successful 1980 rebellion spearheaded by Master Sergeant Samuel Kanyon Doe, who was a member of one of the local tribes, the Krahn. As a native he was restricted from becoming an officer, but he had showed such competence that he was given Special Forces training in the United States. Doe led a group of soldiers representing the various ethnic groups marginalized by the Americo-Liberians. He became the first Liberian head of state not to be a member of the Americo-Liberian elite.

In 1985, elections were held to legitimize Doe's regime. The U.S. administration was happy to view the new government as a democracy. When he was defeated at the hands of Jackson Doe (no relation), Samuel altered the election results and declared victory. When those he had cheated protested, his government repressed its opposition, killing thousands of civilians. Then he quelled a coup led by Thomas Quiwonkpa, a former soldier and ally of Doe's who had split over Doe's abuse of power. The dictator suppressed the revolt and continued to rule, repressing all opposition even more adamantly than the Americo government once had.

The dictatorial atmosphere bred discontent, which resulted in the onset of the first Liberian civil war in 1989. Americo-Liberian warlord Charles Taylor led a bloody insurgency that resulted in Doe's assassination and Taylor's eventual ascension to the presidency. But Charles Taylor was not rebelling to create a democracy; he simply wanted to gain power for himself and his cronies. His government soon proved to be equally dysfunctional. Its autocratic policies led to a resumption of violence when the second Liberian civil war began in 1999.

Finally, the United States had to accept that the nation they had given birth to was moving away from, not toward, democracy in any form. American and Nigerian troops intervened in 2003 to protect the extensive corporate interests in the country and to prevent further war crimes. Meanwhile, a movement called the Women of Liberia Mass Action for Peace staged numerous protests in an attempt to garner concessions from Taylor. Faced with international condemnation, dwindling public support, military challenges, and widespread protests, Taylor attended peace talks and eventually resigned. He was later convicted in the Hague of crimes against humanity. In total, approximately two hundred thousand Liberians perished during the two wars.

Today, Liberia is a mixed-success story. It is led by Ellen Johnson Sirleaf, the first female to be elected head of state in an African country. The country has made efforts to bring justice to those who perpetrated human rights abuses during the civil wars. On the other hand, it is a very corrupt country. It is also extremely poor. While it is intellectually dishonest to attribute all of Liberia's problems to the initial act of American colonization, it is also foolish not to acknowledge the effects of United States action. Tensions between Americo-Liberians and indigenous groups were the driving force behind the coup that precipitated the civil wars. The United States helped create the Americo-Liberian elite.

Whatever good intentions the United States had in the creation of Liberia, there are numerous side effects of that decision that have persisted throughout Liberia's history. The United States should be wary of supporting countries merely because they profess to be democratic or because they have some shared history; after all, Liberia was extremely unequal despite its name. The United States often gets lulled into believing that a nation is improving itself when it offers piecemeal reforms.

The lesson of Liberia is that even an African nation that shares some history with the United States has found that the road to democracy was nearly impossible to navigate and walked it only stumblingly and at a great cost. It cannot be assumed that any government or rebel that mouths the correct words about democracy will be truly democratic. That a nation that for a century has had ties to the world's largest democracy continues to fail in its efforts to create one has to be discouraging.

Africa's Future?

The continent of Africa still faces numerous challenges and has found dealing with many of them difficult or impossible. Most African countries remain riddled with infectious diseases and others suffer from lack of food and rapidly growing populations. Civil war, terrorism, disease, and poverty are the norm for many Africans. War is also occurring in the Ivory Coast, the Democratic Republic of the Congo, Somalia, and elsewhere. With the military might to stop genocide comes a great moral weight. When is outside intervention desirable or even acceptable? What has been the cost of such intervention for those doing it? If America steps in and forces "peace" on warring tribes, how will they view the United States a year or a decade later? It is clear that Western involvement in Africa has been destructive in the past. The irony is that Western inaction has also created problems and continues to do so. Behind it all, the memory of colonial domination and exploitation looms. The situation and potential of Africa make it both dangerous and imperative that something be done. Yet among the myriad of tribal rivalries, dictators, and religious frictions—all in the shadow of colonialism—there seem to be few good choices.

So what does the history of Africa say about its future? It says that change has to occur. History has also shown us that imposed change has not eliminated the basic problems such as tribalism. But it also shows that without some impetus, sub-Saharan Africa is likely to remain a victim. Even nations such as the Democratic Republic of the Congo, with its immense resources, have neither unity nor a consensus to succeed in a way that could be created when the vast national wealth is used in conjunction with peace and cooperation. The more stable and less naturally wealthy Kenya, by contrast, has tripled its citizen's average income in the past two decades.

History shows that the status quo of tribalism, coups, rebellions, and corruption will continue to be a problem. But without an end to these concerns much of southern Africa will continue to suffer. Drastic actions by outside powers have failed. UN observers, such as those in Sudan, have often been unable to mitigate the violence. The richer nations of the world doing the wrong things creates long-lasting enmity, but doing nothing can allow the situation to collapse into total chaos, such as in Congo. So what history says is that the uplifting of many of the nations in southern Africa is going to be a slow, difficult process that has to be inspired from within. Forcing change from the outside has been tried unsuccessfully, so the solution cannot just be imposed. Something inherent in many of the African cultures has held them back. There is a need to get many of the nations of Africa to adopt customs and systems that will allow them to change themselves and their own attitudes enough to win their constant battle against poverty and tribalism. The cultures of Africa can be given the means to enter the modern world with modern values, but the decision to do so has to be made by those people themselves, when they are ready.

CHAPTER FIVE

A Plague on All of Our Houses

Ring a ring o' roses, pocket full of posies, atishoo, atishoo, we all fall down.

—Children's song

R ing a Ring o' Roses" is a folk song many of us are familiar with from our childhood. But the subject matter of the song is something we would rather shield our children from. The song was first printed in 1881, but some think it is derived from children's songs stemming from the 1655 Great Plague of London. Then, people would fill their pockets with pleasant-smelling flowers and herbs to fight off the stench of the disease. Through history, "the plague" has always frightened and killed everyone from pauper to noble. Neither wealth nor status protected anyone. The mere cry of "unclean" in an ancient Roman square would clear it in seconds. Just about everything has been tried when a plague appears; a few efforts even succeeded. Nowadays, antibiotics, antiviral drugs, and vaccines substitute for a pocket full of posies in our disease-fighting arsenal. But with new diseases emerging and global travel occurring at an unprecedented rate, are we creating a situation where the entire human race may soon all fall down?

Why the concern? Some scientists are predicting a pandemic in the near future that could conceivably rival the Black Death during the Middle Ages. The Black Death was a plague that, in four massive outbreaks, wiped out almost thirteen million people across Europe in a single century. Those concerned are not doctors and epidemiologists (scientists who study epidemics) on the fringes of science; the Centers for Disease Control and Prevention in Atlanta has demonstrated its constant concern with this possibility. In spite of huge advances in medicine since that time, the emergence of antibiotic-resistant strains of bacteria, as well as the increase in international travel, may put us at greater risk than ever before of a devastating pandemic.

An epidemic is a rapidly spreading disease that spreads more quickly than is normal or expected. A pandemic is not only an epidemic, but one that spreads widely and often quickly, affecting many nations and populations. In our world, the modernized nations have learned how to deal with most epidemics, but when a disease becomes a pandemic the potential for disaster is greatly magnified.

Plagues such as the Black Death are known as pandemics. These are not uncommon today; almost every year a new flu strain spreads across the world. That makes it a flu pandemic. But what most experts are worried about is not mild illnesses, but the threat of a particularly virulent strain of flu, or some other disease we cannot even predict, sweeping our population.

Most believe that when this cataclysmic "superbug" appears, it could leave tens of millions dead, altering our way of life and dramatically changing the shape of our society's future. Every few years, we are exposed to a new strain of flu that our immune systems are unable to deal with. This single, microscopic super-flu virus has the potential to initiate a cascade of destruction that could impact humanity more than any natural disaster. More than once, plagues have ended empires, lost wars, and irrevocably changed the way people work and live. As history has shown us, the threat is very real and the results have far-reaching consequences. A look at some of the many plagues throughout history can give us insight and guidance that hopefully will help avoid similar tragedies in the future.

Bubonic Plague

When you say "plague," there is a good reason most people think of the bubonic plague. Bubonic plague is a ravaging infection of the lymph nodes caused by a deadly bacteria carried by fleas. The symptoms are horrific: the infected have painful lymph node swellings called buboes (from which the name bubonic, "buboes-causing," is derived), which bleed and ooze pus, and they vomit continuously and cough up blood. They can also suffer from gangrene and necrosis.

Several major bubonic plague epidemics have devastated North Africa, Europe, and Asia. The infections from the Plague of Justinian in the sixth century, the Black Death in the four-teenth century, and the Great Plague of London in the seven-teenth century were all carried along trade routes by rats that stowed away on merchant ships. Hiding on grain ships and wagons, they crossed continents within months, even in the days when a sailing ship or a horse was the fastest way to travel. The number of deaths was staggering. Even today, the cry of "plague" in India, Pakistan, or even in many Balkan and Middle Eastern countries will start a near riot. There is good cause for this fear. The Black Death depopulated entire villages and killed up to half of some nations' populations.

Nor has the danger of this classic disease passed. The bubonic plague is still seen in underdeveloped countries around the world. The last active pandemic ended in Asia as recently as 1959. Another outbreak of the bubonic plague, or some equally deadly disease, in the Americas or Europe is more than just possible. Modern medicine has failed to end the occurrence of the plague, leprosy, and tuberculosis among the teeming populations of India, Indonesia, and the Far East. With air travel becoming more common and affordable, the chance of an infected individual spreading the disease is actually increasing. In recent years a small number of people have been infected with bubonic plague in the western United States. Fortunately, their illness was recognized and the outbreaks were contained. The approach of isolating the infected has been used many times and remains one of the most effective ways to stop the spread of the plague or a deadly flu.

The Plague of Justinian (541–542 CE)

The Byzantine Empire, which more or less comprised the eastern half of the Roman Empire, needed to import much of its grain from Egypt to feed its population. In 541 CE, the bubonic plague was likely brought to Constantinople on a grain ship from Elysium in Egypt in the form of infected fleas riding on the rats in the ship's hold. Rats that had lived off the grain in the Egyptian warehouses simply followed their food onto the ship. (Rats have been a problem on ships throughout history; even modern cruise ships have a metal funnel on the lines when in port to prevent rats from boarding.) Upon arriving in Constantinople, the largest city in Byzantium and the capital of the Byzantine Roman Empire, the rats scurried off the ship and the fleas began biting and infecting those living near the docks. This spread the disease to more rats, whose fleas bit and infected more humans, and so the bubonic plague spread quickly through the city. It eventually devastated most of the empire. Historians of the day did not keep detailed records of the plague's effects on the people, but it was almost beyond conception to someone today. Descriptions exist of bodies being stacked six and ten high and beginning to decay because they couldn't be buried fast enough. Farmers were unwilling to enter the city with their produce, which led to hunger, and a surge of inheritance suits created confusion among the city's administrators. Those who were able to fled the city. Ships sailing from the city carried infected rats to ports all over the Mediterranean, repeating the pattern and spreading the plague.

Byzantine historian Procopius recorded that at its height, the plague was killing ten thousand people each day in the city. Modern historians put the number closer to five thousand, but ultimately the plague killed well over 40 percent of the city's half million inhabitants. In the Plague of Justinian, hundreds of thousands of people died in and around the Byzantine capital. The symptoms of the plague were horrendous and frightening. If someone became ill, the first sign would be a painful swelling of their lymph nodes as the body rallied every effort to fight off the disease and failed. Lymph nodes are most apparent in the neck, armpits, legs, and groin. The buboes would turn dark purple or black and eventually burst. Once the buboes burst open and drained, there was a 90 percent chance of death within hours. The drainage was very malodorous and included rotting flesh and congealed blood. The entire process was extremely painful and left any survivors weak and susceptible to other diseases. While sick, most victims also had a high fever, leading to delirium, disorientation, and muscular pain. The internal bleeding caused by the infection often meant that beyond the buboes there was a good chance of the infected person's lungs filling with blood, which they would then vomit. Many bubonic plague victims literally drowned in their own blood. It is no wonder that even the hint of this plague can generate such fear in the parts of the world it once ravaged.

Most of the attempts made to limit or avoid the Plague of Justinian failed. Medical science did not understand the nature of the plague or that it was rats that carried the infected fleas. Inevitably, some saw the plague as divine retribution. Many turned to prayer and more, hoping to be saved. The most successful effort was an embargo on trade from any city or port known to be infected. This helped keep out the infected rats those ships would inevitably carry. However, it did not keep out those who traveled by land when fleeing the Plague, including some who were already infected. At one point the Emperor Justinian limited all movement in and out of the infected areas of Greece. This was hard on those trapped in the infected areas but helped to at least slow the spread of the plague. Other, less effective efforts included the burning of various chemicals, the use of face masks, intensive prayer, isolating oneself in one's home, and burning the dead bodies. When an infected body was burned, the fleas on it would jump off and begin infecting those nearby.

Several smaller outbreaks of the Plague of Justinian occurred during the next century, often devastating towns and cities. Each evening, carts would move through an infected city, picking up bodies to be dumped in a mass grave. By the year 700, after those subsequent outbreaks of the plague had ended, the death toll for Europe and Asia is estimated to be between twenty-five and one hundred million. As many as one in five died from the plague during these centuries, and everyone in Europe or Asia knew someone or some place that had been lost. So great was the damage and the economic collapse that the Plague of Justinian can be counted as one of the causes of the barbaric era that we now call the Dark Ages.

The Black Death (1347–1351)

The Black Death was one of the deadliest pandemics in human history, responsible for wiping out between 30 percent and 60 percent of Europe's population during the Middle Ages. At the time, it was known as "the Great Mortality," or simply "the Pestilence." There were about two hundred million casualties from the Black Death, worldwide. Numbers for plague victims were always inexact because there was often much chaos and the death toll was so high that few or no records were kept. It was all that a city or town could do to bury the dead. At two hundred million, that higher estimate is more than the entire population of the United States in 1960. The plague began in Asia and spread via merchant ships carrying grain and other foodstuffs from ports on the northern edge of the Black Sea to Europe.

Most of Asia had suffered from the plague before it reached Europe. The first European cases appear to have been recorded at Baikal. By 1347 it may have been first spread along the Mediterranean from the Black Sea to Sicily and Italy by a fleet of Genoese trading ships. It spread all over Europe for fifteen to twenty years, peaking in 1347–1348. It spread quickly and widely between cities. Within a few weeks of the first cases being observed, half or more of the population fell ill, and within eight days, four out of five of those who were ill had died. By the tenth day, 90 percent of those who contracted the infection were dead. Cities were inundated with stacks of rotting corpses, and there weren't enough people left alive who were willing to bury them. As in Constantinople, mass graves became common.

The plague caused massive panic and despondency and forever changed Europe's social, economic, and religious structures. The uncertainty of survival led to an "each man for himself" mentality. Parents abandoned their children, husbands abandoned their wives, and bodies were dumped into the street with no proper burial. Before the Black Death, the population of Europe had exploded and there was a surplus of labor. Just to eat, most families had to accept virtual or real serfdom. There were no real industries, so there was little alternative to working as a servant or on a farm unless you were a craftsman. Since they could be paid in only food and the use of a cottage, the poor remained poor and landless. Then within a few years, half or more of the workers had died. There was suddenly more land than people to farm it. In England, large areas remained uncultivated. Where land had been the basis of wealth and human labor was cheap to obtain, now land was less useful and labor dear. Feudal society was suddenly threatened because the labor force became prized. There was competition for workers, and the former peasant was able to choose where to work and for whom. Soon workers demanded higher wages, and, for a while anyway, the peasant class seemed to disappear, replaced by paid farmers who often became landowners.

Whereas people turned to religion during the time of the Plague of Justinian, many fourteenth-century Europeans eventually looked elsewhere for answers and help during the Black Death. They turned to science and to the universities that were forming all over Europe during that time. In 1340 there were fourteen universities in all of Europe, having been founded over the preceding three centuries. In the next fifty years more than a dozen new universities were founded and the original ones greatly expanded.

Again, through ignorance, most of what was done for protection from the Black Death seems, to our enlightened eyes, useless. Again masks were worn, often even by the medical professionals. Without any understanding of germs or knowledge that fleas carried the plague, even the most advanced scientists were unable to protect themselves. In some areas fear spurred religious fanaticism. Those who saw the plague as divine punishment tried to atone for their and the world's sins. Their efforts would range from prayer to self-flagellation. Groups of flagellants would walk from city to city, whipping themselves until they bled.

There was also a desire to blame the plague on others. Jews, Muslims, and Gypsies found themselves the butt of the fear and frustration. What we would today call conspiracy theories abounded. Tens of thousands were killed and more driven out of the cities. Another creature was blamed for spreading the Black Death as a minion of the devil: the cat. Ironically, since the plague was actually caused by rat-borne fleas, the slaughter of the cats, who would have otherwise decreased the number of rats, actually made things worse.

Flowers, masks, prayer, and pogroms failed to keep anyone healthy. The old methods of embargo and isolation were still the only effective way to slow the spread of the plague. Eventually, the first, fierce outbreak died down, but not before so many deaths caused the economy and social structure of Europe to change. During the next three hundred years ships from Asia or distant, still-plague-ridden corners of Europe would land, sometimes carrying rats with infected fleas. The Black Death would then sweep across one or two of the nations of Europe for a few years. One of the last major outbreaks occurred in Britain.

The Great Plague of London (1665–1666)

In 1658, the first shipments of tea arrived in London to be sold in coffeehouses, and it soon became "the thing" to drink for the nobility. Times were good and fortunes were being made through trade with China. But seven years later, in 1665, the euphoria was destroyed by another import. This has become known as the Great Plague of London. It was a huge outbreak of the bubonic plague all over southern England; in London alone, it killed about a fifth of the half-million population.

At one point, it was killing two thousand people a week in the city. Anyone with enough money or a place to go abandoned London, including the royal family. Quarantine was implemented for all ships going from England to the colonies in North America to keep the plague from spreading. This did nothing for those trapped in the city. Fortunately, the plague was relatively short-lived, ending in less than a year, even as it grew in virulence and the death count rose. What ended the outbreak was the Great Fire of London. The 1666 fire was perhaps the worst cure of the plague that ever happened, but it worked. This is probably the largest example of the traditional method of dealing with a home or village infected with the plague: burning it. On this scale it worked, but when just a home or two burned, it simply caused the rats, and their fleas, to spread.

The Great Plague of Marseille (1720–1722)

In 1720 there was a huge outbreak of the bubonic plague in Marseille, France, killing a hundred thousand people in the city and its surrounding areas. However, it was not a recurrence of the Black Death that devastated Europe in the fourteenth century. At the time of the plague, Marseille was a very important port city, and a ship arrived from Syria with several confirmed cases of the plague on board. The ship had a huge stock of imported goods in its hold, in preparation for trading with the New World and the West Indies.

Although the ship's captain notified the authorities of the infected passengers, city merchants, who wanted to trade the goods, persuaded the government to lift the quarantine. Within a few days an epidemic broke out, the hospitals were bombarded, and frightened people drove the sick from their homes. The heat seemed to spread the infection, with up to a thousand people dying each day. Massive graves were dug, but the gravediggers could not keep up. Bodies were thrown out the windows of homes and left in the streets where they fell. Before long, all the gravediggers had also died and no one was willing to take their place. Soon thousands of corpses were strewn all over the city streets.

The French had learned from past experience that the plague was spread when the residents in an infected area moved out of it. So the French government decided to take an extreme measure to prevent this from happening and in doing so probably saved all of Europe from another outbreak. This was the Act of Parliament of Aix, enacted to forbid any travel, trade, or even the passing of mail between Marseille and the rest of the province. Food was occasionally left just inside the picket lines that isolated the city, but care was taken to make sure that no one delivering it came anywhere near the citizens of Marseille, who later brought it into the city. The French army built a plague wall across the countryside, and if residents attempted to flee the city by climbing the wall, they were shot and killed. Warships blocked the harbor and sank any vessel trying to leave or enter the port of Marseille. The entire plague area was totally sealed off and anyone who managed to get even close to the city was trapped there. No one could go in to help and no one, no matter how important or noble, could get out. Effectively the population of the city was written off in the name of the greater good of France.

Despite all of the precautions, there were eventually outbreaks in Aix-en-Provence, Arles, Apt, and Toulon. These areas were also isolated, and by the end of 1722 there were few cases reported.

By the end of the epidemic more than one hundred thousand French had died. This total included more than forty-five thousand residents of Marseille (approximately half of its population) and fifty thousand people living in the areas outside the city. The one weapon that France had against the plague was to prevent its spread, and the vehement and militant attempt at isolation, though not foolproof, eventually worked. Its lesson was not lost fifty years later and on the other side of Europe.

The Moscow Plague (1771)

In 1770, the Boston Massacre took place in the American colonies, and on the other side of the world Captain James Cook first landed in Botany Bay, Australia. But in Moscow, history was taking a much darker turn. In December, an outbreak of a virus occurred in a military hospital. Twenty-seven patients were infected and only five survived. The hospital's surgeon, Dr. Shafonsky, identified it correctly as bubonic plague. He ordered the hospital locked down and quarantined the patients. But his superior, Dr. Rinder, called the report medically incompetent and said it was designed to cause unnecessary panic. The Moscow authorities, relying on Rinder's opinion, ignored the spread of the plague until the following spring, after it had become a full-blown epidemic within the city. Hundreds of residents died each day, including Dr. Rinder, who died that summer.

In February 1771, another mass outbreak hit a state-owned textile mill on the island across from the Kremlin. Factory managers, trying to hide the outbreak so that their employees would still come to work, buried the dead at night. When the workers learned of the outbreak they panicked, leaving the factory and spreading the germs all over the city. Traders who delivered goods to the city also left. The death count rose, and a severe food shortage quickly followed.

Once authorities accepted the fact that an outbreak was underway, the entire city was quarantined, with everything from shops to churches shut down. Contaminated homes and property were destroyed without compensation, and masses of people were forced into the streets as the city's economy came to an abrupt halt. Russian nobility, the rich, and even the governor and the police chief all fled from Moscow.

Even though three-quarters of the population had already fled the city, the plague was killing about a thousand residents a day by September 1771. There were 20,401 deaths recorded in September alone, but that figure may be much lower than the actual number since many residents either buried their dead at night or threw them into the streets for fear that the authorities would destroy their property.

On the morning of September 17, 1771, nearly one thousand residents gathered to demand that the authorities end the quarantines. The authorities admitted there was nothing more they could do. This resulted in rioting that spread across the desperate city and continued for three days. Finally, Catherine the Great sent Grigory Orlov, who helped run the court and was the father of two of her children, to take over the city. He restored public faith in the state's emergency measures by improving the implementation of the quarantine. Orlov did this by varying the duration of the quarantine for those people who had been exposed to the plague but were still healthy. He also compensated those citizens for their quarantine stay by giving them a small payment from the treasury for their "service." This not only allowed the masses to buy food, but also gave them a sense of having a stake in the city's efforts. Finally, he put skilled laborers back to work and provided food and shelter for those who had none. Eventually, the quarantine worked and the plague was limited to the Moscow area. Like most plagues, this one finally died out because of a combination of isolating and even burning down infected areas and the fact that the weak and vulnerable had simply all died. Grigory Orlov was hailed as the savior of all Russia.

The Moscow Plague had run its course by the summer of 1772. The estimated death toll ranged from fifty-two thousand to one hundred thousand of the three hundred thousand residents. But several positive developments occurred as a result of the plague. For the first time, a serious and scientific look was taken at the causes and spread of plagues. Local research in disease prevention was expanded. Even in religious Russia, plagues were no longer seen as a punishment from God. The idea that the disease had to come from somewhere and be spread somehow was finally accepted.

In this case, it was determined that the first plague appeared in places involving trade with certain areas. A scientific consensus emerged that these epidemics were brought into the country from southern Europe and Central Asia. Genetic research today confirms these conclusions. Consequently, border quarantine checkpoints were vastly expanded and any incidents of plagues in countries that were trading partners were immediately reported and goods from those countries embargoed . . . in much the same way that countries stop buying beef at the first sign of mad cow disease today. Also, authorities banned any burials inside the city limits, pushing new cemeteries outside existing boundaries. In 1798, Russian doctors writing about the plague brought it to the attention of scientists and academics all over western Europe. The first specialized antiplague research facility was established in Saratov, Russia, in 1890.

Bubonic Plague Today

Science has given mankind a better weapon than fire or isolation for fighting the Black Death. The bubonic infection is still a serious problem in some underdeveloped countries, but it can be cured in 85 percent of the cases if treated promptly with antibiotics. New research has suggested that the bubonic infection is now lying dormant. We are not seeing many new cases, but this fits the pattern of history. The plague will retreat and then reappear a hundred or more years later. Modern medicine may be able to help control the plague or prevent its spread, but the threat remains.

Smallpox

Smallpox is a highly infectious disease unique to humans.
Unlike with the bubonic plague, the carrier is other humans,
not fleas. It is caused by one of two types of the variola virus.
The symptoms of smallpox begin with a rising fever and a mild
backache, about two weeks after the victim is infected. A headache follows, and that leads to a feeling of severe fatigue and
exhaustion. As the disease progresses, the weakness increases,
the fever becomes more intense, and the backache turns into
severe pain. Often the victim is nauseous and has diarrhea,
leading to dehydration and weakening him or her further. All
this can happen within a day or two, and then the red spots
appear. They normally show up first on the face, hands, and
forearms, but spread quickly all over the body. Within a few
days these spots turn into small blisters, called pustules. As the
infection worsens, the content of the pustules changes from
clear to white pus. A little longer than a week after appearing,
the pustules will break open and begin to drain. They then scab
over, almost always leaving a deep scar.

Not all of the victims live. Variola major has a mortality rate
of 30–35 percent, while variola minor kills less than 1 percent of
its victims. Variola major is what is normally referred to when
speaking of a smallpox plague. Side effects for survivors can
include blindness, scars on the skin, and infertility in males.
The weak, the elderly, and children are the most susceptible
to smallpox. When the disease was introduced into the Americas in the seventeenth century, often by the Spanish and on
purpose, it encountered an entire population with no immunity or natural resistance. Often whole communities and even
areas were totally depopulated. The death rate among Ameri-

can natives was often double those cited above, at 70 percent. But Europe itself was not exempt. In the eighteenth century alone, smallpox killed tens of millions of Europeans, including five reigning monarchs. Since smallpox spreads via human contact, the disease became even more deadly as the population increased. Most cases appeared in poor and undeveloped nations that were least able to treat the disease. In India, between 1868 and 1907, nearly five million people died from a series of smallpox outbreaks. Even in the 1950s, an estimated one million were infected by smallpox, mostly in Africa and Asia, and almost 15 percent died from the disease.

The Antonine Plague (165–180 CE)

The Antonine Plague was an ancient pandemic, of either smallpox or measles, brought back to the Roman Empire by troops returning from campaigns in the east in 165 CE. It claimed the lives of two ruling emperors: Lucius Verus died of the disease in 169 CE, and Marcus Aurelius Antoninus succumbed to the illness in 180 CE, depriving Rome of its last great leader. It was recorded, in some depth, by Galen of Pergamon, a Greek physician. He described it as an illness involving fever, diarrhea, and an inflamed throat, as well as pustules covering the skin. At its peak, the plague caused up to two thousand deaths a day in Rome, killing a quarter of those infected. The death toll has been estimated at five million. The disease killed as much as one-third of the population in some areas. The plague was also a major factor in the weakening of the entire Roman Empire, as the decimated Roman army began to struggle against the barbarian tribes invading the empire from the east and the north.

Native American Smallpox Epidemic (Sixteenth Century)

Some experts say that the deaths of 90–95 percent of the native population in the Americas were caused by initial contact with Europeans and Africans. Since the ancestors of the Native Americans crossed over the Bering Strait somewhere between thirty thousand and forty thousand years earlier, there had been no real contact between Eurasians and Americans. Diseases that had come and gone in Europe were unknown in North America. This spared the first Americans the plagues discussed above, but also made them vulnerable. When the foreigners brought over their Old World diseases, the natives had no immunity to them at all.

Many European settlers in the Americas hated the Indians. In 1763, during the French and Indian War, Lord Jeffrey Amherst, the British commander at Fort Pitt (now Pittsburgh), discussed giving the Indians smallpox-infected blankets to kill them. The fort was under siege from Chief Pontiac's forces. It is not known whether the plans were carried out, but what is certain is that the Delaware Indians living in that area began to spread the disease soon after those discussions occurred. But there is also a record of smallpox appearing among the garrison. Whether by intent or not, by the late 1800s, smallpox and other diseases such as influenza, which the natives had not been exposed to previously, had killed more than half of all Native Americans in eastern North America and at least 30 percent of those living in the American Northwest.

The ethnographer Charles Hill-Tout interviewed a very elderly Squamish tribesman in the 1890s and recorded this account of one smallpox outbreak on the Fraser River that had been passed on to him.

[A] dreadful misfortune befell them. . . . One salmon season the fish were found to be covered with running sores and blotches, which rendered them unfit for food. But as the people depended very largely upon these salmon for their winter's food supply, they were obliged to catch and cure them as best they could, and store them away for food. They put off eating them till no other food was available, and then began a terrible time of sickness and distress. A dreadful skin disease, loathsome to look upon, broke out upon all alike. None were spared. Men, women, and children sickened, took the disease and died in agony by hundreds, so that when the spring arrived and fresh food was procurable, there was scarcely a person left of all their numbers to get it. Camp after camp, village after village, was left desolate. The remains of which, said the old man, in answer by my queries on this, are found today in the old camp sites or midden-heaps over which the forest has been growing for so many generations.

—From Robert Boyd,
The Coming of the Spirit of Pestilence

How Smallpox Is Handled Today

Until the twentieth century the only defenses that a nation had against smallpox were isolation and the rapid destruction of the corpses. In the twentieth century alone, the disease caused an estimated three hundred to five hundred million deaths worldwide. However, smallpox was the first disease for which a successful vaccine was invented. As far back as 1796, Edward

Jenner was publicizing the vaccine. But since each person had to be individually immunized and the expense was at first significant, it was not in use worldwide until after World War II. Finally, by the 1960s, inoculations became widespread enough that the smallpox outbreaks were easily contained and isolated. The disease appeared less and less frequently and anyone near a case was immediately vaccinated. Because of the aggressive vaccination programs, the World Health Organization certified in 1979 that smallpox was eliminated. The virus that causes smallpox exists today only in a few laboratories. It is humanity's one great victory over plague. Smallpox is the only infectious disease in humans that has been completely eradicated from the planet.

Typhus

Epidemic typhus is caused by the bacteria *Rickettsia prowazekii*. When a victim is infected a dull red rash appears, normally on the chest. This rash darkens as the disease worsens. The next symptoms are coughing, high fever, chills, joint pain, headache, and often low blood pressure, which leads to dizziness. As the disease progresses the symptoms intensify to severe muscle pain, delirium, or even a near-senseless stupor.

Typhus outbreaks are now uncommon in the modern nations, though small outbreaks have occurred in the southern United States. It is more often seen where people spend a long time indoors and are infested with the lice and fleas carried in by squirrels and similar small animals when the weather gets colder. A lack of personal hygiene allows the pests to remain on the victim, ensuring infection. Typhus is often found in crowded urban areas where the lice and fleas are able to move between victims easily. Such was the case 2,500 years ago.

Plague of Athens (430—427 BCE)

It began, by report, first in that part of Ethiopia that lieth upon Egypt, and thence fell down into Egypt and Africa and into the greatest part of the territories of the king.
—THUCYDIDES (460–395 BCE),
HISTORY OF THE PELOPONNESIAN WAR, BOOK 2: 2.48

In the early years of the Peloponnesian War, the Greek city-states Athens and Sparta were battling for dominance. Neither Athens nor anyone else could defeat the Spartan army on land. But Sparta had virtually no navy or naval tradition. When Sparta marched into Athens in 439 BCE they expected an easy victory. The Athenian army expected to lose, too, so they were convinced by their brilliant leader Pericles not to fight back at all. The entire population retreated into the city, where the walls prevented any real attack. The situation soon degenerated into the Athenians using their navy to raid Sparta while the Spartan army sat outside Athens's walls. By the second year of the war, an Athenian victory seemed within reach. With tens of thousands of farmers and laborers withdrawn behind its walls, the city was densely populated.

Athenian merchant ships traded with the Mediterranean basin and suddenly, a deadly and highly contagious disease entered the city through its port community of Piraeus. It likely came from one of the Egyptian harbors, as Egypt was the city's main source of grain. This turned the massively overcrowded city into a plague breeding ground. Originally, scholars thought that it was an outbreak of the bubonic plague in one of its many forms, but a reexamination of the illness and its symptoms has led most scholars to conclude that it was an epidemic of typhus.

The historian Thucydides was in Athens and succumbed to the disease, but survived the plague. This was his account of what it was like:

They were taken first with an extreme ache in their heads, redness and inflammation of the eyes; and then inwardly, their throats and tongues grew presently bloody and their breath noisome and unsavory. Upon this followed a sneezing and hoarseness, and not long after the pain, together with a mighty cough, came down into the breast. And when once it was settled in the stomach, it caused vomit; and with great torment came up all manner of bilious purgation that physicians ever named. Most of them had also the hickyexe which brought with it a strong convulsion, and in some ceased quickly but in others was long before it gave over. Their bodies outwardly to the touch were neither very hot nor pale but reddish, livid, and beflowered with little pimples and whelks, but so burned inwardly as not to endure any but the lightest clothes or linen garment to be upon them nor anything but mere nakedness, but rather most willingly to have cast themselves into the cold water. And many of them that were not looked to, possessed with insatiate thirst, ran unto the wells, and to drink much or little was indifferent, being still from ease and power to sleep as far as ever. As long as the disease was at its height, their bodies wasted not but resisted the torment beyond all ex-

pectation; insomuch as the most of them either died of
their inward burning in nine or seven days whilst they
had yet strength, or, if they escaped that, then the disease falling down into their bellies and causing there
great exulcerations and immoderate looseness, they died
many of them afterwards through weakness. For the disease, which took first the head, began above and came
down and passed through the whole body; and he that
overcame the worst of it was yet marked with the loss of
his extreme parts; for breaking out both at their privy
members and at their fingers and toes, many with the
loss of these escaped; there were also some that lost their
eyes. And many that presently upon their recovery were
taken with such an oblivion of all things whatsoever, as
they neither knew themselves nor their acquaintance.

—*HISTORY OF THE PELOPONNESIAN WAR*, BOOK 2: 2.49

The illness spread quickly. By the time the plague had run
its first course, more than half of those packed into the city
had been sick and one in three Athenians were dead. It also
killed a quarter of the Athenian troops, including their cel-
ebrated leader Pericles. Many who survived were too weak
to work, fight, or row. But with its army camped just outside
Athens, it was not long before Sparta, and much of the eastern
Mediterranean, was also hit by the disease. The war effort on
both sides stalled, and what had appeared to be certain victory
for Sparta became a stalemate that would not end for more
than two decades.

The Athenian typhus plague was less dealt with than endured. Trapped in their city, there was little the population of
Athens could do. The plague returned twice more, in 429 BCE
and in the winter of 427–426 BCE.

Typhus Today

In the 1930s a vaccine was discovered to prevent typhus. With prompt antibiotic treatment and fluid replacement, the patient will likely recover completely. Typhus often appears in situations such as after the Haitian earthquake in 2006, where people become crowded into refugee camps and sanitation facilities are destroyed. If left untreated, 10–60 percent of those infected will die. Today, typhus still kills about 1,400 people per year, worldwide.

Influenza

Influenza, commonly called the flu, is caused by a virus that also affects birds and small mammals. In less virulent strains of influenza, symptoms are limited to sore throat, muscle pain and headaches, fever and coughing. Most flu infections are not life threatening for those who are healthy. For susceptible groups, like the elderly and those with compromised immune systems, the flu can often lead to dehydration or pneumonia and death. Occasionally a strain of flu mutates into something that is much more deadly.

During the twentieth century, tens of millions of people died from four major influenza pandemics: the Spanish flu of 1918, the Asian flu of 1957, the Hong Kong flu of 1968, and the Russian flu of 1977. A new strain of virus was the cause of each outbreak. Generally, new influenza strains do not mutate in infected humans. Typically, a new virus emerges in humans when an existing virus, seen only in animals, mutates so that it is able to spread to humans. The danger of flu spreading has increased greatly with air travel. An infected person can travel across the world before he or she has any symptoms.

The Spanish Flu Pandemic (1918–1920)

During the climax of World War I, a shockingly virulent strain of Influenza A swept the world, spreading quickly to regions as far apart as Asia, Australia, North America, Europe, the Pacific islands, and even the Arctic. Nearly one-third of the world's population contracted the virus. This flu has been described as "the greatest medical holocaust in history," and this strain of "just" the flu may have killed more people than the bubonic plague ever did.

This was flu like none other. Whereas most flu epidemics affect weaker populations, such as infants or the elderly, this one involved a mutation that allowed the virus to overtake the immune system and turn it against the victim's body. This resulted in a much higher mortality rate among the otherwise young and healthy, whose immune systems were stronger. It was not just the elderly or children falling ill; half of those who died were the healthiest and the strongest. This meant that families lost their breadwinners and factories lost their workers. So the Spanish flu not only was one of the most widespread epidemics in history, but also took a truly devastating toll on economic productivity.

As many as half of those who caught the Spanish flu died within a few days; the rest died from complications and secondary infections caused by their weakened immune system. Fear dominated, and no one wanted to go anywhere they might be infected. This meant anywhere they might come into contact with anyone beyond their own family. Everyday life stopped, schools and shops closed, and even gravediggers were too sick to bury the dead. In some cases, mass graves were dug using steam shovels, and hundreds of bodies at a time were buried without coffins.

The pandemic spread all over the world and affected almost every nation. At the time, most of the world was just recovering from World War I. The war had claimed eighteen million lives, but the influenza that swept the globe during that time claimed the lives of between fifty and one hundred million. The influenza epidemic of 1918, which gets little mention in U.S. history books, caused more deaths than all the combat deaths from all the wars in the twentieth century. Everyone knew someone who died and dozens who were ill. Well over half a million Americans died within just a few months.

Influenza is spread by a virus gotten from those already infected or from objects the infected have touched. Throughout history, the treatment for influenza pandemics has been to avoid the infected. This is rarely possible for any extended period in the modern world. Modern epidemics have changed in that, while many are infected, few die, and antibiotics prevent the deadly secondary infections that follow the weakening caused by the disease. But for those who are already ill or have a compromised immune system, the almost annual local outbreaks of some form of influenza can prove deadly. What officials fear is another mutation that creates a flu as deadly as the Spanish flu, which modern transportation could spread worldwide within days. For a few months there was a fear that the "bird flu" might be the next such epidemic, but it was not. It remains the case that society has found a way to survive, but not prevent, flu pandemics.

Influenza Today

There is a reason that even in the United States the Centers for Disease Control and Prevention advertises heavily to encourage flu shots. Even today there is no cure for the influenza virus. It spreads in seasonal epidemics, resulting in 250,000 to 500,000 deaths worldwide, every year. It has the potential to kill millions of the weak and elderly during severe outbreaks, such as the four pandemics mentioned earlier. The importance of good hygiene, such as hand washing, is now recognized as vital in preventing the spread of influenza.

Every year, vaccines are created to prevent the most-likely strains the public will be exposed to during the upcoming flu season. However, these vaccines do not protect people from any new viral strains that can emerge right before or during flu season. Each type of flu creates its own immunity, and often being immune to one has no benefit when exposed to another strain. Because there are so many influenza viruses and it is necessary to first develop then mass-produce any "wide spectrum" vaccine, it takes at least six months to create a vaccine for a new strain. Since new strains of influenza can develop rapidly, the immunity received from a prior year's vaccine or illness will not necessarily protect anyone from the following year's variety. This makes everyone vulnerable every year.

This is why people are remonstrated to get a new flu shot every fall. It also means that since it is prepared beginning six months in advance, the annual flu vaccine is just based upon the best guess of which influenza strains will prove the most dangerous and widespread. This is why those concerned with influenza at the Centers for Disease Control and Prevention and elsewhere are on alert, constantly monitoring the new strains. Sometimes even they guess wrong.

Tamiflu and Relenza are antiviral drugs that can reduce the severity of flu symptoms and help prevent its transmission. These drugs do not actually kill the virus as antibiotics kill germs, but instead prevent it from multiplying. Ideally, those antivirals are administered as soon as the onset of flu symptoms occurs. If given too late, medical science's best tool against influenza can be ineffective.

The lesson history gives us is that new strains of influenza appear every year. Modern medicine can moderate the effects, but nothing will stop the new mutations or their spread to humans. This is inevitable and occasionally a new influenza can—indeed, history shows that it *will*—be very deadly.

Ebola Virus

In recent years a new disease has appeared that, because of its virulence and near 100 percent mortality rate, is giving health authorities nightmares. Ebola is a ravaging virus that causes a disease called viral hemorrhagic fever. Those infected have damage to the cells that line their blood vessels, making it difficult for their blood to coagulate. Victims usually bleed to death, often internally and most painfully. The virus was first discovered in humans in 1976 in the Ebola River Valley in the Congo. Ebola hemorrhagic fever has been reported in humans only in Africa, typically in remote areas. This is because the animal source for the virus appears to live in jungles and forests. Bats, monkey, spiders, and some insects are suspected, but the carrier has yet to be found. New strains of the Ebola virus occur regularly. Very few humans have any immunity to the virus.

Ebola has the highest mortality rate of any human pathogen, causing death in 90 percent of those infected. For this reason, there is concern among security experts that it could be used in a bioterror attack. If it mutates to being spread by human contact or in the air, it will not need any human assistance in killing millions.

What Would a Modern Plague Look Like?

There really is no doubt that there will be another widespread plague in the future. It may be a mutation that appears in modern hospitals or something emerging from some dark corner of the Third World. But with modern transportation, the historical first option, isolation, will have dubious success. With cross-country travel by jet being commonplace, and international travel almost as common, any new diseases will be difficult to isolate. The potential for quick, widespread transmission of a deadly new virus is fairly high. Despite two decades of drastic efforts, overwhelming reactions like stopping the purchase of beef from entire countries, and huge economic incentives, mad cow disease reappears regularly. It has even recently been found in cattle in California and France. By the time a nation's health authorities are aware of a dangerous new plague it is likely to be already in their country. The question is: What form will the plague take and how well can we control the symptoms and mortality?

A majority of health experts also agree that another pandemic of influenza is inevitable. Typical influenza pandemics had mortality rates ranging from 0.1 percent to 2.5 percent. The devastating Spanish flu of 1918, which killed 3–6 percent of the world population, had a mortality rate of around 10–20 percent, with an infection rate of 28–50 percent. The scenario might play out something like this: A new strain of flu could emerge with the high mortality rate of the avian flu (bird flu) combined with the ease of transmission of the relatively recent swine flu. Avian flu has a 60–75 percent mortality rate. Swine flu is easily transmitted by an airborne virus between individuals in the same room. That combination could re-create the millions of fatalities of the Spanish flu, despite modern medicine.

So a new strain of pandemic flu, with characteristics of both avian and swine flu, has the potential to overwhelm both preventive and curative efforts and wipe out a measurable part of the world's population. If some highly virulent and dangerous new flu mutation spread as quickly as the Spanish flu, it could infect half the world's population within weeks. If there was a 60 percent mortality rate, then this superflu would have the potential to kill 30 percent of the population. That would be more than two billion dead. This would be as world changing and destructive as the Black Death ever was in Europe.

What Measures Can Be Taken Now to Prevent a Pandemic in the Future?

Old-fashioned quarantines, like the ones placed on ships coming to America from England during the Great Plague of London, may no longer be possible with our increasingly global society. Nor is isolation a viable choice for more than a small village or a single case. The modern age has introduced new problems that make the historical solutions difficult to repeat successfully. But it has also created some new ways to monitor and control the spread of a disease.

Although there are measures available to prevent pandemics or better control them, these can be costly and intrusive. For example, thermal imaging at airports can detect elevated body temperatures in humans. Of course you would also then be stopped if you were late and had run for the gate. If another pandemic occurs, these machines could be used in airports across the world to keep infected people from traveling. But because of cost concerns and travel logistics, there is no mechanism in place for the universal usage of these machines.

The first modern medical technique that really made a difference was vaccinations. These have helped control some diseases and limited the damage done by others. Only one classic plague, smallpox, has been completely eradicated, but many, such as mumps and measles—diseases every child was expected to catch at one point in history—have become so uncommon that a few hundred cases occurring in a state is newsworthy. Recent history has also shown that this very success has become a problem. Parents, for a range of reasons, including some bad science, can be led to believe that inoculations are no longer necessary. But almost inevitably, when even a few percent of the children are not immunized, these illnesses reappear.

During the twentieth century, the creation of antibiotics drastically lowered the threat of several infectious diseases. This success has also led to their overuse. Excessive use and misuse of these potentially lifesaving antibiotics has caused some people to develop a resistance to them. And because one of the side effects of antibiotics in animals is faster weight gain, this has encouraged overuse in cattle and other food sources. Because of these choices, many diseases themselves have developed a resistance to treatments with certain antibiotics. Throughout history, the plague would revisit every century or two when a new strain was able to bypass the old immunities. Today, we are artificially speeding up this process, allowing new strains that are antibiotic resistant to appear in decades or even years. These superbugs are treated by new drugs, and some are already mutating to become unaffected by them. One of the most deadly is the MRSA virus (methicillin-resistant *Staphylococcus aureus*), for which medicine does not have an effective treatment. At one time, hospitals could control staph infections with antibiotics, but now they are helpless when this deadly form appears. If this trend of antibiotic overuse continues, there could well be a resurgence of infections most people think of as being controlled very effectively by antibiotics.

Some governments in Europe have begun to demand that their food sources come from animals that have not consumed antibiotics. The United States currently has no such policy in place. Farm lobbyists have spent millions defeating such laws, saying it would be too costly to prohibit farmers from treating animals with antibiotics. If this increases the chance you or your children will die from a disease that was previously easy to control, can we afford not to?

Controlling Pandemics versus Prevention

The way organizations approach disease control globally is a bit like what cardiologists were doing in the 1950s, which is pretty much wait for the heart attack and then do your best to treat it. The reality is, just as with cardiology, there is a whole range of ways we can try to prevent pandemics.

—Nathan Wolfe, epidemiologist, NIH Director's Pioneer Award winner, and member of *Popular Science*'s "Brilliant 10" for 2005, as interviewed in *National Geographic Traveler*

After tracing the history of infectious diseases through the centuries, scientists have concluded that most viruses have emerged in humans after interactions with animals. It has also been discovered that most of the microbes that have caused pandemics over the ages originated in animals from specific regions around the world. These places are known as viral hot spots. They vary over time, but include many locations in Africa, Asia, and the American West. Ebola appeared in the Congo, bird flu in Vietnam, and other flus that can transfer to humans have arisen in hot spots all around the world.

Based on historical studies of infectious diseases and their own "pilot study" in Cameroon, Nathan Wolfe and his colleagues Claire Panosian Dunavan and Jared Diamond propose an idea that warrants serious consideration and could help us predict and perhaps even prevent pandemics in the future. Their theory is that scientists could discover lethal microbes right before they make that cross-species jump. By examining potentially mutating viruses in the infected animals, medicine may be able to prevent their spread to humans. Wolfe and his colleagues propose creating a worldwide "early warning system" for contagious diseases. This early warning system would require periodic testing of groups of people who come into regular contact with wild animals, such as hunters and zookeepers living in viral hot spots.

By collecting specimens from both hunters and their prey, for example, these researchers have discovered previously unknown viruses that have made the cross-species jump from animals to humans. In fact, during their study, one of their subjects contracted a gorilla retrovirus that had never been seen in humans before. A retrovirus is one whose genes are encoded in the virus's RNA instead of DNA. These viruses need to combine with a normal cell before replicating themselves and spreading the infection. The process is different, the effect often the same.

These human-animal interactions have also shaped history. A notable example, as mentioned earlier, is why Native Americans were much more vulnerable to European settlers' diseases. The settlers had exposure to their own infected domesticated animals prior to traveling to the Americas and had long before developed immunities. The Native Americans had no previous encounters with those types of animals.

By monitoring people with regular animal contact in viral hot spots, scientists can discover the exact moment when the viruses enter the human population. This critical information could help predict, and maybe even prevent, future pandemics. But the cost is high, though history shows it would be a much lower price than another worldwide plague.

The recent swine flu pandemic seemed to come out of nowhere. But in fact, it was mutated from an existing virus. It took just a few days to spread far enough to make containment impossible. If a monitoring system, like the one proposed, had been in place at farms in Mexico, where this outbreak emerged, they might have been able to identify the point where it crossed over to humans. This would have resulted in a much quicker response. Thankfully, this time the flu virus did not cause widespread fatalities, although it did cause widespread panic.

NASA Technology

NASA's Applied Sciences Program currently uses satellite remote sensing technology to monitor the Earth's environment. With the data retrieved from a special series of fourteen satellites, scientists can now better predict and prevent infectious disease outbreaks across the globe. Climate, precipitation, and vegetation changes in the Earth's environment will often determine whether or not an infectious disease can thrive and spread. Even the movement of refugees from infected areas can be followed, showing where to deploy the medical response teams. By combining that information with potential hot spots, scientists can use this remote sensing technology to predict an outbreak of some of today's most common infectious diseases, such as typhus and the deadly Ebola virus.

Using satellite images, a scientist today can measure the amount of rainfall, how wet the soil is, the temperature of the ground, how fast vegetation is growing, and even the migration of large herds of animals or flocks of birds. They can also observe and estimate the growth of villages, camps, or cities and changes in the population density. Even the number of fresh graves in a suspected area can be monitored. Information obtained daily from the satellites is sent to the Centers for Disease Control and Prevention and the Department of Defense. Experts compare what they find to past outbreaks. These agencies then use this data to predict and track outbreaks of infectious diseases and make public-health policy decisions based partially on that information.

The remote sensing technology can also be used to identify and track plague-carrying vectors, like insects and rodents. Scientists can analyze the precipitation, vegetation, and slope of an area to predict whether the food supply used by these animal vectors is available or capable of attracting or sustaining larger numbers of infected creatures. This helps them to determine the threat to the human population, and based on this information, they can institute preventive measures to control the plague-carrying population.

The highly infectious disease malaria is one of those targeted by NASA. There are more than three hundred million people already infected, and they are only a small part of the 40 percent of the world's population at risk from this mosquito-carried disease. NASA technology is currently being used by researchers and government agencies in Thailand and Indonesia under the Malaria Modeling and Surveillance Project. This allows a targeted response, instead of a widespread one covering hundreds of miles with pesticides in the hopes of including the viral hot spots. The satellite surveillance now gives public health organizations an earlier warning of an outbreak. And since malaria is carried by mosquitoes, the same information also helps prepare and utilize fewer pesticides more effectively. This in turn leads to less damage to the environment and the appearance of fewer drug-resistant strains of the disease. The monitoring of the environment by these satellites is also critical now that global warming has caused such drastic changes in habitats and diseases like malaria are commonly seen in previously low-risk locations.

NASA's remote sensing technology has been a huge weapon in the fight to both control and prevent pandemics of new and existing diseases, even in places where these diseases had never been seen before. It remains to be seen how the recent drastic cutbacks in the NASA budget will affect the agency's ability to help prevent the next deadly pandemic.

History's Lessons

Perhaps because the threat is so general and even leaders are at risk, we seem to have learned many lessons from history about preventing or stopping epidemics. The days of ignoring or hiding an initial outbreak of a virus or infection, as happened with the Moscow Plague, are long gone. Today, information is shared across continents, and monitoring can be done on a worldwide scale. Even otherwise antagonistic governments normally see their own self-interest in cooperating.

This is particularly important in our increasingly global society. Advances in medicine and disease prevention may have lessened the likelihood of a pandemic that could threaten the very existence of humanity. But these medical and technological advances may not be enough to offset the risk posed by modern travel. With increasingly larger segments of the population traveling both locally and globally, the likelihood of quick, widespread transmission of a new and deadly infection is higher than at any other point in history. Humanity may survive—it always has—but millions or even billions could perish.

Men can use disease as a weapon. The Spanish settlers in North America may have given out smallpox-infected blankets. The Russians used to have literally tons of weaponized anthrax, and maybe still do. Weapons technology and easy global travel have made us more vulnerable than ever to bioterrorism as well. History has shown that even rudimentary attacks of bioterrorism can be effective, such as with the suspected distribution of smallpox-infested blankets to the Native Americans. Bioweapons are much easier and cheaper to develop than a nuclear bomb. When Saddam Hussein shot Scud rockets at Israel, there was a real concern that they contained bioweapons. They did not, but in the future this is a real possibility.

There are many things that have worked in the past to contain or stop the spread of a pandemic and numerous examples from history of mistakes that have also exacerbated the problem. Currently, we focus most of our resources on identifying a pandemic early and trying to contain it. This "solution" may not be sufficient in this modern world of global travel if a new strain of disease emerges that is easily transmissible and has a high mortality rate. Governments are reluctant to pour money into scientific research and the development of disease prevention or the monitoring of humans exposed to animals in viral hot spots. Yet these are the actions that could eventually lead to preventing pandemics from ever occurring to begin with. Smallpox is an example; humanity can win the battle against the plague.

CHAPTER SIX

How You Say It

What we have learned is that people who speak different languages do indeed think differently and that even flukes of grammar can profoundly affect how we see the world.
— LERA BORODITSKY (1976–),
*HOW DOES OUR LANGUAGE SHAPE
THE WAY WE THINK?*

In What Language

A debate is raging across the United States as to what language or languages should be used in official functions and education. The rapid increase in the Hispanic population (now 18 percent of the U.S. population), along with a tendency for ethnic isolation in communities of immigrants from Islamic countries, has led to efforts by individual states to designate English an "official" language. They have even forbidden the use of languages other than English in schools. All through history, language has been used both as a way for the elite to set themselves above the masses and as a means of acculturating new members of a society. In twelfth-century England the nobles spoke Norman and the peasants Saxon. The educated spoke and wrote in Latin. The question is this: Does history show if such efforts have succeeded, and if so, will these efforts to require English force quick adaption of the younger non–English speakers into American or European culture?

When Rome conquered another nation, it did not attack the local language or customs. This added to the stability of an empire that lasted hundreds of years. But it did require that all the official business and notices be done in Latin. This effectively made it advantageous for anyone who wanted to be anything or anyone important to learn Latin. As a result, the Latin language became the lingua franca (also a Latin phrase) for the Western world. It was, by the second century CE, the common language of the Mediterranean world. Even when the empire collapsed, the Roman Catholic Church, true to its name, retained the Roman language as its official language, both for written use and in ceremonies. This provided in a fragmenting Europe a common tongue for all churchmen, and later for scientists and statesmen as well.

What Difference Does Language Make?

There are built-in attitudes and cultural assumptions in any language. The language people use and think with does affect both how they view the world and what their thoughts are. If there is no word for something, then it is unlikely a thought about it will occur. This is based on what is called cognitive psychological theory. (All psychology is theoretical; we still don't have a detailed and working model of how the human mind works.) Perhaps the easiest way to explain this is that if a culture had no word at all for "lies," then telling the truth would be the norm. Most people would not understand the concept of lying because there would be no way to think about it.

If your culture is surrounded by and interacts constantly with snow, as the Inuit are, you would have many words for the different types of snow. This is because any language both reflects and facilitates the speaker's environment. There is likely no commonly used word in Inuit for palm tree, so when you say "tree" to an Inuit speaker it is safe to assume that palm is not the type of tree he or she will picture.

The Tuareg of North Africa have many terms for different types of dry terrain that range from loose sand to boulder fields. A New Yorker would simply lump them all together as being a "desert." But that same New Yorker has as many words for elements of his environment—specialty stores, delis, roads—as the Tuareg's language (actually a group of related dialects) contains for parts of their deserts. If you are raising a Tuareg child in New York City, then to have them think in a traditional Tuareg manner, they would have to learn to think in their Tuareg tongue first, or perhaps only. That might be somewhat inconvenient since there are a lot of things in New York City that there is no Tuareg word for. If the Tuareg children think first in English, then they will begin to have the same thought/word patterns that other New Yorkers have. This would include many thoughts that there are simply no Tuareg words to express. This is why some ethnic groups prefer to isolate themselves in closed neighborhoods where only their native language is spoken. Because they want to overcome this isolation and encourage integration, some educators dislike multilingual education. Since, like speaking Latin in the provinces of Rome, there are real advantages to speaking English when living in America and severe disadvantages if you can't speak English, English can be very difficult to discourage. Simply said, language is one way that a nation absorbs immigrants. Its use eases them into adopting the culture's way of thinking and attitudes by providing the framework needed to think and speak as part of it. Learning and using the group's language allows ethnically diverse newcomers, or at least their children, to move easily into a society.

Can Language Be Repressed?

Is it possible to completely change the language used in a nation? It appears the answer may be "yes," with a big "but." The dark corollary to this question is that accomplishing this requires a level of repression that would be abhorrent to a Western government today. In fact, the heavy-handed and often violent way this was once done in such nations as Ireland, where Gaelic was all but obliterated, still causes emotional resistance all over the world to "official language" laws in general.

At the time of the Norman invasion in 1171, Gaelic was spoken in all of Ireland except the area adjacent to Dublin, known as the Pale, where English was already used. By the time of Thomas Cromwell, during the 1530s, England had begun to actively suppress both Irish culture and language. Use of Gaelic was forbidden. Just owning anything written in Gaelic was illegal. The Potato Famine of 1845, and the subsequent breakdown it caused to Irish society and culture, also contributed to the collapse of Gaelic. By 1871, the repressive language laws were eased, not because of tolerance, but because Gaelic was no longer the common language of the isle and the laws were deemed unnecessary.

While today in Ireland you can again find those who speak Gaelic, English is the language used for virtually every function. In schools Gaelic is now often taught as a second language and is popular all over Ireland. Patriotism and interest in Irish culture have caused this modern resurgence of Gaelic speakers, surprisingly in greater numbers among the younger age groups. Fifty years ago only a few thousand Irish were fluent in Gaelic and there was a concern about the language dying out entirely. Now more than one hundred thousand Irish use Gaelic, mostly in the western Gaeltacht counties of Cork, Donegal, Galway, Kerry, and Mayo.

Even more amazing is the number of Irish who can again at least speak the language. According to the census figures from 2002, released by Ireland's Central Statistics Office, there were 1,570,894 Gaelic speakers in the country as opposed to 2,180,101 non–Gaelic speakers.

So the simple answer to the original question then is that if you ruthlessly repress a language as part of your destruction of a culture, and do so long enough, you can at least almost succeed. Since the nineteenth century, virtually all Irish business and governmental duties have been done in English. The British did succeed in effectively replacing Gaelic with English as the language used in commerce. Even those who spoke Gaelic felt compelled to learn some English as well. James Joyce wrote in English. Still, even after four centuries of repression, the English were not able to fully eliminate Gaelic.

Why English?

English is used worldwide. It is the language of science, air traffic control, and diplomacy. Schoolchildren from Japan to Egypt are taught English in their early grades. A language dominates because it is useful. This may be a political reason, as was the case of Latin, or it may be just because it fills people's needs best. One of the many reasons for the far-flung use of the English language is its adaptability. You can describe a very wide range of environments and concepts in English. English now contains about twice as many words as any other European language. The language is also well suited for science and technical discussions and has become the accepted language used for the publication of all scientific papers. If you need to think about the degeneration rate of certain quantum particles, you need to think about it in a language that has a word for quantum particle. If you need to be concerned with currents and fish, then a Micronesian language would serve you better. But if you want to set up a GPS for your boat, hope the instructions are in English.

Because American English is a conglomerate language, based on Anglo-Saxon but filled with terms and concepts from many other languages, it is arguably the most adaptable and flexible language on the planet. Its popularity is not only because of the combined influence of the United States and Britain, but also because it works. The joke that linguists tell about American English is that it waits in the dark and mugs other languages to get their best words. Today, it is also busy mugging the jargon of technology all over the world, as well as stealing from the more traditional languages.

This is not the first time this pattern has occurred. The commerce and government of the Roman Republic were done in

Latin. But science and literature all over the Roman Empire appeared in Greek. Most literate Romans felt they had to speak Greek, just as most literate Europeans now also speak English. During the eighteenth and nineteenth centuries, the language of science and diplomacy was French. The upper classes and educated of Europe and the Americas learned French as a necessity. Today, the French may occasionally resent it, but they, too, often learn English.

Perhaps the best current example of a common language being vital to a nation even when its people speak many languages is India. There are more than two dozen distinct and separate languages spoken on the Indian subcontinent. But for two centuries of British domination, English had been the language used for commerce and government. Despite English being a reminder of their colonial state, the newly free nation found it was not able to eliminate the use of the former occupier's language. Because the Indians speak in more than two dozen languages and hundreds of dialects, they had to have a common tongue, and English was what most of those making the decisions already spoke. Even today, the two recognized languages used for the Indian national government and business are Hindi and English. Both are widespread enough that they are jointly the "official" language of that giant nation's government and courts. There was an attempt in the 1950s to phase out English, calling it a remnant of the colonial masters, but this never gained momentum. With only about 40 percent of all Indians speaking Hindi, and the large number of other languages spoken locally, there simply was no alternative.

India's Official Languages Act of 1963 and subsequent laws have continued to include English. Even a language imposed from the outside by colonial powers has proved impossible to repress because it serves a purpose and does it best. The British colonial government forced English on those they dealt with.

The use of English as a common tongue has since proved a necessity. It appears that if a language becomes established in a nation, it is very hard to eradicate it. It's so hard, in fact, that even in 1947, during their first flush of national pride, the newly independent people of India could not do without English.

What does this say about the language questions being asked in America and Europe? If a small part of the nation is speaking a foreign language only within their community, this is likely not something that will continue for generations. Eventually, because a language is used to communicate, the one that communicates best in that environment will prevail. So Farsi in Sweden, barring a lot more immigration, will not be a permanent addition to the languages spoken by Swedes when viewed over generations. On the other hand, a very large number of people speak Spanish in the United States and there is, because of the proximity to other Spanish-speaking nations and the interaction of individuals between them, a real benefit in speaking Spanish. It is unlikely that Spanish would prevail over the more widely used and useful English, but Spanish is likely to contribute much to American English in the coming centuries. And judging from historical cases, it is not going to disappear even if immigration slows drastically. Like English and Gaelic in Ireland, or English and Zulu in South Africa, or even Latin and Greek in Ancient Rome, a second language that serves a purpose is likely to be around for a very long time no matter what "official language" laws are passed.

Keeping a Language Alive

There is no question that a language can be retained when it is not the main language of a nation. This is shown not only by the diversity of languages in nations such as India and the former Soviet Union, where Russian competed with local tongues, or the retention of both Pashto and Dari in Afghanistan. But there is an even more striking example that is so accepted most people do not realize the novelty of it. Even when the Jewish people had no nation and no land of their own where their language was spoken since the rise of Islam, Hebrew survived. In fact, not only did it survive (and evolve), but a rich literature was produced in the nearly two thousand years there was no separate Israeli nation.

There are many reasons for this. One reason was the often forced segregation of Jews in Europe. Not only could Hebrew be spoken daily, but it allowed them to converse without the other locals understanding. When there are thousands who already speak Hebrew, and the native population avoids most contact, the language of the ghetto will continue. Another cause was the combination of both cultural and religious importance given Hebrew by the Jewish people. Certainly there was no question that a constant and conscious effort was made to retain Hebrew and keep it alive.

This is not to say that Hebrew was not affected by the languages and lifestyles around it. Yiddish is a good example of such an intermingling. Yiddish evolved beginning in Germany around 900 CE. It was primarily a spoken language used by the Jews of Europe. Its speakers already had both Hebrew and German to write with. There was no written use of Yiddish among the German Jews except for in literature. Still, at the language's peak in the early 1900s, eleven million Jews spoke Yiddish. Most of them also studied, read, and spoke Hebrew. Today, Yiddish is rarely spoken; most of its speakers were lost to the Holocaust. But Hebrew did not have the same fate and has been retained even after the losses and exiles. All Jews are still culturally encouraged and religiously required to learn at least some of the language. What this shows is that even with a geographically divided population, a group, if they retain a strong cultural identity, can keep a language alive and active, be it Hebrew, Gaelic, or Romany. For the first time since the Romans drove the Jews from Judea in the first century CE, Hebrew is again (since 1947) the national language of a nation, Israel.

A Problem That Solves Itself

Historically, major languages have amazing resiliency and power. Perhaps the greatest conclusion we can draw from history is that languages evolve or are retained to fit the situation. This is despite the efforts of governments and politicians. If a group has a good reason to keep a native tongue, it can and will. Even the most stringent efforts to eliminate Gaelic were not effective. If there is a good reason or need to speak a common language, that language will become or remain widespread, as English has in India and effectively worldwide. If there is a need for Spanish in the United States, then it will continue to be widely spoken and will spread as a second language, as Greek was used among the Romans. If just English is better suited for everyone in the United States to speak, then laws to force this are not needed, just patience. It will happen with or without laws.

There is a lot of noise and debate about forcing the use of only one national language. The record for artificial manipulation of language use is unpersuasive. The United States and its states can pass all the language laws they want, but the most any of those language laws may do is accelerate the rate at which immigrants living in America learn English. In the span of history, we see that languages really are a tool we communicate with and that they can, in return, mold those who speak them. People will find the most efficient way to talk to each other no matter what laws temporarily constrain them. The purpose of any language is to communicate, and eventually the language or languages that communicate best dominate. Nor will a language that serves a purpose disappear. A culturally based language can be retained even under great pressure, and a useful language will spread despite resistance, à la Big Mac.

CHAPTER SEVEN

Speculation and Crashes

For greed all nature is too little.
— LUCIUS ANNAEUS SENECA (4 BCE–65 CE),
ROMAN STATESMAN

It rather goes without saying that massive economic collapses do widespread and lasting damage to a nation and its families. In the last twenty-five years the United States has suffered from three such incidents. These have profoundly affected the wealth and attitudes of the average American. Surveys taken in 2012 show that for the first time, many Americans doubt that their children will live better than they have. Three crashes so close together are uncommon, but the pattern of speculation and collapse is an old one, and one that other nations have dealt with in the past.

So what is a speculative bubble? It is really a simple process driven by common emotions: greed and competitiveness. A speculative bubble occurs when investors want something so badly that they will pay a high price for it—a price that is more than the item or stock is worth. When you have people paying more than the true value of something, that is the beginning of a speculative bubble. These purchases create the illusion of value, which often allows for even greater increases in the perceived value, but not in the real value, of whatever is involved. The result is that something is purchased not for what it is really worth, but for what the buyer thinks they can sell it for later. This can be a tech stock, a house, or a tulip bulb.

So why is a speculative bubble a destroyer of homes and nations? Well, first of all, it's a pure market phenomenon. Not just the stock market, but "market" in the sense that all commerce is affected. It is an economic disaster that has happened many times and each time deeply affects the lives of everyone in the economy, not just investors. Whether you invest, or save, or do just about anything—other than live in a shack, wear animal skins for clothes, and raise your own food—you will feel the severe effect of the next speculation bubble and the crash it causes. The burst of a speculative bubble often devastates a nation financially and plunges it into a depression. In 2008 that is exactly what happened to the United States.

Any speculation bubble is basically driven by one simple motive: greed.

The desire to have more money, more things.

The desire to want more money and get it quickly.

These speculative crashes that destroy lives and livelihoods have been around for as long as there has been greed, which means probably back to the earliest homes: caves. One of the most striking occurred just as the Americas were being settled.

Flower Power

The end of the sixteenth century was an exciting time to live in Holland. Having the only viable sea routes to Asia, that nation was at the center of much of the world's trade. Ships making the two-year journey around Africa to India or China would return full of spices, silks, and exotic goods. A successful voyage would make those who invested in it as much as 2,000 percent on their investment. Men became rich, or much richer, in one night when "their ship came in." Holland's navy was successfully meeting in battle, and often defeating, that of much larger England. One Dutch fleet actually sailed up the Thames and threatened London itself. But by the 1600s Holland was a land of merchants, and everyone was enjoying newfound wealth and prosperity. One of the benefits for Holland of being the leading trade center for Europe was that new and exotic imports arrived there first. One of these came in 1593, and that was the tulip. Boom times can lead to indulgence, and the garden centers of Holland were able to charge a good price for this new flower. This put tulips out of the reach of the general population but made them a luxury item that even the middle class could enjoy. However, in this case, that indulgence mushroomed into a speculative bubble.

Tulips were first a wildflower that grew in the steppes of Central Asia. They were found in Turkey as early as 1000 CE. Dutch merchants brought them to the Netherlands by the 1590s. Those who were well-off planted them in their gardens, and for a few years that was that, just a little snob appeal, similar to raising orchids. Then a most unusual disease struck the bulbs and plants, actually destabilizing the DNA of the tulips and creating mutations. As is normal, most of those mutations killed or hurt the plants by creating weak stems or shriveled leaves. But a few of the mutations did something different: they affected the tulips' colors and patterns. From being first found in just a few solid colors, suddenly tulips could be found that had five or six different colors on one plant's petals. New colors never before seen appeared as well. People were fascinated by the exotic new color combinations and even the petals' shapes. Those with money were willing to pay a premium for the best of the new varieties.

The way the speculative bubble grows really hasn't changed in five centuries. To show how this starts, let's begin with a tulip bulb dealer who has some newly arrived bulbs. These have a blue flower, which is a totally new and beautiful variety. He shows these to a rich customer who wants to have a unique garden and she buys them for double the normal price. That customer tells a friend who is a real hard-core gardener. He would really like a blue tulip, and the bulb dealer has the only ones he has heard of. So he offers to buy one at double the price his friend paid for it. The dealer makes a quadruple profit and talks with another bulb dealer about all the guilders (Dutch currency) he made on just one sale. That dealer goes to the next ship to arrive with tulip bulbs and buys three more of the mutated blue bulbs. He sells these to another gardener who wants blue flowers because his rich neighbor has them and this dealer more than doubles his money, too. As word gets out that easy money can be made on blue tulip bulbs, everyone in the bulb business swarms the bulb importers and cleans them out of the mutated bulbs. Once all the blue are gone, other new colors sell, too. Most of these dealers then sell their bulbs at a good profit.

A few speculators begin buying the bulbs from these dealers, not to plant, but to sell again at a profit. Soon, more and more people are hearing about how others are making money on tulip bulbs. (Substitute for tulip bulbs other products, such as dot-com stock, magic cards, lots in Florida, houses, etc., and the results are the same.) So now lots of new people are buying tulip bulbs and that drives the price up. This means that some people make a lot of guilders when they resell their tulip bulbs. Auction houses start selling the bulbs, and investors bid up the price.

Everyone who owns tulip bulbs makes money on them, and this attracts even more people to buy bulbs as an investment and with no concern to their real value or actually planting them. In fact, no one is actually thinking about the real value of the bulbs, just what they can make buying and selling them.

For a few months, everyone wants to buy tulip bulbs. At every auction the prices go higher and higher. The value of the bulbs becomes totally unrelated to anything material. From 1634 to 1637 the value of a desirable tulip bulb increased more than tenfold. Some single bulbs cost more than a house in Amsterdam. One bulb sold for 5,200 guilders, at a time when a laborer was paid at most 1 guilder per day. That would be about $500,000 for that one bulb, in today's dollars. At the end of 1636 a single bulb might change hands ten times in one day, with each owner selling it for more money. Some men mortgaged those houses in Amsterdam just to invest in tulip bulbs.

Then, in the winter of 1637, the tulip bubble burst. One day a merchant offered his entire stock of tulip bulbs at auction. Only weeks previously the collection would have been worth millions of today's dollars. But on this day, not a single person bid. Word spread, and within just a few hours everyone began dumping tulips at a half, then a quarter, then a tenth of their previous value. Within a few days you could not sell tulips at any price. People who had spent their life savings or borrowed small fortunes to invest in the bulbs were suddenly destitute.

Men who had sold everything hoping to get rich reselling exotically colored tulips found they owned nothing but a small bag of bulbs suitable only for planting in their garden.

With the tulip bubble's collapse, about 32 percent of the entire nation's wealth simply evaporated. With so many people suddenly poor, and so much of Holland's wealth disappearing in the matter of a few days, a depression was inevitable. So many merchants had lost their money that the Dutch government passed a law allowing tulip debtors to pay off what they owed for the now valueless bulbs at pennies on the dollar. Even those who never invested in tulip bulbs suffered. The economy slowed. With less money available, less could be invested in voyages to Asia and trade slowed. With slower trade, merchants needed less help, bought less in stores, and the recession was on. It took several years for the Dutch economy to really stabilize.

Tulipmania and its collapse set the pattern for every speculative bubble to come. Once people see only the money they can make by investing in something and pay no attention to the real value of the item or stock, the bubble begins to inflate. Those who sell early make money, others follow making more, and seeing the easy and quick profits, more buyers push the price up unrealistically. When the bubble gets too big, everyone, not just the investors, pays for their foolishness.

South Sea Vacation

The next big speculative bubble began inflating in 1711, only seventy-five years after the tulip crash. The setting was England, and the times were again good. Having taken over as the maritime power, Britain ruled the sea and controlled the world's trade. Merchants in London and the English ports now made fortunes importing goods from both the Orient and the Caribbean. These same merchants then spent their new wealth on more ships, clothes, coaches, and all of the accoutrements of wealth, and showed it off. This helped create a class of craftsmen and storekeepers who supplied the wealthy. This growing middle class had money but daily saw those who had much more. The East India Company was delivering dividends that made its investors the richest men in Britain. But like the other "stock" companies of this day, it was owned by fewer than five hundred men. Everyone else just watched as these few lucky "stockholders" became richer and richer. Everyone wanted in on the opportunity, but there were no stocks to buy.

The British government had its own concerns. It had run up a lot of debts fighting wars, maintaining the Royal Navy, and generally doing what governments do when founding and running a worldwide empire. The Exchequer, the British treasury, was borrowing money from the wealthy and the banks to keep things going. The Crown was ten million pounds in debt. They saw no way to pay it back without crippling taxes, and the kingdom would not stand for that. So when a group of entrepreneurs approached the government with an offer, the Crown could not refuse it.

"Sell us the same rights to the southern seaports such as Fiji and the Mariana Islands as you sold to the East India Company." The East India Company had been formed in 1707 to exploit trade with India. Every investor in this joint stock company had made back several times his investment in just the first four years. Eventually this private company virtually controlled the subcontinent and made its stockholders very rich. These new and hungry investors wanted a chance at the same success.

They offered to form the South Sea Company, sell stock to the public, and pay the very broke British treasury ten million pounds for the right to do so. The problem was that the Spanish controlled all of the rights, as most of the islands were their colonies and had Spanish garrisons on them. Spain also forbade all of its colonies to trade with Britain, so there could be no trade, much less exploitation as occurred in India, without starting a war. The fact that the entire premise was false and the plan could not work at all does not seem to have deterred anyone, from the British government to investors. All they could see was the money that others were making with the same kind of joint stock trading company and not that the two were in near opposite situations.

So despite its unrealistic agenda, the South Sea Company was formed. It announced to the public that the stock for the ownership of the new trading company was going to be for sale. Having seen the East India Company make others rich, anyone who could raise the money for a few shares was determined to get them. So the stock went on sale, and very quickly the price of a share jumped from one pound to a thousand pounds. This just convinced everyone that it was valuable. Then the rumor spread that the Spanish were about to sell Britain the trading rights to four ports in Chile and Peru. With that rumor and the approval of the government, a stock-buying frenzy occurred. Shares in the South Sea Company doubled in value, and then doubled again.

Other stock "trading" companies arose and sold stock at escalating values, often disappearing within weeks and taking their investors' money with them. Finding that they could buy stock in the morning and sell it at a profit that afternoon, everyone began buying up the stock in new companies that suddenly appeared—mostly for the purpose of issuing stock and nothing else. Each new joint stock company had its own scheme for making a fortune, but the reality was, they were formed just to sell stock. Here's a look at the announced purposes from eleven of these companies' charters. They range from the impractical to the absurd.

- To supply the town of Deal with fresh water.
- To trade in human hair.
- To assure seamen's wages.
- To insure horses.
- To make improved soap.
- To improve London gardens.
- To import walnut trees from Virginia.
- To pay pensions to widows at a small discount.
- To make iron using pit coal.
- To effect the alchemic transmutation of quicksilver into fine metal.
- To make a perpetual motion machine.

The frightening thing is that all of these companies succeeded in selling their stock.

Still, the value of the South Sea Company grew as more and more people were sure it would make them wealthy. No one considered that the company did not own even one ship; in fact, no one seems to have asked. Nor did anyone question whether it had any real rights from the Spanish, who controlled the southern Pacific ports. The South Sea Company was easily able to pay the government the promised ten million pounds, literally paying off the entire British deficit in a few months. The French suspected the English had invented a secret process to

create great wealth and soon were trying to mimic the South
Sea Company.

For eight years the South Sea Company stock kept on selling at higher and higher prices. The company never paid out
a penny, but began to announce in 1719 that a dividend would
be paid soon. It had made so much money issuing new stock
that the company had gathered more wealth than anyone else
in Britain, perhaps the world. The company was so wealthy
it outbid the Bank of England and bought thirty-one million
pounds of government debt that year. It is interesting that the
speculators in the South Sea Company spent their own money
on the safest investment, notes backed by the ability to tax the
British, while selling their own stock that had no basis at all
for its value.

No dividend was paid, ever. A few people began to notice that
the "trading" company wasn't doing much trading. It did not
own ships or have agents in the South Seas to purchase goods. If
you went to Fiji and looked for some trace of the South Sea Company, you would be out of luck. In fact, it wasn't doing much of
anything except issuing more stock and making its founders
richer. So in 1720, no one wanted any more stock. People who
had invested millions of pounds into the South Sea Company
found that not only were they not going to see a profit on their
shares, but they could not sell these shares at any price. Within
days, the bubble collapsed. Tens of millions in sterling simply
disappeared. A recession, of course, followed.

Only the British treasury gained. The reaction to the bursting of this bubble was so strong that for the next century the
British banned the sale of any stock certificates. Because of the
South Sea Bubble, not a single share of stock was sold in England
from 1720 to 1825.

Land in Florida

One of the greatest bubbles in the United States was neither stock nor flowers; it was land. The buying frenzy began with the same scenario. In the 1920s, America was booming and lots of people were making some money. They were also hearing about a few people, speculators and corporate heads, who were making a lot of money, and they wanted in on the bonanza.

Americans had discovered their own tropical paradise: the sunshine state of Florida. The price of land crept up and builders flocked down, putting up houses and buildings they knew would make them a big profit. Prices rose and rose. A house that went for $800,000 in 1920 sold for $4.5 million in 1926 (at a time when a workingman made $20 a week). Prices and profits obviously had no relationship to the cost of construction and land. They were too high for anyone to pay for a house and actually live in it. But the fact that they were building, and speculating on land on which to build, houses no one could afford to live in was ignored by those who could only see the opportunity. Everyone in Florida and thousands who never even saw the state hurried to take advantage of the boom and began to speculate in land. The atmosphere was much like a gold boom . . . without the gold. (There was a bubble in 1980 when gold reached more than $2,000 an ounce in today's dollars, but it was short-lived and limited in effect.)

Everyone wanted to buy land in Florida and make their fortune. Con men saw this and bought up swamps and broke them into lots. Overconfident investors gobbled them up, sight unseen. This is the source of the phrase "selling some swampland in Florida," which is still used, almost a century later, to describe cheating a gullible mark. It really happened, and for a while it happened a lot. Prices quadrupled from 1920 to 1924, and then they really took off, often going at ten or twenty times their 1920 price.

No one knows who, one day in 1925, said, "Enough!" But suddenly the buyers went away. People all over the United States had paid top dollar for Florida land they had never seen and could never use. But now no one wanted it. The bubble deflated, then recovered slightly, then collapsed completely. Hundreds of thousands of investors lost everything. Prices dropped below where they had started in 1920. Millions of dollars were simply gone, and the economy began to slow. There were many other causes in the late 1920s that led to the Great Depression, including an even greater speculative bubble, but the Florida real estate bubble has to be considered one of the factors that brought down the world's economy.

The Biggest Burst

Even after the Florida real estate bubble burst, there was an air of optimism about the American economy. Investors ignored everything and stocks continued to increase in value. (Anytime you think this seems similar to modern events, you are correct. That is why this book is titled *Doomed to Repeat*.) Everyone knew that stocks always went up. They had been doing just that for more than a decade. It didn't matter what the value or size of the company was, its stock was going to go up. There has been a lot written about the Crash of 1929, when a simple speculative bubble in stocks collapsed. People had bought stocks at values that had no real basis in the actual value or profits of the company. Then one day someone, or rather lots of investors, recognized this and the bubble burst. People with portfolios worth tens of thousands of dollars, back when a nice house sold for less than $2,000, were penniless. The "Depressions and Recessions" chapter in this book describes this crash in depressing detail. But by any measure, the stock bubble of the 1920s was a significant cause of the Great Depression of the 1930s.

In the aftermath of the Great Depression, a series of new laws were passed that limited speculation and prevented such entities as banks from making the same mistakes and buying into bubbles with an account holder's money. Prominent among these was the Glass-Steagall Act, which prohibited banks from speculating, buying on margin, creating highly speculative bonds and other paper, and investing the savings in them in speculative things like the stock market and high-risk, high-margin investments. But the 1990s were boom years, and everyone was making money in the stock market (sound familiar by now?), except the banks. So they spent millions lobbying Congress who, conveniently for the banks, decided that those old protections weren't needed anymore. The result of this wisdom, or lack thereof, resulted in the housing bubble.

Dot-com Crash

In the year 2000, there seemed to be no limit to the money you could make with a company that used the Internet. It was as much a part of the new millennium as the Y2K bug. Certainly every company that did business over the Net was a potential gold mine. It was a heady time, characterized by twenty-year-old "dot-com millionaires" and everyone wanting in on the profits. Established companies soon rose to have valuations of several hundred times their profits, if they made a profit at all. Stocks sold when the Internet companies went public, with initial public offerings (IPOs) being snapped up by investors with no regard for the company's viability or business model. It was a time filled with jargon and publicity, where the "new paradigm" of information technologies made obsolete little things like real corporate valuations, sales projections, and good, old-fashioned common sense. A good example is Yahoo!. The company had a search engine that millions of people used each day. This meant that those millions would see advertisements and the search engine would get paid when they did. What most people did not realize about Yahoo! was that this was all the company did—and there were only so many people who would use Yahoo! each day, and no more. Also, Yahoo!'s very success spawned competitors, eventually including Google. In 2000, the market value of Yahoo! stock rose to just over $500 a share. This made the company more valuable than General Motors or Ford, even though its real assets were just the search engine and some office furniture. The normal rules for stock value were ignored when the Internet was involved. It did not matter if there was no profit; the stock price kept on going up because an investor could buy it in the morning and sell it at a profit in the afternoon. (Sounding familiar?) Similar unrealistic valuation meant that AOL, which basically owned only websites and servers, was valued more highly than all of Time Warner, including *Time* magazine and Warner Bros., when the two merged.

By 2002 the bubble began to burst. Many of the companies that had their stock rise to ten or twenty times their first IPO value announced they were now showing massive losses and that attempts to expand their products into new areas such as games, news, and online sales were failing. On October 9, 2002, the stock market crashed, led by the total deflation of Internet stock values. Yahoo! lost more than 90 percent of its value, which means that anyone who had just bought Yahoo! stock lost

90 percent of his or her investment in less than two days. AOL was no better, and even Intel and IBM saw massive drops. Stories abounded about dot-com millionaires taking jobs as janitors, but the real losers were the millions of Americans whose pension funds and investment portfolios lost half or more of their value. The economy followed with the traditional recession.

The Housing Bubble

Many social and political factors contributed to the crash and burst of 2007 to 2009. By this time, all of the world's economies were intertwined and dependent on each other. The housing crisis was generally a U.S. and British concern, but the stock market collapse and credit disaster became a worldwide event, affecting every nation.

To begin with, it was a boom time all over the world. In the United States, home prices were climbing every year, and credit was so loose that almost anyone could be approved for a home mortgage. The problem was that just about everyone bought a house, even those who had no way to maintain the payments or upkeep. Lots of exotic investment instruments were created (just like in the South Sea Bubble days) and were sold to anyone who wanted to invest.

Among the new ways to invest were mortgage-backed securities. These were investments in the holding of mortgages with the assumption being that either everyone would make their mortgage payments or the values of the homes would continue to go up so quickly that a repossessed house could be resold at a profit.

Not only did the individual investor buy into the housing

boom, but banks did as well. And those banks did so by using your money on obscene margins. The bank would speculate by buying bonds or debt, paying only two cents for each dollar purchased. If the value increased by two cents, they could sell and double their (your) money. But buying on margin works only if the value increases. That is why it is so speculative and dangerous. If the value of the investment goes down more than, for example, the two cents (dropping to ninety-eight cents from one dollar), the bank is on the hook to make up the difference. And if the investment is in something, say bad mortgages, that goes down fifty cents, then the bank that bought the investment for two cents has just lost twenty-five cents for every penny initially invested, and is still expected to make up the difference. Investment plans were created where a bank or investment house would use a highly marginalized investment to buy yet another highly marginalized investment, with both being based upon the value of mortgages that they never looked at. So they spent two cents to buy one dollar in the portfolio that was itself two cents on yet another dollar in another portfolio, and sometimes going yet another two-cent round before reaching the actual investment item, which was itself of questionable value at any price, such as a dubiously given mortgage. That is a 2 percent of 2 percent of 2 percent margin, or $0.000008 invested for every actual dollar of debt purchased. So there was no room for the value to go down at all, even though the debt purchased was mostly from questionable loans made on the assumption that housing values (like tulip prices or Florida land) would never go down.

The banks and investment firms then insured these investments against large losses with other companies. But to handle the amounts involved, the insuring firms also were dependent on other marginalized investments in the housing bubble to cover any losses. If one firm lost money, this system worked, but because they too were buying on large margin to raise the money to cover the insurance claims, the insurers could not make good on many banks' losses when the housing bubble burst.

In 1999, when Bill Clinton was president, the Glass-Steagall Act was lobbied against and rescinded. This was mostly the work of the larger banks that saw other companies making big money by buying debt on margin and reselling it, and wanted in on the massive profits being made. Their argument was that times were different and the restrictions unneeded. Finally, both President Clinton and his Congress agreed and rescinded all the restrictions that had been put in place after the stock market crash of 1929. The stupidity of this decision is shown by what followed.

Companies such as Goldman Sachs and JPMorgan Chase created billion-dollar funds with questionable mortgages that the United States backed. But the banks and investors didn't care because shares could be resold at a profit. (Sounding even more familiar?) Money flowed, and the Dow Jones Industrial Average, which measures the value of stocks being sold on the New York Stock Exchange, approached the 14,000 level. Banks showed immense paper profits, and mortgage loan rates were kept low to encourage home ownership. This also discouraged saving and encouraged "investing" in the stock market. The government even mandated that, depending on the bank's location, a few percent to 20 percent of all mortgages had to be given to the less privileged. This effectively forced the granting of home loans to those who could not afford them. But the banks did not object, as even those loans could be the basis of more inflated mortgage-backed securities. The ratings agencies, who valued for the general investors the soundness of the new bank instruments based on the guaranteed bad loans, went along with the game. These agencies competed to be paid a percentage of an investment's value to rate it, so they never pointed out that it was a house of cards (if they had, then they would not have gotten to make million-dollar evaluations on the next offering).

Then one day someone stopped paying a higher price for a house than the seller had bought it for. Then everyone began playing less for real estate than the same home or building had been worth the year before. Instead of increasing, the value of a house began to slide. The real estate securities that the banks and hedge funds had bought with massive margins became first questionable and then worthless. Billions of dollars in value disappeared almost overnight, and the biggest banks, the ones that had forced the rescinding of the Glass-Steagall Act, were in exactly the situation that they said could never happen. Credit disappeared. Without credit, construction stops, new businesses can't start up or expand, and sales drop. When sales drop, jobs go away. The bubble burst all over the economy.

In a few months, the stock market lost half of its value. Ordinary investors lost literally trillions from their pension funds and savings. Credit went from easy to get to nonexistent. (If you are interested in reading more, there are a number of good books laying blame and analyzing exactly who did what to whom in order to exploit everyone else.)

The question now is this: Can the world's governments, particularly the United States and more directly, Congress, actually learn from this recent history and restore true protections and limits? Perhaps we *will* learn from history this time. Perhaps U.S. regulators such as the Securities and Exchange Commission and the Federal Reserve will learn to act when the value of a stock or investment soars far out of proportion to its profits or assets. But to date, there is little to show that this is happening.

Groupon, a company that has lost money each year, has never shown a profit, and owns no physical assets to mention, was valued at $1.2 billion in April of 2010. Stock in Facebook, which has never paid a dividend or shown a profit, gave the company a valuation of a whopping $20 billion when it went public in 2012. The rationalizations of these valuations do seem to sound unpleasantly like those rationalizations made for tulips, Florida land, the dot-com stocks of the 1990s, or even the South Sea Company. Simply put, the stocks are being valued at what the market might bear and bought by those who hope to resell at a profit. This is happening while even the ratings companies ignore the normal standards for valuing a company, such as what the company actually owns or might pay its shareholders in dividends.

What history seems to give us today is questions, not solutions. Are those who benefit from speculation too influential in Washington, London, and Berlin to allow for true reform? If so, we are doomed for the cycle to repeat itself. Are the elected officials capable of looking not just at the distant past, but at the speculative bubbles of the last two decades and preventing the same mistakes? Can those who manage the companies that handle the money learn from history and resist short-term greed that is at the cost of a future recession? The record is not good.

CHAPTER EIGHT

Too Much Money?

The first panacea for a misguided nation is inflation of the currency; the second is war. Both bring a temporary prosperity; both bring a permanent ruin. But both are the refuge of political and economic opportunists.

—ERNEST HEMINGWAY (1899–1961)

The United States government did not create its Federal Reserve Board in 1913 to assist in recovery from depressions. It was started to control and prevent inflation. Even during the long recession starting in 2008, the primary stated purpose of the "Fed" is to make sure inflation is kept at a low level. Why is this? Why is there so much concern with inflation, even over recession? Because you can have too much money. Well, maybe not you personally, but a nation can actually have too many dollars floating around. So more correctly, there can be simply too much money in circulation. Too much currency—whether it be printed dollars, puka shells, coins, wampum, or numbers recorded in a Federal Reserve computer—can create inflation. When the amount of money in circulation increases but the amount of goods that the money can be used to buy stays the same, the result is "inflation." The cost of everything inflates larger and larger, like a balloon being blown up. Unfortunately, like that balloon, an economy can be burst by too much inflation.

From Ancient Rome to twenty-first-century Zimbabwe, inflation has brought many a nation to its economic knees. It was not that long ago that inflation crippled the U.S. economy. In the early 1980s the inflation rate surged until it reached a staggering 13 percent. That meant that everything cost, on the average, 13 percent more than it did the year before. It also meant that someone on a fixed income, like an elderly retiree on a pension, could buy 13 percent less food, fuel, and clothes compared to a year earlier. Since then the inflation rate has been much lower, so many of us are ignoring the topic, but that is a mistake. Inflation, in the classic form of higher costs for basic goods, is again a threat. The increased cost of gasoline alone shows how inflation can affect every single person in a nation.

Inflation has several causes, but often it happens when the economy expands too quickly. Credit and cash are plentiful, and people borrow and spend freely. That creates a demand for more goods and services, so the prices on these items and services inflate. This is often reflected in the decreasing value of the dollar (or any currency) compared to the money of other nations.

Inflation can be put in two categories: monetary and price. When there is too much money in circulation—monetary inflation—then there's too much money chasing too few goods or services. This results in price inflation, an increase in the cost of those goods and services.

Inflation is typically measured by the Federal government by excluding the volatile prices of things like food and gas. This "core inflation rate" is what the Federal Reserve considers in determining whether inflation is escalating. This measurement is sometimes controversial because the items excluded from the core inflation rate are many of the very purchases that consumers make daily. When gas and food prices go up dramatically, this is called "headline inflation." A dramatic rise in those costs makes headlines, but they are not considered in the official number.

Why Inflation Hurts So Bad

When inflation was high in the early 1980s, there was no wage stagnation. So the money earned from wages, savings, and investments made up for the higher cost of living. This meant that Americans could still buy about the same amount of food, etc., as the year before. They didn't necessarily get ahead, but they had a chance to break even over the long run. This is no longer true. In 2011 the inflation rate was just under 3 percent, but if you added in gasoline and some other costs that the government just happens to leave out, the real rate was at least double that at over 6 percent. In 1981 the banks were paying 16 percent on a six-month CD and the inflation rate was 10.3 percent. This meant that if you saved your money in a bank, you gained over 5 percent after inflation. Thirty years later, money market rates are hovering around 1 percent. This meant that, in 2011, money on deposit in a bank lost at least 2 percent of its buying power by just sitting there. To make matters worse, because of the economy and political uncertainties, many private sector workers haven't seen a cost-of-living adjustment in the past several years and cannot get a raise to keep up with rising costs. This includes just about everyone. Few private workers in 2010 or 2011 received increases in pay, which effectively means they were paid less in "real dollars."

In its simplest form, what inflation always does is make things cost more. If there is a rate of inflation of 100 percent per year, then a loaf of bread that costs $1 today will cost $2 next year. The people who are affected the most by inflation are those who receive a set amount of dollars or euros each month, an amount that does not go up when inflation raises their real cost of living. These are people who are living off their savings, as well as anyone who is getting social security (which is adjusted only once per year) or relying on a pension. This can mean that in a place or time where the inflation rate becomes high, someone who retired at age sixty-five with enough money to live comfortably will find out at age seventy that the same amount of money is not enough to live on. The tragedy is that there is often nothing this retiree can do about it. Stories about the elderly who go from buying roasts to secretly eating dog food are painfully real in times of high inflation.

A high rate of inflation also steals the value of any money you have in the bank. Banks rarely pay a rate of interest high enough to balance out rapid inflation. Inflation is the enemy of savings. If you save your money, as the government encourages, but that same government allows a high rate of inflation, then you will actually lose money saving it in a bank (or under a mattress). In 2012, as it had for several years, the Federal Reserve's policy forced banks to pay virtually nothing, often as low as 0.25 percent interest on savings. The intention was to force everyone to make risky investments to earn more, such as in the still highly volatile stock market. The reality is that this means the money in everyone's savings accounts is losing real value each year. It also means that where before a retiree could live off the interest on their savings, today they have to use the savings itself to live on, and so lose doubly with higher prices and no safe way to counter that inflation. This below-inflation interest rate was also supposed to allow banks to loan money more easily, but regulation and bank greed have prevented that from happening.

In the United States, food, gas, utilities, health care, education, and insurance costs are rising rapidly. If these prices continue to increase and the current rate of inflation goes up even slightly, consumer spending could drop off significantly. We could then be headed for another recession—a double dip—just as this country is trying to recover from the last one. The livelihood of Americans is once again in economic peril.

"I Can't Eat an iPad"

The average American family is falling behind in terms of what they can purchase with the money they have. Over time, this can cause a family to take a hit on all their long-term investments and possibly run out of money for retirement. In the short term, it can make it difficult to pay everyday bills without going into debt. Saving for college, vacations, or a new car becomes nearly impossible.

At the start of 2011, wholesale food prices rose by 3.9 percent, the highest monthly increase since November 1974, and they went up 7.3 percent in the twelve months ending in June 2012. Food prices are at their highest levels since the United States began tracking them in 1990. This means food costs more in the advanced countries, and it is also becoming dangerously more expensive in those nations where most of the population earns very little. Yes, inflation can contribute to starvation in the Third World.

U.S. consumers have watched food and gas prices ravage their household budgets. A recent survey showed that 75 percent of American consumers are spending less because of the higher gas prices. In February 2011, the consumer price index (CPI) showed food-at-home prices rose 2.8 percent in the past year, with the cost of certain items, such as beef and pork, surging 9 percent and 16 percent, respectively. Airfares climbed 12 percent in 2011, the cost of used cars was up 15 percent, and gasoline prices climbed a whopping 19.2 percent.

Many economists believe that the United States is once again headed for a high inflationary period. Two years into the economic "recovery," when the prospect of high inflation is coupled with the recent unemployment figures, the economic forecast looks alarming. Unemployment in the first half of 2012 was once more increasing and the real rate of unemployment remained in the double digits. Industrial growth, home building, and new factory orders have shown little or no growth. But costs continued to increase, including dramatic new increases in such necessities as health insurance and heating oil. When the costs go up but there are fewer current dollars to pay those costs, you have a situation called "stagflation." Stagflation occurs when the poor consumer is seeing prices rise due to inflation but her income remains the same. This really means that during stagflation everyone loses ground, and when it ends their money does not go as far. It is income stagnation and price inflation, the worst of both worlds. One sign of stagflation is the many empty storefronts seen all across the Western world. Stagflation is now a legitimate concern that could catapult the U.S. economy into a full-blown depression, causing the collapse of the already battered economies of many advanced nations across the globe.

William Dudley, president of the Federal Reserve Bank of New York, recently got a taste of the public's frustration with higher prices. In the early spring of 2011, he spoke to a crowd in Queens, to address food-inflation questions. Dudley told the audience that while some prices rise, other products are cheaper—like Apple's latest iPad.

"Today you can buy an iPad 2 that costs the same as an iPad 1 that is twice as powerful," said Dudley. "You have to look at the prices of all things."

One frustrated audience member had this to say to Dudley's comparison: "I can't eat an iPad."

The Great Recession

The main reason for the most recent economic crisis, now called the Great Recession, was that the housing market in the United States heated up too fast, as explained in the previous chapter. Credit was easy—really, too easy; some in the industry were saying that if you had a pulse, you could get a mortgage. There was little oversight, and so-called subprime mortgages were readily approved with little or no verification of income and sometimes no down payment at all. More than 80 percent of those mortgages were adjustable-rate. More people than ever before "qualified" for loans, all the new borrowers created more demand, and housing prices inflated rapidly. Many existing mortgage holders borrowed against their newly acquired equity, using their houses as virtual ATMs. A sizable chunk of people moved up to bigger, more expensive houses that they would not have qualified for just a few years prior.

By mid-2006, housing prices had peaked. The subprime mortgage crisis that resulted when the housing bubble burst forced a huge cash infusion to all the banks that were "too big to fail." Trillions of dollars have been lost in home equity, and many of the long-term unemployed were in construction and real estate. Investment banking firms, heavily invested in risky subprime mortgages, began to topple like dominoes. The stock market plummeted, and unemployment soared in all sectors across the board, with the exception of government jobs. Those jobs increased in order to implement all the government programs designed to get the financial crisis under control.

Concern over the soundness of the U.S. financial markets caused global investors to restrict credit, and slow growth began to occur outside the United States as well, spreading to European countries and causing a global recession.

Many experts are deeply concerned about the size of the 2008 bailout. Adjusting the amounts to equal today's dollar, the costs from all American wars, from the American Revolution through Iraq and Afghanistan, coupled with all the major government programs—the New Deal, the S&L crisis, and NASA's entire budget—total less than the amount of the 2008 bailout. Since those bailout dollars were mostly borrowed, the problem is complicated by the interest payments taking dollars away from future needs. And then there was the federal stimulus money and other fiscal policies implemented to pull the country back from the brink of depression. This money disappeared in June of 2011. But will the policies that have been put in place to keep us out of the Second Great Depression threaten to create soaring inflation, coupled with a recessionary economy that would make the crippling stagflation of the 1970s look mild by comparison? One sign of this happening is the cost of gasoline, which has doubled since the bailout.

Funny Money

Government is the only agency that can take a valuable commodity like paper, slap some ink on it, and make it totally worthless.

— LUDWIG VON MISES (1881–1973)

Where did the billions of dollars that funded the stimulus package to pull the country out of the Great Recession come from? Well, it wasn't from raising taxes. The money was created with a stroke of a pen and some thin air. That got the printing presses started, and the dollars, which seemed to magically appear, were then spent—sometimes before the ink was even dry on them. The magic continues, getting trickier to perform each time, until every dollar is worth less and less. The U.S. government is now printing a lot of new money. The value of the dollar has dropped against foreign currencies: 17 percent since 2009. The current magic show will be over when the resulting monetary inflation cripples the U.S. economy.

During World War II, after the Great Depression that started in 1929, the economy was jump-started by the manufacture of items needed for the war effort. Unemployment dropped from 14.6 percent in 1940 to just 1.2 percent in 1942 in the wartime economy. Such a recovery due to military spending is no longer possible. The United States has outsourced so much of its manufacturing that these jobs aren't coming back. Similarly, the nation's housing market by 2012 had lost more of its value than it did during the Great Depression. What's even more troubling, in

2012, three years into the economic "recovery," housing prices are expected to rise very slowly or drop further before bottoming out. That would put some areas of the country in the range of a 75–80 percent loss in the value of homes from the peak in 2005–2006.

What has been the government's solution to get the economy nursed back to health? Borrowing more money and printing more money—the two crucial ingredients guaranteeing inflation.

A Long Tradition

Perhaps the earliest form of inflation can be found way back in Ancient Rome. Nero, of fiddling fame, was not a very good money manager. Unfortunately, he was also emperor. After the great fire in 64 CE destroyed most of the city, Nero decided to rebuild in marble and stone. The problem was that marble and stone were expensive. About halfway through the rebuilding of Rome, Nero's government ran out of money. Nero personally ran out of money, too, since he controlled every last cent in the treasury.

Money in Rome consisted of coins, mostly made of precious metals. These coins were the aureus (gold), the denarius (silver), and the sestertius (bronze). This meant that unlike today, Nero could not just print more money as he needed it. But it also meant that those Roman coins were accepted anywhere in the "known" world and set a standard for all other coinage. After all, a silver denarius was worth exactly that: one denarius in silver. But Nero was out of silver, and gold, and bronze. He needed more coins to pay the workers, the stonemasons, and the costs of the elaborate stage productions he himself starred in. He came up with the idea to use cheaper metals to make the denarius. But then it would not be a real denarius, and it would be worth less. So he was careful to fill only the center of the coins with lead or tin and leave the silver on the outside, so they looked like real silver coins.

This is called debasing the currency. Basically it is a government version of bait and switch. This worked at first, but soon everyone realized that some of the denarii weren't worth as much as others. And if you can't tell which coins are real, then the only solution is to assume that all the denarii are debased coins and raise your prices to balance this out. Prices rose, and since things cost more, the emperor had to create even more coins with less silver on the outside of each denarius to pay for the more expensive marble, food, and so on. But more cheap coins forced the prices up again. Nero very creatively found a way to cause inflation even in an economy using precious metal coinage.

Modern governments have it much easier. They just start the presses and print more money. However, the effect is the same. If a government, any government, prints too much money, the result is inflation. This can vary from a few extra percentage points each year to a runaway disaster that makes everyone's money valueless. With more dollars chasing the same number of goods, the cost of everything from food to automobiles goes up. Sometimes a government prints too much money because it is financing a war or trying to jump-start a slow economy. Sometimes a government does it because of circumstances it cannot control.

Worst-Case Scenario: Hyperinflation

Can you imagine going to your favorite coffee shop, and in the time it takes you to down your first cup of the day, the price for a cup of coffee has already doubled? This is an example of hyperinflation. In Zimbabwe, 50 percent inflation or more was a daily experience for years. Eventually, hyperinflation was so bad that the government was issuing money with the denomination of $50 billion. Bread cost a billion—yes, *billion*—times more than it once had. When the economy is in a period of extreme inflation, the price of goods can rise so fast that the money you have in your pocket or bank account or wheelbarrow when you wake up that morning can be almost worthless by dinnertime. Zimbabwe's solution was to effectively give up control of its currency and link it to the South African rand.

It is interesting to note that hyperinflations have never occurred when a commodity, like gold or silver, has served as money or when paper money was converted to a commodity. In the United States, we are on the "fiat system," where the dollar is controlled by a discretionary paper-money standard. This means there are no natural constraints on the currency. The Feds can just fire up the printing presses at their discretion, making inflation increasingly likely and the risk of the United States experiencing a period of devastating hyperinflation a real possibility in the future.

The first recorded instance of hyperinflation occurred during the French Revolution, when monthly inflation shot up to 143 percent. This was caused by the French National Assembly printing and issuing hundreds of millions of livres several times over the course of 1789 to 1791 with nothing to back them up. At one point they had printed 40 billion livres, and the cost of goods had gone up to more than a hundred times in a decade. When he became first consul, Napoleon Bonaparte tightened the currency and brought down the runaway inflation. A century later, France wasn't suffering from hyperinflation . . . however, the French were the cause of it in Germany.

In the Treaty of Versailles ending World War I, Germany agreed to reparations. Those were payments to the countries Germany attacked, mostly France and England, compensating them for the cost of the war. The trouble was that the economy in Germany was already in shambles because of the war. It quickly became obvious that there was no extra money to pay the demanded reparations. But France and other nations insisted the payments be made, so the German government simply printed more money and used that to pay the penalty. This started an inflationary spiral, which means that as the rate of inflation goes up (and the buying power of each dollar, mark, pound, peso, etc., goes down just as quickly), the government prints yet more money even faster to pay its bills.

Post-WWI Germany had terrible inflation. Its money became so worthless that it took a basketful of money to buy a basket of food. There was a story told about a German woman who had to buy a lot of food for her family. To have enough money to pay for her purchases, she had to fill two large baskets with bills. When she got to the store, she put one basket down so she could open the door. Then she went in carrying only one basket. Remembering she had left the other one outside, the woman hurried back. She was afraid that the basket of money would be stolen, and she was partially right. There on the ground was her money. The thief had stolen the basket and dumped out the almost worthless cash.

The dark side of such a crippling inflation is that it makes people desperate. Not long after inflation destroyed the German economy, the Nazi Party was elected to take over the government. More recently, we have seen Egypt and other poor countries have significant political and social unrest partially because of high inflation.

The United States has never experienced a period of hyperinflation, although it has come close during two notable periods: during the American Revolution and right after the Civil War. However, in both examples, inflation never surpassed the hyperinflation threshold of a 50 percent monthly inflation rate.

The American Revolution

Inflation is a problem that has dogged the American economy since before the colonies won their independence. The United States actually has a tradition of cyclic bouts of inflation that goes all the way back to the American Revolution. The Continental Congress needed money to pay the soldiers fighting for them. When in June of 1775 the British army occupied New York, and eventually most of the colonial cities, the Continental Congress still needed money to pay its army but had few places left to tax. They solved the problem that year by printing currency, called the Continental, that they promised to cash in for specie, precious metals like gold, after the war was won and the United States was an independent nation. Whenever they needed more money, the Continental Congress just printed more promises. The trouble was, as the number of Continentals grew, their value diminished. Congress made up for the value going down because of inflation by printing even more Continentals. Even after the war was won, inflation had destroyed the value of the money that had been issued to finance it. The phrase used to mean "totally worthless" was "not worth a Continental." Even after independence, inflation dogged the Continental currency. Continentals remained the currency of the United States until 1785, when they were replaced by the dollar and much greater fiscal constraint. Backed by gold, the new dollars were far less subject to inflation, and that stability aided in the explosive growth of the nation.

American Civil War

At the start of the Civil War in 1861, the Confederacy began to fund the war by issuing treasury notes. These were bills used as money (which is what every American has in his or her wallet today), and were secured in value only by cotton that could not be sold. Later Confederate money was backed only by the promise to make it good with gold or silver after the war was won. The wealthier groups of Southerners, like rich cotton growers, still demanded payment in gold and silver coins. They had to pay overseas for their seed, machines, and everything imported with real money, and so used their position to obtain it. This used up what hard currency and reserves the Confederacy had. The middle class and poor were immediately forced to accept the new paper money in exchange for the goods and services they provided. As the war dragged on the Rebel government printed more and more money. It was still backed by nothing but hope, even as they were obviously losing the war. Four years into the rebellion it took 1,200 Confederate dollars to buy what had once sold for just one dollar. But by 1865 even that minimal value was an illusion. After the Battle of Gettysburg and Sherman's March to the Sea, it was apparent that the South had little hope of victory. The average Confederate soldier's family went hungry because merchants simply no longer accepted the Confederate dollars. The soldiers would send them home, but with the war as good as lost, the Confederacy's promise to make good on them once it was won was valueless.

The 1970s and Early 1980s

During the 1970s, inflation was very high in the United States, but the economy was sluggish. Both housing and manufacturing growth had slowed, and competition from Asia had begun to affect American employment. This produced stagflation. The problem with stagflation, as mentioned earlier, is that it creates a spiral of decreasing growth and income. If people have to pay more for an item but have less money, then they buy less. If everyone buys less, then factories close and stores stay empty. This created a dilemma for the federal government: If it lowered interest rates, inflation would rise. But if it raised rates, it would create even more of a strain on the economy by forcing inflation even higher. After trying just about everything, including government-mandated wage and price controls, they chose growth over their concern for further inflation. The Federal Reserve raised the interest rates to a whopping 20 percent in January 1981. Satirist Art Buchwald said of this period that it was cheaper to borrow from the Mafia than from the local bank.

Mortgage rates went through the roof, and many people were priced out of the housing market completely. The stock market went into a nosedive, and people on fixed incomes were financially devastated.

Historically, it's common for a period of high inflation to catapult the country into a recession. Money becomes too expensive for businesses to use to expand or to buy new equipment, housing loans cost too much for anyone to afford, and new businesses have to pay too much for startup capital. The monstrous inflation of the 1970s didn't end until the recession of 1980–1982 emerged. This stopped the rise in costs by simply and drastically lowering demand because people could afford less and unemployment had increased. For a while this created a balance between inflation and growth. When the economy rebounded from that recession, the stock market soared in what would become one of the longest bull runs in history.

Tightrope Walking

A recession occurs when the economy goes in reverse. Companies make less than they made the year before, so they stop hiring employees or lay off existing ones, meaning there are fewer jobs. Consumers then spend less money because they have no work, and so the companies make even less money, and the recession cycle continues.

As mentioned above, the Federal Reserve's primary job is to keep inflation under control while preventing a recession. This can be a constant balancing act. Alan Greenspan, the Fed chairman from 1987 to 2006, believed in laissez-faire economics: no micromanaging, just accomplishing the overall goal of stimulating the economy while avoiding high inflation. During the 2001 recession, he began lowering interest rates to alleviate the economic crisis. But by 2004, amid inflation concerns, he began to raise them again. However, in order to keep the economy from slipping back into a recession, he kept stock market investors apprised of his intentions, which encouraged them to keep investing. Some experts feel that the deregulation and lack of oversight of the financial institutions during the Greenspan years created a fertile ground for corruption and the ultimate collapse of the entire banking industry as well as the overall economy.

Since 2007, the Federal Reserve, under current chairman

Ben Bernanke, has taken a much more proactive and creative approach to managing the economy, especially after the housing market collapsed. Bernanke implemented many innovative programs to pump trillions of dollars into the fragile U.S. economy. It has been theorized that these actions prevented the United States and the rest of the world from falling into a global depression.

The United States has again been printing a lot of new money in order to ease the financial crisis brought on by the Great Recession. The government has printed more money in the past several years than at any other time since the American Revolution, when it was printing out empty promises—not worth a Continental—to fund the war. And as history has shown from that time, printing excessive amounts of money almost pushed our brand-new nation into hyperinflation and economic collapse.

The Federal Reserve has also recently implemented a controversial policy called "quantitative easing" (QE) to stimulate the economy, which means that the Feds will print more money to buy treasury bonds from the public, and the T-bill holders will receive the proceeds from those sales. Some economists think that will cause inflation. It certainly fits the definition of inflation: putting more money into the system rapidly. They have done two rounds of QE, with a third round now being implemented since QE2 ended in June 2011. The Fed massively increased the money supply again in 2012 and expected to do so far into 2013.

Another important fiscal measure that the Federal Reserve has at its disposal to stimulate a weak economy is to lower interest rates to encourage buying. But interest rates are currently near zero. They have reached the bottom, and there's nowhere to go but up. Bernanke, however, is very wary of raising interest rates. He was a student of the Great Depression and he doesn't want the shaky economy plunging back into economic crisis when interest rates are raised. However, the most common fiscal policy employed by the Fed to lower inflation is to raise interest rates. He also has been quoted as saying that the most important job of the Federal Reserve is to give the American public an expectation of moderate pricing. Looking back on the 1970s, Bernanke feels that the high inflation of that period created more volatility in the economy because the public planned for higher prices and changed their behavior accordingly. If the Fed can show moderation, the public's confidence in the economy will remain high, reducing the likelihood of economic volatility. It is almost inconceivable that the Fed, under Bernanke, would ever raise interest rates to anywhere near the staggering 20 percent of the early 1980s. But if he is leery of raising interest rates, which his predecessors did with some regularity, how will he strike the right balance between price moderation and economic growth?

With all the new dollars being put into the economy, coupled with a soaring national debt and rising costs of goods and services, the perfect inflationary storm is brewing. So what happens when the Fed has to do the inevitable and raise interest rates to curb runaway inflation? As mentioned above, that action could stall an already anemic economy, plunging the nation into another devastating recession. Economists disagree as to the best course of action given the current poor economic conditions. However, one thing is acknowledged across the board: The Federal Reserve is balancing on the tightrope between the rising risk of inflation and the looming threat of another recession. But this time, there seems to be no safety net in sight.

The Collapse of an Economic Superpower?

Just how bad could inflation get over the next few years in the Unites States? Well, two things that add fuel to the inflationary fire are piling up: the national debt and an excess of new money in circulation. We have an astronomical national debt of over $16 trillion. That is an amount equal to the total annual gross domestic product. That simply means it would take every penny everyone makes for a year to pay it off. This level of national debt has never before been reached. The total national debt in 1977 totaled $1.75 trillion in today's dollars ($706 billion then). The current national debt is more than an eightfold increase in twenty-five years. The debt is twice as high as it was in 2007 and increasing at a higher percentage than even occurred during World War II. As mentioned earlier, the U.S. government hasn't printed money at this rate since the United States was fighting to become an independent nation. With so much debt and a surplus of new currency in circulation, the dollar is being devalued like never before. Current Treasury Secretary Timothy Geithner said in 2012 that his policy has been and will always be that a strong dollar is in our interest as a country. But compared to other currencies around the world, the dollar has depreciated a troubling 17 percent since 2009. The Canadian dollar cost seventy cents to buy in 2000 and now is worth more than the U.S. dollar. That means everything costs more in the United States and less in Canada because their money has inflated less. In the 1960s a British pound sterling was worth about ninety cents; today buying one would cost $1.55.

In 1912 a loaf of bread cost a nickel and gold sold for $20.17 an ounce. Now bread costs at least $2 and gold sells for $1,600 an ounce. This is because since 1913, the year the Federal Reserve was created, the dollar has lost more than 95 percent of its purchasing power. That is both a striking example and the definition of the effect of inflation. To be as rich as a millionaire was in 1913, you would have to have more than $20 million today.

The fragile recovery from the recent Great Recession has been a jobless recovery, with technological advances and globalization eliminating or moving jobs out of this country. Historically, most recoveries after an economic downturn result in a period of high growth and low unemployment. But this has been an unusually weak recovery. Some economists feel that the current U.S. housing market, having lost more of its value than in the aftermath of the Great Depression, will never come back. What if a weak housing market and high unemployment is the new normal? What can history tell us about controlling inflation under this new normal?

Tighter regulatory control and closer oversight may have prevented some of the economic crisis the country is still trying to dig itself out of. Current Fed Chairman Bernanke seems to prioritize preventing another financially catastrophic event by keeping inflation tightly reigned in. Yet some economists suggest creating a mild increase in the rate of inflation to encourage economic growth. So far Bernanke has resisted that approach.

Some economists suggest that Bernanke do what former Fed Chair Paul Volcker did in the 1980s, keeping a tight control of the money supply and interest rates. In part because of Volker's fiscal policies, inflation dropped from 13.5 percent to 3 percent in just three years.

The traditional control on inflation was linking your money to the nation's gold reserve. The amount of gold limited how much money could be printed. When President Nixon took the country entirely off the gold standard in the early 1970s, inflation exploded. Until the United States stopped issuing dollars as "silver certificates" that could actually be exchanged at the Federal banks for actual silver, there was a limit as to how many dollars could be printed. What about the United States returning to the gold standard instead of paper money backed by nothing? With the amount of money in circulation around the world there is not enough gold, or even gold and silver combined, to go back to this. Tie money to some commodity? Oil dollars for real? Coffee dollars? Dollars you could change for land?

Perhaps a problem is that we are not really seeing inflation now in the same way we looked at it in the past. In light of the housing bust, some experts suggest changing the way the inflation rate is calculated to include home prices instead of just rental costs. Others go further and suggest that to really get a realistic rate of inflation the index must include fuel and food prices at a minimum—even if spiraling health care costs and rising educational expenses are still excluded. A more inclusive index would give the government a more realistic picture of inflation, in order to monitor it more closely and prevent it from getting too high. Still others argue that the CPI is a completely bogus index which lacks credibility because it has been "improved" upon twenty-four times since 1978. If the older methods of calculating inflation from just twenty-five years ago were used now, the inflation rate would be a scary 10 percent today.

After several years of falling interest rates to offset the economic downturn, inflationary pressures are starting to be felt. What will the federal government do now? If it raises interest rates to offset inflation, it could wreck an already fragile economy, catapulting it into something that could become known in history as the Second Great Depression.

Is the problem with the political system and not the economy? Historically, a unified government with a strong will is needed to battle inflation. In the political arena, candidates promise things to their constituents in order to win elections. But once elected, they are unwilling to raise taxes on the bulk of the people in order to pay for those promises. The easy way out is for the government to print more magic dollars to maintain the political status quo. This is what happened in Zimbabwe on a massive scale, and something no different in nature—just size—is being done by the United States.

In Nero's time, when the Romans accepted the initial diluted denarii, the first recipients of those coins thought they were as good as the real ones. But when the word got out, the coins became worth less. The same thing is happening to the U.S. dollar. Over time, citizens, as well as foreign countries and investors who hold our debt, may come to the realization that they need wheelbarrows full of dollars to buy what a single dollar used to. Then no one will buy the debt at any rate and the U.S. economy, if not fixed, will implode.

The American economy is just emerging from the worst economic crisis since the Great Depression, and inflation is heating up. There is a growing fear that we will see another period of stagflation like the one in the 1970s. Some economists are worried that in an attempt to avoid a catastrophic 1930s-like depression, the Federal Reserve's policies will give us a crippling 1970s-like economy.

To some extent the United States is in uncharted territory. No economy this large and so prominent in the world has taken on such debt. To avoid the trauma the European Union is going through, the United States must do more than governments have done in the past.

As history has shown us many times, excessive inflation can be the catalyst for another recession or depression that may make the most recent economic crisis look mild by comparison. Periods of high inflation seem to cycle in and out with economic

downturns. The question is no longer whether we will see another period of high inflation. The past has demonstrated that
a rise in the inflation rate is inevitable as the nation and world
recover. The Federal Reserve Board feels this inflation can be
controlled, and hopefully they will do more than just redefining
the calculation a twenty-fifth time. No one feels it can be eliminated. The United States, and many of the nations of Europe,
have entered a period where they are plagued by massive debt
and deficit spending. Those have always been the harbingers of
damaging inflation. The only question remaining seems to be
whether or not the next inflation rises so high and so fast that
it triggers a collapse of the U.S. economy to rival the fall of the
Roman Empire. As we have seen, the lesson from history is that
this can happen, and the results can be catastrophic.

CHAPTER NINE

Unemployment

An "acceptable" level of unemployment means that the
government economist to whom it is acceptable still
has a job.

— AUTHOR UNKNOWN

I n the United States, the Bureau of Labor Statistics (BLS)
measures and calculates the nation's unemployment rate.
Every month the BLS surveys sixty thousand U.S. house-
holds. There are many questions asked of each person of working age. However, they are not directly asked what they think
their own labor force status is. Then they are classified into one
of three categories: Employed, Unemployed, or Not in the Labor
Force. The number of unemployed persons is then divided by
the entire labor force, and that is how they determine the unemployment rate.

Many economists believe that the "official" unemployment rate isn't even close to the actual rate of unemployment. They argue that the actual rate is probably twice as high as the official rate because of the way the government classifies people. For the "unemployed," the BLS counts only those people not working who have seriously tried to find a job in the past four weeks.

First there's the problem with how they classify the underemployed. If someone is laid off from his full-time job and all he can get is a job flipping burgers for one hour a week, that person is put in the "employed" category. Obviously, he can't make a living, and at an hour a week, it's hard to even call it a job. These underemployed individuals keep the unemployment rate artificially low. It is important to keep in mind that it's in the interest of whoever is running the country to show the lowest unemployment figure possible.

One way to massage the number is to find a reason to remove workers from the "unemployed" category. A large number of people excluded in order to lower the official unemployment rate are those frustrated workers who get classified as "not in the labor force." They want a job, but they feel it's pointless to continue looking when the job market is so limited. They may have searched for a year or more, but they've given up on finding work for the time being. By counting these people as "not in the labor force," it lowers the unemployment rate. Since they will begin looking for employment once jobs are available again, the validity of this exclusion is questionable.

Temporary workers are also counted as "employed," even though they are working at temp positions because they can't find permanent employment.

Self-employed people who were forced to start their own businesses when they couldn't find a replacement for the job they lost are also not counted as "unemployed." They can be struggling just as much or more than the underemployed crowd. They may not be making enough profit to come even close to supporting a family, but are considered fully employed.

To see what a difference the classification into categories makes, we can use employment figures from the "recovery" period after the Great Recession of 2008–2009. In June 2011, the official national unemployment rate was 9.2 percent. In June 2012, it was still hovering near 8 percent with a massive twenty-six million Americans having retired or given up looking.

Unemployment and History

There actually was a period of several hundred years after the fall of the Western Roman Empire during which unemployment was not a concern. But the reason there was no unemployment in Europe was not a positive one: it was because there wasn't any money to pay workers with. During the Dark Ages, people basically bartered. A piglet was traded for some corn. Money, in the form of coins, was hard to get and rare except among the nobles.

It wasn't until the population began to move from farms into cities that people needed money to buy food from an outside source instead of growing or catching it themselves. By definition, a serf or a slave cannot be unemployed, only downtrodden. If you weren't a serf or a slave you might be a yeoman farmer, self-employed with no other option. Once the massive casualties caused by the Black Death changed the social and economic structure of Europe (see the chapter on plagues), workers became scarce and therefore valuable and had to be paid. The best pay was in the new and growing cities. But you can't grow crops when you no longer live on the land, and so the new working class needed money to pay for housing, food, and just about everything else for themselves and their family. But it was very possible to go to a city only to find there were no jobs or to lose your job. Consequently, the earliest examples of unemployment occurred when the cities began to grow all over Europe and people first developed a dependence on the income from their jobs to buy food and shelter.

Perhaps the first recognition of unemployment as a social problem came in sixteenth-century England. During the first part of that century, there was no distinction made between vagrants and the unemployed. But a combination of factors contributed to a rise in the number of people unable to find work, and they were faced with an awful choice: break the law or starve. There was even a law passed allowing vagabonds to be hanged. And they were. Not having a job could get you killed. This is rather a far cry from today's extended unemployment benefits. An estimated seventy-two thousand vagabonds were executed as vagrants during the rule of King Henry VIII alone. In 1601, one of the earliest welfare programs was enacted by the English government. The Elizabethan Poor Law distinguished between those who wanted work and those who refused to work. The law created workhouses for unemployed people to live and work in. These workhouses were miserable and paid virtually nothing, but they were an alternative to death or imprisonment. They were, for their time, considered a generous and forward-looking social program.

Nobody but those out of work saw unemployment as a serious problem until industrialization had firmly taken hold in urban areas. In the 1800s, the population shifted from the rural farmlands to the cities. There simply were a lot more people than were needed to work the farms. By the end of the nineteenth century, after the Industrial Revolution, unemployment began to rise. Many laborers had their jobs replaced by machines, and many other types of jobs became obsolete. A good example of this process was the harvester. Before the harvester was invented, it could take a dozen men weeks to pick the corn or reap the wheat on a large farm. Once there was a mechanical device, the same amount of crops could be gathered in days by just a few men and horses. As productivity and agricultural output per worker increased dramatically, the price of goods decreased. The same process has continued ever since in the factories as well. Today we see the ultimate example of this where robots have replaced most of the workforce needed to manufacture an auto. But when people are not employees, they are also not consumers. And if they can't afford to buy the products of the factories, soon no one has a job because there is nothing to manufacture. This cycle of unemployment and diminishing markets has caused many businesses to fail even while on paper the economy was still growing.

Cause and Effect

The single greatest cause of unemployment is for the economy to slow down. Whenever that has happened, unemployment numbers have skyrocketed. This has been particularly true for the Unites States over the past century.

The Great Depression

"Life is just a bowl of cherries"
—"LIFE IS JUST A BOWL OF CHERRIES,"
LYRICS BY LEW BROWN, MUSIC BY RAY HENDERSON

In early 1931, the most popular song was "Life Is Just a Bowl of Cherries." Six months later, the song played on the radio the most was "Brother Can You Spare a Dime?" That pretty much says it all. As you read what happened then, if you see any parallels to today's problems, feel free to be nervous. We may now be living in the prime economic example of having not learned from history.

In the United States during the 1920s, many investors and businesses took on too much debt. Investors could borrow money to buy stocks. Banks were willing to loan investors $9 for every $1 in assets. During the Roaring Twenties, times were good. But eventually investors panicked and began to sell their stocks so that they could pay off their loans. In 1929 the stock market crashed, losing 89 percent of its value during the next three years.

In 1929 U.S. unemployment was at 3 percent. But just four years later, across the United States, 25 percent of all workers and 37 percent of all nonfarmworkers were unemployed. In the 1930s, the Great Depression created massive unemployment throughout the world. By 1932, Germany also had national unemployment rates of around 25 percent. In some cities across England, unemployment reached 70 percent. Back in the United States, in Ohio, unemployment topped 60 percent in Cleveland and reached a devastating 80 percent in Toledo. During that time, two million homeless people moved across the United States looking for work. And more than three million out-of-work men were put in federal work camps to keep them off city streets.

In Germany, massive unemployment left a nation ripe for the rise of the Nazi Party. In the United States, it caused many social programs to be enacted under President Franklin D. Roosevelt. His New Deal policies were created to provide some financial protection to American citizens. These same policies greatly increased the size of the federal government and involved it in every aspect of our society. Unemployment and the Great Depression were the parents of Big Government.

Unemployment remained high throughout the 1930s, first generally falling, then actually increasing again in 1937 when there was a second "dip." There is no way to know just how long the Great Depression might have lasted if World War II had not intervened. By 1939 America was moving toward a wartime economy, and by 1942 there was no unemployment left because of the needs of the war. The surplus of men changed to a shortage, and millions of women joined the workforce to replace those men who went off to fight.

The 1973–1975 Recession

Unemployment rose to 9 percent during the mid-1970s. Two outside forces triggered the recession that caused this: a surge in oil prices by OPEC (a quadruple increase) and much higher government spending because of the Vietnam War. This in turn created stagflation. It is easy to see the similarities between that time period and today. Again the United States has seen a doubling of the cost of fuel and has been borrowing massive amounts of money to support overseas wars.

The Early Eighties Recession

Unemployment rose to a high of 10.8 percent during the 1981–1982 recession. Inflation was carried over from the previous decade because of the 1973 oil crisis and the 1979 energy crisis.

Inflation, whose control is the technical reason for the Federal Reserve to exist and set interest rates, was considered to be damaging the entire economy. The recession was caused primarily because of tighter monetary policies put in place by the U.S. government to get inflation under control. This included raising interest rates and making credit harder to get, and by doing so slowing home building, limiting major purchases like furniture and cars, and discouraging business start-ups and expansions of larger corporations by making them more expensive. This made it harder for new graduates to get jobs, for anyone to find a job, and put out of work those who built homes or structures and those who supplied the builders. The threat of inflation ended, with several million new unemployed not worrying about there being too much money.

The Great Recession of 2008–2009

The next bubble that formed and then burst was in the U.S. housing market. Because housing values rose so high from 2001 to 2007, many believed the U.S. economy was much stronger than it actually was. Like the pre–Great Depression years, when money and credit were extended to investors to buy stocks, money and credit were freely given for home purchases. In 2008, several economic disasters hit the United States and then the rest of the world, causing a massive global recession. First the housing market collapsed, and then the construction industries soon followed. Millions of mortgages had been resold to creditors worldwide. Many banks and hedge funds had borrowed billions of dollars to buy these repackaged mortgages, and they became "toxic," with no buyers in sight and values unknown.

Some of the largest banks in the United States and Europe collapsed. Congress voted to give the U.S. banks $700 billion in bailout money. For the first time ever, the U.S. government took major ownership in the country's largest banks. The same banks that had been giving credit so easily to almost anyone just a year before were now cutting off loans and credit to consumers and businesses. It was a major ordeal just to get a car loan. The stock market fell 40 percent, and housing prices fell 20 percent. Trillions of dollars in personal wealth evaporated. By late 2008 the crisis had spread to the auto and retail industries, and the Big Three U.S. automakers (GM, Chrysler, and Ford) were about to go bankrupt.

Many economists are concerned about the $787 billion stimulus package that was signed by President Obama in 2009 in an effort to jump-start the ailing U.S. economy. Experts worry that it will cause future inflation and a crippling debt the government can't get out from under.

In this increasingly global economy, the U.S. recession pushed the rest of the rich industrialized nations into their own steep recessions. Between 2007 and 2010, twenty-five million people in the world's wealthiest countries lost their jobs. During the Great Recession, more than 10 percent of the U.S. workforce was unemployed, with some areas of the country hovering at a 25 percent unemployment rate. The government's broader U-6 unemployment figure was a frightening 20 percent. The U-6 figures include people who are no longer looking for work but would take a job if offered one and those who only work part-time. If you work only one day a week at McDonald's, making fries for minimum wage, then you are on the U-6 index as "underemployed." This is often felt to give a better picture of the national situation than the U-3 figures used by the government, which cover only those who are actively looking for work and have none at all. Our one-day fry cook is listed as "employed" for U-3 purposes.

The "official" date when this most recent recession ended was June 2009. But two years into the "recovery," the unemployment rate averaged over three full percentage points higher than the average unemployment rate during the recession itself. And this is the very narrow, official unemployment rate: the real U-6 rate being as high as 16 percent unemployed and holding. This has been the worst recovery from an economic downturn since the Great Depression.

It is still too early in the recovery from this new Great Recession to determine if the jobs will come back in significant numbers. Most economists agree it will take many years—maybe a decade or more—to recover all those lost jobs. Government decisions seem to be having a significant effect on this. Whether that will be considered a good thing or a bad one in the long run has yet to be determined. Just as there was in 1937, when Roosevelt misjudged the economy and tightened it prematurely, there is a chance of a "double dip" into another official recession. Or even as the world situation changes, triple or quadruple dips may occur over a greatly slowed and extended recovery. Long-term, perhaps even permanent, high unemployment seems to be more possible and even more commonplace now than at any time before. When you combine the current U.S. economic situation with the exporting of jobs, there is no guarantee there will ever be a "full" recovery. Some economists are worried that the United States will be forced to accept an 8–9 percent U-3 unemployment rate as the new normal. History has said this will not be the case—almost every period of high unemployment is followed by one with less—but never before has the world economy been so linked, free enterprise so fettered, and technology changing so quickly.

Effects of Unemployment

Shakespeare, being Shakespeare, described unemployment in distressingly lyrical terms: "You take my life when you do take the means whereby I live."

Unemployment can have devastating effects, putting the physical and emotional health of all family members at risk. It affects everyone, even those fortunate enough to escape job loss directly. Every time someone loses his or her job, that is one less person who can pay local, state, and federal taxes. These people will also cut back on their discretionary, or nonessential, spending. That will contribute to a further decline in tax revenues, and in some cases, destroy the social and economic fabric of entire communities. Unemployment has built into it a feedback mechanism. When fewer people work, less money is spent, causing businesses to falter or fail and more people to lose their jobs. It can be both a cause and an effect of a recession.

Additionally, many of the newly unemployed will draw state unemployment benefits instead of paying taxes. As unemployment within the state increases, the state begins to operate at a deficit. If unemployment gets too high, a state may have no choice but to raise taxes, which costs virtually everyone a loss of income. It may also have to lay off state workers. Then those newly unemployed spend less, so sales tax revenue continues to decline. They also draw unemployment, which strains state resources even further. In a long period of high unemployment even the benefits can run out, pushing formerly stable families into poverty. This strains the state's resources further. More needs to be done with even fewer taxpayers, so taxes increase.

This discourages job formation and the cycle of unemployment then continues.

Many of the jobs that were lost in this recent recession are never coming back. They may have been outsourced overseas, or now one overworked person does the job of two or three people. Technology can also lead to high unemployment. When mechanical looms began appearing in England at the start of the 1800s, tens of thousands of weavers could not compete and became unemployed. This led to riots and even terrorist groups attacking the new factories.

Unemployment can cause personal debt to soar. People have to rely on credit to pay for everyday necessities.

Unemployment causes a big increase in bankruptcies.

High unemployment destroys home values, making it difficult for you to relocate for another job or borrow against the value of your house when you need the money to pay for essentials.

Less revenue for schools means the quality of your child's education declines.

Less revenue for law enforcement, coupled with more people in desperate financial straits, means the crime rate rises.

Unemployment affects a wide range of industries in the private sector, from retailing to auto to housing.

Even average rates of unemployment can destroy small businesses.

Long-term high unemployment rates can cause a mass exodus of people fleeing entire communities, leaving virtual ghost towns.

Unemployment causes homelessness. During the most recent recession, tent cities cropped up in urban areas with high unemployment. Nowhere in history is there an upside to unemployment for the worker or the nation.

What History Can Tell Us

Looking back at history, can we predict our economic future? Will the United States continue to be an economic superpower or will the recovery from the greatest financial crisis since the 1930s falter, leaving an entire generation under- or unemployed for the rest of their lives?

The United States lost 3.2 million manufacturing jobs between 2000 and 2007. Like the period of time after the Industrial Revolution, when people were replaced by machines, the tech revolution during the 1990s and early 2000s was the catalyst for the elimination of many manufacturing jobs. And just like the jobs lost during the Industrial Revolution, most of the manufacturing jobs lost over the past decade will never come back. During the Industrial Revolution, workers were forced to retrain or leave the industry they were in entirely. That may be exactly what an entire generation of laid-off American manufacturing workers will have to do.

If we look at the previous two recoveries, after the 1990s recession and the early 2000s recession, they were both considered "jobless" recoveries. And just like the period right after the Industrial Revolution, productivity increased after these two recent recessions. The same thing appears to be occurring in this current recovery: productivity has increased with no corresponding increase in jobs. As Klaus Kleinfeld, chairman and CEO of Alcoa, said recently: "We've found ways to do more with fewer people." That trend is now being seen in businesses all across America. Even though productivity is increasing and healthy profit margins are starting to emerge, it has been done without rehiring those employees who were laid off during the

Great Recession. One person now does the work of two or three people. Those laid-off workers have been replaced by sophisticated machines and technological advances. In fact, the United States was producing slightly more goods and services in 2011 than it was in 2007, but with seven million fewer workers. Even slight drops in productivity in early 2012 did not produce more jobs.

As any nation claws its way out of the Great Recession, it has to do it in an increasingly global environment. All nations now have one world market for many goods and services. In the past ten to fifteen years, four hundred million skilled workers have entered the global workforce from countries such as China, India, and South Africa. They can produce some goods or provide services for one-tenth of the price of those same goods and services made in America or Germany. This outsourcing has increased profits of U.S. corporations, but it has ravaged areas of the country that once had large manufacturing bases and millions of blue-collar, unionized positions.

Nor is education any protection in the twenty-first century. In the white-collar computer industry itself, which created so much cutting-edge technology, countless jobs are being outsourced to Third World countries like India, where U.S. companies can hire five programmers for the same amount of money it would cost to hire one U.S. worker. American computer experts have to work to their strengths, imagination, and creativity, finding new solutions, in order to remain competitive at the higher cost.

Professional services jobs always seemed safe from outsourcing. But now even some medical doctors' jobs have been outsourced. This means a radiologist in India may read the brain scan of a patient in Houston, Texas, uploading a report and diagnosis in minutes from across the world. Technology can even allow doctors to virtually assist in the operating room while working from another continent.

Technology has also transformed jobs in the legal profession, resulting in some legal skills becoming obsolete while others are regularly outsourced. For example, software created to streamline document production and massive search engines developed for legal research have allowed many law firms and government agencies to reduce the number of lawyers they must hire. That same software enables many Americans to produce simple legal forms themselves, using a $30 software package instead of a $300-an-hour lawyer to draw up a will and other common documents. Virtual depositions and other interviews can now be conducted via the Internet by America-trained lawyers who moved back to their native Third World countries and are willing to work for wages lower than what most paralegals in this country would get paid.

Back in the 1930s, President Franklin Delano Roosevelt created the New Deal, a series of social programs designed to help the unemployed and other low-income groups recover from the devastating effects of the Great Depression. The New Deal significantly increased government spending, as opposed to creating jobs. Economists are split as to whether that lengthened and deepened the Depression. A sizable number of economists believe the creation of those entitlement programs burdened the fragile economy, and government resources could have been better used for job creation. Many experts and historians believe that it was not the New Deal policies and increased spending that spurred job growth, but rather the start of World War II and the demand for goods and services to support the war effort.

In 2009 President Obama passed a massive stimulus pro-

gram designed to help pull the nation out of the severe recession. And like the 1930s post-Depression era, economists and
politicians are split over whether the stimulus has created jobs
or jeopardized the fragile recovery from the Great Recession.
Administration supporters argue that as of June 2011, Obama
was doing better at creating jobs than FDR and Ronald Reagan
at this time in their presidencies and parallel recessions. They
remind people that before Obama took office, 4.4 million jobs
had already been lost in 2008. When Barack Obama was inaugu-
rated in January 2009, the economy was still in free fall, losing
seven hundred thousand jobs per month. By the time the levels
bottomed out in late 2009, 4.3 million more jobs had been lost.
A staggering 8.7 million jobs were lost during that two-year
period. The problem is that the programs have not significantly
lowered the number of unemployed. If twenty-four million have
left the workforce, then five people are no longer seeking employment for every one person who has found a job since 2009.
Some may be retirees, but many are simply discouraged, and
the unemployment rate is likely more than double that of the
official U-6 numbers. This is both the classic example and the
definition of a "jobless recovery."

Historically, how the money was spent is very different, and
unlike in the 1930s, some of the government money went directly to job creation, not to entitlement programs. However, a
sizable portion of the stimulus funds was earmarked for more
government spending on social programs, such as an extension of unemployment benefits, food stamps, Medicaid, and
low-income housing. There were also numerous new tax credits
given to many of the working Americans, to encourage spending and hopefully spur economic growth. But a recent study
showed that most Americans used those tax savings and re-
funds to lower their personal debt or save for the next down-

turn, rather than putting money back into the economy in the form of increased spending. Likewise, there's evidence that many state and local governments simply lowered their debts with the stimulus money, rather than creating new jobs. The stimulus also gave grants to many state and local governments to temporarily prevent layoffs of educators and certain other government employees. Now the grant money is gone, and the states are still broke and will have to enact widespread layoffs. It's a vicious cycle, since the burden of large unemployment has kept tax revenues down while these financially strapped governments have to pay out ever increasing amounts of unemployment benefits.

It's challenging to get an exact number of jobs created under the stimulus program because the different political sides vary in their interpretation of those numbers. Critics of the current administration have argued that President Obama should have focused solely on creating new jobs, with little or no money going to social programs. They also say that favoring certain groups with stimulus money hurt other industries. For example, private businesses using or creating green technology got large amounts of money to compete with companies that employed workers in industries harnessing traditional energy sources, like coal and oil. The results were layoffs in the traditional industries and fewer factories built in this country. Critics also argue that if you take into account the population growth in this country, there was a net loss of 1.4 million jobs in the twelve months ending in May of 2011, and little improvement in 2012. To the critics, the stimulus was a trillion-dollar black hole.

Supporters of the administration argue that the passage of the stimulus program was absolutely critical in keeping this country from entering a Second Great Depression. And although the unemployment levels are still high, they would have been catastrophically high if the stimulus program were not in place. Supporters also argue that the $787 billion package needed to be larger in order to create enough new, permanent jobs.

As if the current unemployment problem weren't enough, many experts are worried that we are now headed for another economic downturn reminiscent of the stagflation of the 1970s. During that period in history, inflation was high and so was unemployment. Inflation seems to be heating up now, with price increases on food, fuel, education, and health care. The recession in the 1970s was triggered by high government spending from the Vietnam War and high oil prices. While trying to recover from the Great Recession, we are still fighting a war in Afghanistan, and we are also militarily involved in other unstable regions across the Middle East. And as in the 1970s, our oil-dependent country is at the mercy of this volatile area of the world to feed its addiction. During the 2011 Arab Spring, oil prices soared. They have since retreated, but given the unpredictability of that region, they could spike again at any time, wreaking havoc on the fragile U.S. economy.

Since World War II, most recession recoveries have followed a similar progression. The economy bounces back in short order, growing at about 6 percent, while unemployment declines steadily and significantly in the aftermath. Even the two recessions preceding the Great Recession were followed by solid growth, though they didn't recover many of the jobs lost during the downturns. This current "recovery" is different. Growth is less than 2 percent, and the job numbers are depressingly weak, with a near record of only eighteen thousand new jobs created in June of 2011 and erratic growth since.

Given that the most recent recession is now on record as being the worst recovery since the Great Depression, it seems unlikely that many of the jobs that were lost during that recession will come back. The number of jobs we need to create just to keep up with population growth is huge and varies depending on the participation rate of the labor force. Many people dropped out of the workforce during the recession because they were unable to get a job. If they start up their job searches again, the participation rate will increase and so will the number of jobs needed just to keep the employment rate steady when accounting for population growth. And if we consider that most of the new jobs created since the recovery were part-time jobs, the actual number of Americans without permanent, full-time jobs is mind-boggling, over twenty-four million.

Solutions

Everyone, at least every elected official, has an opinion on how to lower unemployment. In 1929, President Herbert Hoover felt that the economy should be left alone to heal itself. That did not work out so well. The shantytowns that filled with the unemployed and homeless became known as Hoovervilles. He was most definitely not reelected, losing to FDR.

President John F. Kennedy, when speaking about the issue of unemployment in America, once said, "We believe that if men have the talent to invent new machines that put men out of work, they have the talent to put those men back to work."

When JFK was president, more than half a century ago, computer science was in its infancy, space exploration had yet to put a man on the moon, and the term "outsourcing" wasn't even a recognized word in the dictionary, much less the business model used by many American companies. But even back then, there was concern about the number of American workers losing their jobs to advances in technology.

We have far too many talented people out of work in this country. The new legions of unemployed include countless people whose jobs have been outsourced or made obsolete. Many of these individuals are people who were creating the machines and technology to advance science and industry long before many Americans had even heard the terms "Internet" or "globalization." Many literally trained their replacements.

Kennedy had an excellent point that the leaders of this country should pay heed to. One of the most important solutions to this country's unemployment problems is the creation of numerous job training (and in many cases, retraining) programs. Noted international affairs expert and author Fareed Zakaria has recently proposed what he calls a "flight plan" to help repair the U.S. economy. He says that an entire generation of middle-aged workers, particularly in the automotive manufacturing industry, will never get their jobs back. To be a viable solution, the job retraining program should be similar in size and scope to the GI Bill (the bill that paid for veterans to go to college after World War II). This should include educational programs that stress innovation and creativity, so the United States can once again be the world's leading exporter of goods instead of jobs.

Leading up to the Great Recession, we had a growing U.S. trade deficit with China. During the years 2001–2008, 2.4 million American jobs were lost because of that deficit. China now has a trade surplus of $22.3 billion; that's how much their exports outnumber their imports. The United States is gobbling up Chinese-made goods, but the Chinese don't seem to be as hungry for American-made products.

What citizens in China, Japan, and many other foreign countries want are things that represent our American culture. They love American movies, television shows, and music, for example. They love to visit American cities as tourists and get their advanced degrees in American universities. Zakaria suggests that we identify growth industries, such as products directly related to American culture, and dramatically increase our exports of those products. Some countries, like China, have restrictive policies on those types of products. But Americans purchase huge amounts of Chinese imports, and the U.S. government needs to put pressure on China to ease those restrictions. Zakaria also notes that we are one of the few wealthy nations in the world without a department of tourism. Tourism creates millions of jobs in this country, and if the government can provide funds for some kind of coordination of efforts, it could create many new jobs.

There are alternative suggestions put forth by experts and politicians based on how other countries are successfully lowering their unemployment rates and enhancing job creation. For example, many countries have a national bank to fund infrastructure projects, in part with private sector money. Studies have also shown that most new jobs from 1980–2005 came from companies that were less than five years old. The government can ease regulations on these fledgling new businesses and encourage capital funding for the start-up environment.

When putting together his budget for America, President Obama and his economic team operated under the assumption that the U.S. economy could create twenty million jobs during the next ten years. Unfortunately, if you simply look at the past decade, only 1.7 million new jobs were created during that time period. It seems almost impossible for the economy to produce anywhere close to the number the president suggests.

History has always repeated itself when it comes to economic downturns. The unemployment levels fluctuated as the economy cycled in and out of periods of expansion and contraction. But with this most recent economic crisis, the situation differed from past downturns from the very beginning. The set of circumstances bringing the country to its economic knees was something we had never seen before to that extent. And the so-called recovery period has also been unprecedented in its lack of real economic growth or job creation. Although they may disagree on how to stimulate the economy and create jobs, experts all agree that high long-term unemployment can destroy families, communities, and entire nations. With that disturbing certainty, the only thing left to do is agree on how to fix the unemployment problem.

The country's leaders must come to a consensus on how to stop the hemorrhaging of American jobs, or the only thing increasing will be the size of the deficit from lost tax revenues, which means more unemployment benefits are paid out. If we ignore the problem, or try to pass it on to the next generation, or spend years bickering over tentative solutions, it will mean the ultimate collapse of the world's greatest economic superpower. Rome, late-eighteenth-century France, and the Ottoman Empire were all economic leaders that faltered and collapsed. It was not in a day, not even a decade, but if a nation loses the ability to use and maintain its workforce, history is full of warnings about what will, not just can, result.

CHAPTER TEN

Depressions and Recessions

But with the slow menace of a glacier, depression came on. No one had any measure of its progress; no one had any plan for stopping it. Everyone tried to get out of its way.

—FRANCES PERKINS (1880–1965),
U.S. SECRETARY OF LABOR, 1933–1945

Simply put, discussing the topics of economic depression and recession is painful at any time. It is, well, depressing emotionally. More so at this writing, since the entire world is not recovering from the last recession caused by the housing bubble, and it seems constantly poised to begin another plunge. There are many definitions of a recession and of a depression. Most involve the size of the gross domestic product (GDP), which is an esoteric economic term that means the value of just about everything that is made, bought, or done in a nation. Perhaps the simplest and most obvious way to define a recession is when this GDP, the total wealth of the nation, "recedes"—when the total amount of wealth, money, and the value of everything else in the nation becomes smaller. Negative growth affects everything, from jobs to interest rates. And if the recession continues for too long, the cumulative negative effects of a loss in wealth create a "depression." Some say two years of recession defines a depression. Politicians, many of whose policies create the problems, try hard not to use either word.

It is good to remember that even when the economy remains unchanged, it is already losing ground. Every day, more people are born and more enter the workplace needing a job. The number of people is growing, and if the amount of wealth does not expand to match this population growth, then the result is, quite simply, that there is less for each person to live on. So when there is a recession and the amount of wealth decreases, that smaller amount of wealth is also constantly being divided by more and more people, a double whammy. Economic growth is needed in every country of the world just to stay even. As in Lewis Carroll's Red Queen's race, "it takes all the running you can do, to keep in the same place. If you want to get somewhere else, you must run at least twice as fast as that!" In a recession, the entire structure of jobs, business, manufacturing, and banking is losing the race with population growth. In a depression, it keeps losing ground for a long time.

In the short run not everyone loses when the economy stalls. There will always be those who benefit from the financial ruin of others. During the Panic of 1907, depositors with failing banks had to stand in line to get their money out of the banks before those banks ran out of money. It was a "first come, first served" kind of mentality. Some exhausted depositors, who had stood in line for days on end, paid people $10 a day to stand in line for them. And in 2011, as the economic recovery began to stall, alcohol sales in the United States shot up. While mortgage lenders, real estate agents, and construction workers scramble to make a living while living through what is still a housing depression, attorneys specializing in bankruptcies and foreclosures are making a fortune off the misfortune of others.

Recessions come from many causes, some of which have been discussed in other parts of this book. But when you look at them, the real cause is abuse and greed. The actions of some affect the entire economy enough that everyone pays. This may be the government, which can both cause and extend the misery. Another group can be those companies that handle the key parts of the economy. Unfortunately, both are in such a position of power that they may cause the recession but tend to suffer less than the average person from it.

The question is, then, have we learned economic honesty from the recent high price everyone is paying for the actions of Wall Street and the banks? Arguably the most powerful investment firm in the world, U.S. brokerage house Goldman Sachs (yes, the same firm that was a major player in the packaging of toxic mortgages that plunged our country into the worst recession since the Great Depression) did some creative accounting and a complex derivatives deal back in 2002. This was done to help the free-spending and -borrowing Greek government mask the extent of its debt so it could join the European Union. Goldman Sachs arranged agreements relating to the exchange of interest payments and principal denominated in two different currencies that are now maturing, swelling the Greek deficit and plunging that country into bankruptcy. Because of the deal brokered, Greece handed over its public assets to the International Monetary Fund (IMF; the organization that backs up the banks and even national treasuries), while Goldman Sachs got a sizable cut from the Greek government for managing to "legally" get the debt-ridden country into the EU even though it violated the 60 percent deficit limit. Now the euro is in trouble, but Goldman Sachs got its money and is doing fine. The real losers are the Greek people, who did enjoy their government spending all that borrowed money on them, but now are facing unprecedented levels of austerity and taxation. Because the disastrous condition of the Greek economy was exposed, the IMF now "owns" the Acropolis of Athens and other prime Greek real estate. Of course the Acropolis might need updating—after all, it is 2,500 years old. Maybe the United States could lend them some unemployed American construction workers; there certainly are enough of them available since the housing bubble burst in 2008 from all those toxic mortgages Goldman Sachs and others prettied up, then repackaged and sent down the road—or even across the Atlantic—again, after taking their hefty brokerage fees.

There is a running joke among economists that when your neighbor loses his job it's a recession, and when you lose your job it's a depression. There is no single agreed-upon definition for either of these terms, but the standard definition for a recession is a decline in the GDP for at least two consecutive quarters. Many economists don't like this definition because it doesn't consider things like consumer confidence or changes in the unemployment levels—two variables that certainly contribute to the collective pain felt by Americans during an economic downturn. It also makes it difficult to determine start and end dates, and using that traditional definition may ignore short recessions altogether.

Some economists feel that the Business Cycle Dating Committee at the National Bureau of Economic Research (NBER; the federal government's source for hopefully unbiased monetary research) provides a more comprehensive and accurate definition. They say that a recession occurs when business activity has reached its peak and then begins to decline until it bottoms out. When it starts to pick up again that is called an "expansionary period." Business activity includes the employment levels, industrial production, and wholesale-retail sales. Under NBER's definition, the average recession lasts about a year.

Most Americans think all this number crunching is bogus. Two-plus years into the "recovery" from the Great Recession, more than 80 percent of Americans surveyed in an August 2011 poll said they believed the country was currently in a recession. Thirty-three percent of those surveyed felt it was "severe." And why wouldn't they? The August 2011 job report showed zero, zip, nada job growth. Since then it has run from 250,000 jobs per month to again almost none. The last time zero job growth was recorded for nonfarm jobs was in February of 1945. And Americans have every right to be depressed about the prospect of the United States tipping into a full-blown depression. After all, the latest news has been nothing but depressing. In August 2011, for the first time ever, the credit rating of the United States was downgraded. This means even the United States, once a safe haven for foreign money, now has to pay extra to borrow it.

Before the Great Depression in the 1930s, all periods of economic downturn were called recessions. But after the Great Depression, there needed to be a way to distinguish the severity of these periods of economic decline. A depression is now thought of as any period where the GDP declines by more than 10 percent. As of 2011, the last depression in the United States was in

1937–1938, when the GDP declined by a staggering 18.2 percent. However, that number pales in comparison to the period of the Great Depression, just a few years earlier, when the GDP declined at a horrific 33 percent. It's significant to note that many economists feel that the Great Depression lasted from the 1929 crash until we entered World War II in late 1941. There was only a gradual recovery over those twelve years, and even that was partially reversed by the 1937–1938 decline that was caused by FDR deciding he could raise taxes. Then even after twelve years of government programs that outright hired millions of workers, it basically took the full employment and massive spending of a world war to end it. So history gives not the best of signs for a government-driven recovery.

This is not to say that all actions by the government are ineffective. Certainly President Hoover showed that by doing nothing as a policy, thinking the economy could heal itself. Things just got worse, and FDR won the 1932 election by a landslide. Having learned from this history lesson when the subprime mortgage industry collapsed in the fall of 2008 and the United States seemed poised for the first depression since the late 1930s, the federal and state governments acted. Through a series of drastic actions, the economy was pulled back from the brink, but we still ended up with the most severe recession in history. The Great Recession of 2008–2009 was seen as a huge relief compared to what many economists believed we were headed for: an epic depression that could have struck the global economy with the force of a tsunami, washing away entire countries and causing the complete collapse of the world's economic superpower. Or perhaps history is repeating itself. Certainly if you ask average Americans whether they think we are headed toward another recession, they overwhelmingly respond that they don't think we are out of the first one yet. The hope is that we have learned enough that this one lasts less than a dozen years, and a less drastic ending can be found.

A Long History

Since 1790, there have been about forty-seven recessions in the United States alone (depending on the definitions used). The more recent U.S. recessions have caused global economic downturns, since we are now more economically entwined with foreign countries than at any time in the past. What we are experiencing now, as fallout from the Great Recession, is plummeting consumer confidence levels—another factor triggering economic downturns. This jargon translates as: people aren't buying because they are afraid of another recession or job loss, but if they don't buy, their fears become self-fulfilling prophecies because there is less sold, so fewer jobs are needed and the recession worsens.

Let's take a look at a select group of recessions and depressions in the past. How they ended can give some insight into solutions available today.

Panic of 1797

This was the first recession recorded in the United States. There was extensive land speculation during the 1790s. The Bank of England was experiencing severe deflationary pressures from its involvement in a war with France. England was still heavily tied to the new American economy, and the deflation wreaked havoc on the real estate market in the United States. Numerous businessmen, congressmen, and even a Supreme Court justice found themselves pursued mercilessly by creditors. In fact, Justice Wilson left Pennsylvania and fled to Maryland to hide from creditors. Eventually, he was found and spent time in a debtor's prison.

After the panic, there was political pressure to pass some laws protecting debtors—particularly when some of the most notable ones were those who made or interpreted those laws. In 1800 the first bankruptcy act was passed, primarily because of huge debts incurred as a result of the land speculation on the western frontier. The act was repealed in 1803, mainly because of abuses from high-rolling debtors who used it to discharge their debts only to then turn around and start all over, knowing they could discharge the new debts almost as soon as those debts were incurred.

1821 Depression

In 1791, Congress created the First Bank of the United States. It was responsible for about 20 percent of the country's money. It acted like a modern central bank, and it was created to help manage and finance the country's needs. The bank's charter lapsed in 1811, but it was soon replaced by the Second Bank of the United States.

In order to finance the War of 1812, the government borrowed heavily. After the war ended in March of 1815, inflation began to skyrocket. Panic ensued when banknotes plummeted in value because of that inflation. This excessive borrowing caused a strain on the bank's reserve specie (gold and silver).

In 1814, the federal government stopped the specie payment. During that time, the U.S. government did not honor the obligations to their depositors. Not only did this cause economic instability, but it triggered a surge of new banks and the expansion of banknotes—paper money. When the printing presses started working overtime, monetary inflation soon followed. With all that excess currency—basically, easy money—risky investments soared. The government did it again in 1819, refusing to pay their depositors and creditors in gold and silver. This caused widespread panic and a deepening of the depression that had been going on for the past four years. By this time, hundreds of thousands of people were thrust into unemployment. In large cities like Philadelphia, unemployment reached 75 percent. Tent cities were set up in urban areas all across the country. Real estate prices plummeted and banks began to fail. Sound familiar?

Panic of 1837

Andrew Jackson was elected president in 1829. He opposed the Second Bank of the United States, calling it unconstitutional, corrupt, and dangerous. He kept the bank's charter, which was due to expire in March of 1836, from being renewed. This caused the number of state and wildcat banks to explode. Money was readily available and investors borrowed heavily in order to fund their cheap public-land purchases. Small farmers, manufacturers, traders, and merchants all borrowed lots and lots of money. And rather than paying off their debts as they were incurred and then financing new projects, businesses kept borrowing more money to invest in speculative purchases. They all assumed that they would make a lot more money that way than if they paid their debts off first.

But it wasn't just cheap public land that was being gobbled up by investors; the value of private land in urban areas began to skyrocket. One speculator from Hartford, Connecticut, related that he was making 75 percent annually on his initial $1,000 purchase in Michigan. The property values in New York City increased by 50 percent within five years. But the land bubble was about to burst.

Jackson believed that the government should be paid in gold and silver currency only—no paper money. He and his supporters thought that the paper money was the cause of the high inflation gripping the young nation. He watched with growing concern as the paper money, not backed by anything, was printed to aid speculators. The country's first recession in 1797, which occurred mainly through funding excessive land speculation, was long forgotten by this time.

In the early 1830s, the economy grew rapidly, primarily because of the construction of new railroads and canals. Land speculation proceeded at a manic pace, and the government sold millions of acres of public land to feverish buyers, who were counting on that land to go up in value as new settlers moved into the areas near these railroads and canals. A new tariff was passed in 1833 that encouraged massive amounts of foreign imports to flood the economy. This tariff eventually caused a huge trade imbalance, as imports far exceeded exports. This imbalance resulted in a loss of specie for the states. Initially, however, all the land sales and the tariff caused the U.S. treasury to have a huge surplus. By 1835, the federal government was able to pay off the national debt. Jackson was thrilled, and most modern politicians would also be ecstatic over retiring the national debt on their watch.

But Congress was under pressure (lobbying apparently never goes out of style) to give the state banks some of that surplus so that the states could fund projects such as more new railroads and canals. Most of those states preferred to hoard their gold and silver and pay their debts off using state banknotes. Jackson was worried about all the federal land being purchased with paper money, so he had the treasury secretary issue an order called the Specie Circular. This order, which occurred right before Jackson left office, mandated that the Treasury no longer accept paper banknotes (or "rag" money) as payment for the land sales. The purchases had to be paid for in gold or silver after August 15, 1836.

A huge financial crisis was brewing in early 1837 for the incoming president, Martin Van Buren. Banks began limiting credit, and depositors started making a run on those banks, trying to get their money out. State banks, now forced to pay in gold and silver instead of paper money, didn't have enough specie to pay their debts. With the loans drying up, construction companies were unable to pay their obligations, so numerous canal and railroad projects failed. All those land speculators, who were counting on that construction to raise the price of the land they had already purchased, could not sell the land for anywhere close to what they had paid for it, much less sell it at a hefty profit. The banks began calling in their loans. Unemployment became rampant, and there were riots over food in several major cities. Eight states went bankrupt in addition to thousands of individuals. The banking system collapsed.

Out of 850 banks, 343 failed and 62 closed partially. The state banks never fully recovered.

Van Buren was opposed to direct government action to alleviate the crisis, which is the likely reason he was not reelected in 1840. President Obama had his reelection hanging in the balance primarily because of the awful economic situation. But while Van Buren was seen as not doing enough, some accuse Obama of doing too much fiscal experimentation and too much spending to try to fix the economy. It's that "damned if you do, damned if you don't" mentality, which persists today.

Panic of 1857

It was the year of the Dred Scott decision and the Crimean War was raging. The depression of 1857 was caused primarily by the declining international economy and an overexpansion of the domestic economy. Foreign investors, who were heavily leveraged because they had bought on margin in the domestic railroad industry, became worried about the overbuilt industry and the solvency of banks in the United States. Any serious drop in their stock's value would be ruinous. Many British investors sold out and took their money to Britain. But simultaneous events seemed to cause the initial panic. First there was embezzlement discovered at the Ohio Life Insurance and Trust Company. On the same day the Ohio company ceased operations, the *Central America*, a merchant marine ship carrying fifteen tons of gold, sank. News could travel quickly with the widespread use of the telegraph. American investors on the New York Stock Exchange panicked, as did British investors, who quickly began pulling their remaining money out of the market. This was an early taste of what could go wrong in a global economy. News in one part of the world, San Francisco, triggered an immediate reaction in London that crashed the American Stock Exchange. This depression quickly spread to Central and South America, whose economies were highly dependent on trade with the United States and Britain.

More than five thousand businesses failed during the first year of the panic. Some of these were railroads—the tech stock of its day—and many of the railroads, the ones that had been built to sell stock rather than to fulfill a transportation need, failed. Massive protests were held in urban areas over unemployment. There were several attempts to rectify the crisis, including creating a bank holiday in October of 1857. The secretary of the treasury also suggested selling bonds and lowering the tariff. By 1859 the country was starting to recover, although the effects lasted until the Civil War began. This war started a period of bank panics and runs on those banks because depositors feared they would lose everything. There was no deposit insurance and if your bank had invested poorly, your savings could be lost. In fact, the Second Bank of the United States did fail, not only destroying tens of thousands of depositors, but leaving the United States without a national bank at the start of the Civil War.

Recovery from the 1857 depression was slow, with the cotton-exporting southern states recovering more quickly than the manufacturing North. This caused the federal government to try to tax exports—especially cotton—more heavily. This increased tensions between the two groups of states and contributed to the split that culminated in the Civil War. The war itself, and the wartime economy, brought an end to the depression.

1873 and the Long Depression

This depression is important because it has many parallels to today's extended and jobless recovery. The year was 1873: the first postcard ever had just been released, and in Canada the North West Mounted Police force was formed. Eight years after the end of the Civil War, growth had returned with a vengeance, particularly in the railroad industry. Railroad stocks became the investment of choice, and in the pattern of bubbles and bursts the stock values quickly became unrelated to the actual profits or even the track owned by the railroad itself. Then the collapse came in 1873 and again banks failed, businesses saw sales cut in half, and unemployment soared. There are many parallels between this depression and that of 2008. Both were tied to a stock bubble—railroads in 1873 and a more general market increase including tech stocks in 2009. A major component was real estate loans going bad. In 1873 the attitude was very similar to 2008 in that those who bought land or buildings did so after over a decade of increasing values. In both cases this raised values to beyond what the real market could bear, with speculation driving up the prices. In 2008 this was complicated by government intervention in the market, forcing the creation of bad housing loans. In both periods the banks bought and sold mortgages, and when the value of the property behind the mortgage collapsed, the banks suffered. Another parallel is that Europe was having severe problems and this spilled over onto the U.S. economy.

The panic began when the largest bank in the United States, Jay Cooke and Company, failed because the foreign money it was dependent on disappeared. Not only was Cooke the top investment banking firm in the United States, it was also the main backer of Northern Pacific Railway and a significant investor in several other major railroad lines. It had invested a disproportionate amount of its depositors' money in the railroads. But most importantly, Cooke handled the majority of the government's wartime loans. The failure of Cooke was a devastating blow to the economy. Of course, if Jay Cooke had been around in 2008, a bank of that size and importance would have been deemed "too big to fail" by the U.S. government, and taxpayers would have bailed it out.

This Cooke bank failure burst yet another speculation bubble that had inflated after the Civil War. The New York Stock Exchange was shut down for ten days after Cooke's collapse to prevent panic selling. Market stops that freeze trading, both in the form of general stops and ones placed only on certain stocks, have been used since. (They were used again in the collapse of 2008, when trading was suspended on a number of bank stocks.) Credit disappeared and factories began closing. Within two years of Cooke's failure, more than eighteen thousand businesses were lost, while a third of the country's railroads went bankrupt. One effect of the high unemployment rate was wage cuts of up to 45 percent. This wage loss, combined with abusive practices and the high unemployment rate, gave impetus to the rise of labor unions.

The government did intervene, and by the time Grover Cleveland became president the nation's reserve had dropped below what most considered a minimum safe level of $100 million. One measure to restore confidence was a return to the gold standard. This helped stabilize stagflation, but did not end the unemployment or credit crunch. The Panic of 1873 caused a severe six-year depression in both Europe and the United States. Even then, jobs did not return and workingmen saw little improvement. In some ways, historians think, the country didn't pull out of this slump until 1897.

Panic of 1893 and Panic of 1896

By 1893 the World's Columbian Exposition, featuring Edison's electric lights, had opened in Chicago. It was the year ice cream cones were invented. Houdini was the greatest entertainer, and the Mormon temple in Salt Lake City was dedicated. It was also the year that saw the beginning of another depression, or possibly the resurgence of one that had not really ended. Like the Panic of 1873, the economic depression that followed in 1893 was triggered by the overbuilding of the railroad industry. The financing of all this railroad building was shaky as well, and a series of bank failures soon followed. Many of the railroads bought up their smaller competitors, compromising their own financial stability. When the mammoth Reading Railroad failed, European investors fled, causing the stock market and the banking industry to collapse.

In addition to the feverish speculation in railroads, the Sherman Silver Purchase Act of 1890 did its share to hurt the economy. In the west, there was overbuilding of the mines and overproduction of silver, so the new law required that the U.S. Treasury buy silver with notes that were backed by gold. The gold reserves fell to very low levels. Wall Street banker J. P. Morgan lent President Grover Cleveland $65 million in gold so that the country could maintain the gold standard. But like President Obama today, Cleveland was blamed for the depression. And so was the Democratic Party. In the 1894 elections, it was all about the economy—wow, that's a familiar refrain—and the Republicans swept the elections in the largest GOP gain in history.

The period between the 1893 Panic and the 1896 Panic was mostly an economic depression with a very brief period of growth right after the first panic. During this time, production shrank with the United States producing less in its factories than it had a decade earlier. Deflation was the order of the day. The economy slowly began to recover in 1897, and it experienced a sizable gold rush in both the western states and Alaska and had ten years of growth before the Panic of 1907 reared its ugly head.

Panic of 1907

The year 1907 began with an exciting change when the rules committee for football legalized the forward pass. At sea, the first modern battleship, the HMS *Dreadnought,* was launched, starting a naval building competition that did not end until World War I. By the summer of 1907, the New York Stock Exchange had already plummeted 50 percent from the previous year's high, and a severe economic downturn ensued. That October, one unscrupulous investor, F. Augustus Heinze, ingratiated himself with the bankers and came close to causing the entire banking industry to collapse when his attempt to corner the copper market failed. In some ways, the October Panic of 1907 was eerily similar to the lead-up to the subprime mortgage industry collapse in the fall of 2008. But in 2008, there was the Federal Reserve Bank to help prevent widespread financial devastation. (Some have argued that occurred anyway.) While they didn't have the Fed in 1907, Wall Street did have financier J. P. Morgan. Yes, Morgan had already come to the rescue during the last panic by lending massive amounts of gold to the U.S. government as mentioned above. But this time, with literally only twelve minutes to spare, he managed to raise enough money to keep the stock market from a cataclysmic crash.

Although the Panic of 1907 wasn't as severe as some of the ones preceding it, a very important change came about in its wake, which we'll get to in a minute. It certainly is obvious from reading about the economic history of the United States during the nineteenth and early twentieth centuries that financial panics and bank runs had become commonplace. Just one important speculator who fell on hard times could cause widespread panic, as investors pulled their money out in an attempt to cut their losses. Remember, there was no federal deposit insurance at the time. To make matters worse, many speculators were also banking officials. So they were the first to know if one of their own was in trouble, and they would immediately pull their money out of any bank that was doing business with that troubled speculator. If a struggling bank had a run on its depositors' money and you didn't make it to the head of the line, you were out of luck. Huge personal fortunes were often lost in a matter of hours, if not minutes. Not only was there no way of getting your lost money back, but there were also no government safety nets at the time. Overnight, you and your family could be out on the streets, begging for food. So it is certainly understandable that during that time there were nervous investors and agitated bank customers.

The Panic of 1907 was a very important event in the financial history of the United States. To reduce or eliminate the panics and bank runs, which seemed to be occurring on a regular basis, the Federal Reserve System was created in 1913.

Recession of 1920–1921

Things happened in 1920 that later changed history. The Nazi Party began, known then as the German Workers' Party. Edsel Ford took over the family business, not knowing his name would later be connected to the worst auto marketing fiasco in history, the Edsel of 1958. The League of Nations had its first meeting in February with great expectations but later failed miserably to prevent World War II or accomplish about anything else. The triggers for the 1920–1921 recession included the massive shift from wartime to a peacetime economy. This recession was only eighteen months long, but it was very steep.

The year 1920 was the most deflationary year on record, at around 18 percent. This was more severe than any single year during the Great Depression. To make the pain even worse, wholesale prices dropped 36.8 percent—the largest drop since the American Revolution.

The causes of these two post–World War I recessions involved more than just adjusting to a peacetime economy. First of all, labor unions were powerful during the war because the government's need for goods, services, and workers was high. Also, with so many men in combat, the year began with a labor shortage, and unions took advantage of it. About 1.2 million workers had been on strike in 1918. But by 1919, four million workers had gone on strike. However, when the war ended, the unemployment rates shot up, and relations between labor and industry quickly improved. Not surprisingly, wages fell while productivity increased.

The brand-new Federal Reserve Bank of New York made novice policy mistakes. At the end of the war, it started raising interest rates, at first by a quarter of a point, and then, a month later, by 1 percent. Six months after that, it was raised to 7 percent. This is the highest interest rate of any period in American history, except for the rates of the 1970s and early 1980s—but those were almost loan-shark rates. Once the rates rose to those new highs, credit dried up for all borrowers—businesses, consumers, and even other banks were unable to get loans.

The 1920–1921 recession ended when the New York Fed dropped the interest rate from 7 percent in July 1921 to 4.5 percent by November. The American economy bounced back with a strong recovery during this era, known as the Roaring Twenties.

1929, the Great Depression

If you were anyone but a farmer, 1929 started well. Farmers were already feeling the financial pressures that would soon bring down the U.S. economy. Many current economists think that we narrowly averted a Second Great Depression in 2008, but thus far no economic downturn in American history has even come close to the scope and size of the 1929 crisis.

Up until the Great Depression, the view of monetary policy held by most economists was that the Federal Reserve had the power and ability to achieve most any economic goal. So when the Great Depression hit and the economy collapsed, most economists were shocked at this catastrophe that they just hadn't seen coming. The depression was so severe and so unexpected that an entire generation of economists was forced to rethink existing theories and develop new ones. The U.S. government created new polices as a result of that new economic thought that helped the economy evolve throughout the twentieth century. As we shall see, this rapid shift in thought and policies also occurred after the recent Great Recession. These new policies are still being debated and evolving throughout the recovery period.

Although most historians agree on the effects of the Great Depression, not all of them agree on all of the causes. Some of the more common theories are discussed next.

On October 29, 1929, the stock market crashed. This date is invariably linked with the start of the Great Depression, although the economy had been in decline for at least six months prior. Yet many greedy bankers on Wall Street refused to acknowledge the warning signs. They continued to borrow money and invest in risky stocks. Eventually, reality hit the stock market and company valuations began to fall. During October, there was intense panic selling and the markets went out of control. Within a matter of days, Wall Street had officially collapsed. It took twenty-seven years for the stock market to recover its losses and return to precrash numbers.

Even though many people think that the crash caused the Great Depression, only 16 percent of Americans had investments in the stock market at the time. Although the crash terrified investors and caused widespread panic, most economists believe that it was neither the sole nor the primary reason for the depression. It appears that it was a combination of several factors, with the bursting of the bubble where business and investors could get easy credit starting the collapse.

Farmers, as already mentioned, were suffering hard times even as the rest of the nation remained almost euphoric. Having enjoyed a booming economy during the 1920s, America had been overproducing goods for which there was a lessening demand. As demand declined, it triggered a slowdown in agriculture and factory production, which caused millions of people to lose their jobs. As people lost jobs, they began to curtail their purchases, which caused demand for those goods and services to decline even further. So production slowed and more jobs got eliminated. The cycle then continued, and as the unemployment rate soared, people who had jobs began to fear losing them, so they also cut back on their spending. If that sounds familiar, it's because that cycle happens with every economic downturn. This lack of consumer confidence is a major reason why economists today are worried that another recession, or perhaps even a depression, is inevitable in the very near future.

By 1933, eleven thousand out of twenty-five thousand banks in the United States had failed. As mentioned above, although the Federal Reserve was created after the 1907 Panic, deposits were still uninsured. Just as in past panics, if the depositor wasn't at the head of the line, he often lost his entire life's savings. As banks began to worry about their own day-to-day survival, they stopped lending as readily. So there was significantly less credit available for investments and purchases.

In 1930, the Smoot-Hawley Tariff was passed in response to the alarming number of business failures during that time. The tariff created a high tax on imports and hurt trade with Europe. This meant we imported much less from them. In retaliation, they raised their tariffs on American goods. Those living in European countries reacted to the higher costs by curtailing their purchases of American-made products. This tariff battle accelerated the economic decline on both sides of the Atlantic because with no place to sell goods overseas, the workers who had made them were let go. Instead of protecting each country's workers, these tariffs destroyed jobs in large numbers.

Though it was not a primary reason for the depression, a severe drought from 1931 to 1936 in the Mississippi Delta devastated countless farmers. In the Great Plains, millions of acres of land became worthless in the "Dust Bowl," as the drought there lasted until the fall of 1939. Families were forced to sell their farms to pay taxes and other debts, losing their livelihoods and their homes in the process. John Steinbeck penned his famous novel *The Grapes of Wrath* about this catastrophic event.

The effects of the Great Depression cannot be understated. As all of this was going on, President Hoover decided to not "interfere" with the market, believing that the recession would end on its own. Hoover was blamed not for causing the depression, but for not acting decisively to end it (which could explain why President Obama acted quickly, if expensively, at the start of the current crisis). He was demolished in the next election by Franklin D. Roosevelt. By 1933, shantytowns, also called Hoovervilles, were cropping up across the country, housing the growing number of homeless. Americans built these makeshift "homes" with scraps of metal, pieces of wood, and cardboard boxes. In 1934, the Federal Deposit Insurance Corporation (FDIC) was created to insure bank deposits and restore depositors' faith in American banks.

At its peak, in 1933, unemployment was at 25 percent. President Roosevelt's New Deal policies were created. Some of them, or their successors, are still in place today, including the Federal Housing Administration, the Farm Security Administration, the National Labor Relations Act, and the U.S. Securities and Exchange Commission. Numerous parks, bridges, and highways were built during the next several years.

1937 Roosevelt Recession

The Great Depression waned, and the economy had recovered substantially by May of 1937. But the recovery was not really complete, and unemployment remained high (as it has after the 2008 recession). By late August of 1937, the economy began to falter again, due mostly to changes in federal policy. By early fall, it was in rapid decline. That is why this later period is sometimes called a "depression within a depression."

The stock market quickly lost a third of its value, and by the spring of 1938, unemployment surged to 1931 levels. The unemployment rate was 19 percent, and corporate profits were down 80 percent from their 1936 levels. Production in industry dropped a dramatic 40 percent, and requests for public assistance in hard-hit places like Detroit quadrupled from those requests made before 1937.

There are several reasons commonly given for the cause of this severe recession. The first is that Roosevelt decided the worst was over and attempted to balance the budget. To do that he had to significantly curtail public works projects. Those projects had provided the economy with over $4 billion in tax receipts by giving hundreds of thousands of people a paycheck and increasing economic growth. Many historians believe that the decision to reduce the public works projects was premature, because the economy had not sufficiently recovered from the Great Depression. Roosevelt blamed businesses for the recession and called it a "capital strike" against his New Deal policies. There was a backlash in the next election, and Democrats lost a large number of House and Senate seats in the congressional elections of 1938.

The Federal Reserve got spooked by inflation worries, so it tightened the money supply. Additionally, declining business profits led to reduced investments. Like today, businesses were unsure as to what new regulations or taxes might be imposed by FDR and this discouraged investment and expansion. More regulations and the threat of new taxes made investors pull back. Finally, the Social Security Act of 1935 had pulled two billion dollars' worth of tax receipts out of the economy. Payments back into the system didn't begin until 1940.

When the country entered World War II in December of 1941, it was still in deep economic trouble. But the war effort proved to be good for the economy. Manufacturing planes, ships, tanks, and other military necessities got the economy growing again. Employment went to near 100 percent as millions of men left the workforce to enlist and everyone else was needed to take up the slack in the factories. Anyone making anything for the war, from auto companies to canning factories, boomed with business as the nation worked three shifts a day to meet the needs of our soldiers and those of our allied countries as well.

After the end of World War II, the American economy had long periods of expansion and, for the most part, less severe recessions than in the past. That held true until 2008.

2008–2009: The Long Recession Begins

The 2001 "tech bubble" and the 9/11 terrorist attacks shook investor confidence and caused a severe emotional trauma to the American psyche. People not only lost faith in the stock market as an investment, but also questioned the future, asking if America was in economic decline. Since 2001 the Federal Reserve has regularly lowered interest rates in an attempt to stimulate the economy. This set a low rate for loans of all sorts, making them more appealing to both businesses and home buyers. Many banks took advantage of these lower rates and the credit began to flow freely.

There was also massive overbuilding during the period leading up to the Great Recession. Like the overbuilding of the railroads in the past and the overproduction of goods in the Roaring Twenties, the housing market became overbuilt. Real estate speculation—as in the lead-up to many of the panics beforehand—was rampant as investors and developers snatched up cheap land. At the height of the housing boom, investors were flipping homes like pancakes—buying cheap, doing a few repairs and some cosmetic work, and then selling for two, three, or four times what they had paid for them.

Everyone and anyone who wanted one could get a mortgage. Credit was easy, easy, easy. The mortgage companies began giving very low introductory rates, even to those buyers who they knew, at their current income, couldn't make the larger payments when the rates increased after a few years.

The adjustable-rate mortgage (ARM) gives a borrower an initial lower interest rate and lower payments because the rate is not set for the entire period of the loan. Instead, the interest rate can increase, or decrease, when the Federal Reserve Rate changes. In 2007 the interest rate increased as credit tightened. When the rates on many of those ARMs started to increase, a lot of buyers lost their homes. The housing crisis began to spiral out of control, unemployment skyrocketed, and the stock market began to collapse. Panicked banks began holding on to their money, and credit for businesses and consumers (even those with good credit) dried up, just like during the Panic of 1907 and the Great Depression.

As the credit crunch put pressure on banks to run their day-to-day business, unemployment rates rose even further, and people with clean credit histories began struggling to repay their mortgages. In 2008, the global stock markets reacted by plummeting around 40 percent.

During the Great Depression there were many bankers and economists who ignored the warning signs only to be stunned when the market collapsed. Free-market proponents argue that the subprime crisis was a direct result of the U.S. government's intervention in the mortgage market and not unbridled capitalism.

In 1990 the Cranston-Gonzalez National Affordable Housing Act was passed so that low-income Americans could have an opportunity to buy homes. These buyers would not have qualified for a mortgage without the passage of the act, based on the credit standards used in the private sector arena at the time. So U.S. banks were basically forced to grant these subprime mortgages. There seems to be a valid argument that the federal act contributed to the subprime mortgage crisis in the sense that there may have been compliance pressure resulting in credit being made too easy. Just as in the years leading up to the Great Depression when anyone could borrow money to buy stock, no matter what the value of the stock, so, too, at the beginning of the twenty-first century, anyone could borrow money to own a home.

We have discussed how, starting in 2002, Goldman Sachs created derivatives to sell that, while technically legal, were so complicated that they could not really be valued. By doing this, Goldman Sachs enabled the Greek government to hide most of the debt that collapsed their economy and threatened the existence of the euro in 2012. Among the derivatives created, which other financial houses quickly traded, were credit default swaps based on toxic mortgages. These were so impenetrable that most rating houses gave them a good score anyhow, encouraged to do so by a system that rewarded them for giving any derivative a good rating.

Derivatives were an unregulated way for the finance industry to make these riskier loans and get them insured. The credit default swaps masked the truth about the financial solvency and creditworthiness of the mortgage's insured borrowers. Once the initial toxic mortgages were in place, the banks could then sell them off to buyers and insurers who were unaware of the extent of financial risk they were taking on. Tens of thousands of Americans have lost their homes—which are now owned by the banks and the government. Greece has lost its 2,500-year-old real estate to the world's bank, the IMF.

The Great Recession, measured by the standard definition of declining gross GDP, lasted eighteen months . . . which is to say it is technically over by the government's definition. That still makes it a longer recession than any other that has occurred since World War II (when the average length of a recession was eleven months). This past recession was also the most severe since that war, with the GDP falling 6.1 percent from its peak right before the downturn began. That compares well with the more than 26 percent drop in 1929, but is worse the 5 percent drop in the 1973–1975 depression, which was the next highest GDP loss until 2008.

The recovery as of 2012 was the slowest and weakest since 1933. The United States hasn't come close to regaining that lost ground with regard to the GDP level. Businesses are recovering more slowly, new business creation is slower, and unlike in other recoveries, the real unemployment remains so high that this "recovery" is often described as being "jobless."

If you examine the past two recessions before this one, some disturbing differences emerge. When the 2001 recession ended, unemployment was measuring 5.5 percent. And after the 1991 recession ended, unemployment was at 6.8 percent. At this point, most Americans would be ecstatic with an unemployment rate that "low."

Even if the current economic indicators don't fall neatly under the definition of a recession, with more than 80 percent of Americans believing we are currently in one, then at a minimum, the country is mired in a psychological recession. It is a strange thing about depressions and recessions: they are self-fulfilling prophecies. If people and businesses believe times are hard and going to get worse, they spend less. If they spend and hire less, the economy does get worse. Simply, when the economy feels painful, people hold off from spending money. When consumers don't spend money, the economy contracts further. The decline begins to create a feedback loop in which the mere fact that things are getting worse and people know it causes the economy to become even worse. The self-fulfilling prophecy can by itself cause the economy to spiral out of control.

So what do we do about it? Well, the psychologically and financially based recession we are in won't end until the unemployed get jobs, the government stops stimulating the economy, the housing values start to recover, and consumers begin spending again. That's a tall order. In the following chapter, we will examine a wide range of political, social, and fiscal policies used throughout history to try to cure ailing economies. Maybe, if we take the best ideas from the past, we won't have the same old economic problems in the future.

CHAPTER ELEVEN

Depression and Recession Cures

Everyone drinks more during a recession; they want to forget.

—CHRISTIAN AUDIGIER (1958–),
FRENCH DESIGNER AND VINTNER

The good news is that countries have been trying to recover from depressions for centuries. The bad news is that we still have them after all that time and effort. A lot of things have been tried; some worked, but many did not.

Experts seem to agree that this current recovery period is unprecedented in history. And there are countless competing suggestions and theories on what we should do to get back on the road to prosperity that the United States had enjoyed for much of the twentieth century. Many economists feel we should look at history and take the best solutions, things that have worked in the past to pull us out of the worst economic calamities, and implement them immediately. Others say that the world has changed and a new order is emerging, one that makes it difficult, if not impossible, to navigate around these daunting challenges, much less solve them.

New York Times columnist and Pulitzer Prize–winning author Thomas Friedman, in his book *That Used to Be Us: How America Fell Behind in the World It Invented and How We Can Come Back*, goes down a list of all the changes this country has experienced just in the seven years leading up to 2011. These include innovations like Twitter, Facebook, LinkedIn, smart phones, and computer tablets. Friedman argues that with all these changes come huge opportunities to compete economically, but first we must learn how to do so.

Historical Hits and Misses

If this next section sounds familiar it's because, if you go all the way back to our nation's birth, you will see the same mistakes being repeated that created the financial crises we are still experiencing today. The solutions evolve, but the mistakes continue to be made. Given the severity and complexity of the current fiscal problems in the United States and in the rest of the world, we may need to try a hodgepodge of things that worked in the past, in combination with some innovative policies now being put forth by leading economists and the politicians whom they are advising.

As far back as 1797, the new United States was grappling with wild land speculation and a massive accumulation of personal debt. The solution that emerged from the Panic of 1797 was the creation of the nation's first bankruptcy act. Before this, there was no legal way to end being in debt. This often led to families becoming impoverished, with no hope of relief. Things had gotten really bad in the nation, and even the formerly very well off were hurting. Thomas Jefferson, for example, had never been really rich and donated much of his wealth. The first presidents were actually required to maintain their residence and entertain foreign leaders on a small stipend from the Congress. This meant most spent a fortune of their own money in office. When these expenditures were combined with the economic problems brought on by independence, many prominent men, even founding fathers of the new nation, were unable to pay their debts to merchants. When you are throwing congressmen, state representatives, and judges into debtors' prison, you know laws will probably change, and quickly. Until the laws were changed, if you failed to pay back a debt you actually broke a law and could be thrown in jail. This was a carryover from English law. One solution was to allow the many debtors to start over with a clean slate. Some simply went into debt again, but for many farmers and businessmen it allowed them to rebuild their lives, and eventually the economy as well.

The Panic of 1837 was the result of an overbuilding of railroads and canals and a shortage of jobs. Think of this as the tech bubble of its day. It had the same effect, with fortunes disappearing overnight and employment dropping almost as quickly. Money was short and there was little credit. The United States was still dependent on foreign money to finance its growth and that investment source dried up. No one was building new factories, which meant more and more Americans were unable to find any place to work.

The solution tried was a new tariff. The idea was that if it cost more to bring goods into the United States, this would encourage foreign investment in American factories. What happened instead was that the money did not come in and few factories were built. In retaliation, most European nations added their own tariffs on American goods. Because of the much higher costs caused by the tariffs, many European companies decided not to bother shipping their goods to the United States and not to buy raw material from the new nation. This created a huge trade imbalance, harming the U.S. economy and dramatically slowing any recovery. Eventually, some of the tariffs were removed and trade returned.

In 1857, a financial crisis was triggered by the unsustainable expansion of railroads, just like the unsustainable new construction inflating the housing market at the dawn of the twenty-first century. At this point, banks were uncontrolled, with no real supervision or limits. Some bank owners used the deposits to invest in highly speculative ventures, which works only when times are good. They bought railroad stocks—the equivalent of hedge funds—which had the same effect as the bad housing derivatives in 2009. The banks ended up losing a fortune of their depositors' money, and then there was no way for them to get it back. Concern over the solvency of even the larger U.S. banks caused foreign investment to dry up and bank runs to occur. In the aftermath of that panic, the National Banking Act was passed. This regulated the banks' activities and allowed them to handle federal notes and bonds. Still, there was no central bank or deposit insurance, so a badly run bank could close and leave its depositors nothing. Because of this, any depositor, including large businesses, would react to even a rumor of problems by withdrawing all of their money. These panics continued until the Civil War began.

After the war, economic growth returned, and with it came prosperity. The unregulated railroad industry boomed as wild speculation and overbuilding quickly returned as the norm. This led to the depression of 1873, discussed earlier. The country had just recovered from this long depression when the overbuilding of the railroads began again. In 1895 the Reading Railroad, which had bought up many of its smaller competitors, went under. If it had been 2008, the Reading would have been a company deemed "Too Big to Fail," like GM or Chrysler. But back then the government was mostly hands-off, so the Reading Railroad and the banks and companies that had invested in it were allowed to fail. This slowed the economy, creating a rising federal deficit and forcing the government to dip into its gold reserves. By February 1895 the gold reserves had fallen to dangerously low levels and there was no more gold to back up printing more paper money. The world held a collective breath, worried that the United States might default on its debt if the gold-based debt ceiling wasn't raised. It was like maxing out your credit card and having to call Visa to raise your credit limit in order for you to buy groceries or pay your mortgage for the month. You know something is wrong.

In 1895 the government acted. As banks and companies began to collapse and the government's gold reserves plummeted, President Grover Cleveland's treasury secretary called J. P. Morgan, a financial genius and self-made millionaire, asking for suggestions to deal with the growing crisis. Morgan said he could put together a group of investors to purchase $50 million in government bonds, with an option to purchase additional bonds. Wall Street calmed down at the news, and the rate of gold withdrawals slowed.

During the summer of 1907, banks faced liquidity concerns. So many trust companies had loaned so much against stocks and bonds that half the bank loans in New York City were backed only by securities, not by depositor cash or gold in their vaults.

Because of this, the major banks didn't keep high enough cash reserves to cover a great number of withdrawals at one time, making them vulnerable to sudden bank runs. They simply did not have enough money on hand to give back to large depositors should they demand it.

Then things got worse, far worse. F. Augustus Heinze had seemed like the "golden boy" of copper. He was the owner of a Montana copper mine, and he came to New York City flush from getting a $25 million legal settlement that he had won against a rival mining company. He began buying up interests in several New York banks. This put a large part of the nation's savings in banks that loaned to and were owned by one man. But no one seemed worried at the time; they were just intrigued with his amazing ability to make money on everything he did.

Many high-profile bankers had seen investing their deposits in Heinze ventures as a way to make quick, large profits. One of the men who wanted to partner up with Heinze was C. W. Morse of Mercantile National Bank. Heinze knew nothing about banking, but that didn't deter Morse. Heinze was named president of the bank.

Then it became known that Heinze had made numerous risky investments and overextended himself trying to buy up the competition. On October 14, 1907, the stock of Heinze's United Copper Company was trading at over $62 a share. But just two days later, it had fallen to $15 a share. In less than a day Heinze had lost $50 million. (That was in 1907 dollars. If you convert it to 2012 money, it comes to 1.3 billion dollars—$1,300,000,000.) Virtually all of the money the banks had invested with him was lost, and many major banks were suddenly insolvent. One man had risked the savings of hundreds of thousands of depositors and nearly brought the banking economy to collapse.

As incredible as it may seem that one man could bring Wall

Street to its knees, it was also a single man who was given credit for bringing the economy back from the brink. J. P. Morgan was seventy years old at the time of this panic. Twenty-five years earlier, he had bailed the U.S. government out of another economic Armageddon, and during the Gilded Age (a huge expansionary period from about 1865 to 1900), Morgan had financed some of the biggest mergers of companies still in business today: AT&T, GE, and United States Steel. He was the original American capitalist. In fact, he resembled the image of that little man on the Monopoly box. People in the finance industry had tremendous respect for him and listened to his advice.

Morgan's partners asked him to return to the city and help the rapidly deteriorating situation. Morgan had his Pullman car attached to a steam engine and, overnight, he rushed from Virginia back to New York City. He decided drastic action was needed, and he was determined to turn things around through sheer force of will. He called top bankers to his mansion to discuss ways to calm the panic, and he created a committee to audit failing banks. On October 22, the day that Knickerbocker Trust went under, the committee began auditing the banks' books to determine their solvency. Morgan had judged some of the banks to be insolvent already, so those were the ones he allowed to fail, Knickerbocker included. But every bank that he decided to save ultimately survived the economic crisis, and this restored the faith of depositors and investors at home and in Europe.

At 1:00 A.M. on October 24, 1907, U.S. Treasury Secretary George Cortelyou and J. P. Morgan announced that the government would deposit $25 million into New York City banks. All morning, men carried boxes of gold and bags of cash from the federal bank vaults and Morgan's bank to the banks approved by Cortelyou. Oil tycoon John D. Rockefeller pledged $10 million of his own money to those troubled banks. That helped the Trust Company of America, one of the big banks whose ties to Heinze had been exaggerated. But depositors were still lining up at those banks that day, and things looked dire as the stock market started crashing when strained trust companies started pulling their money out.

The president of the New York Stock Exchange arrived at Morgan's office at 1:30 P.M., telling him that they had no choice but to close the Stock Exchange. Pointing his finger at the president, Morgan said that it "will not be closed one minute before" the normal time of 3:00 P.M. Then Morgan went to work. At 1:45, he summoned the New York bank presidents to his office. They started arriving at 2:00. They had twenty minutes before the moment of reckoning—the time when the Exchange would, as it was required to do daily, compare the sales and adjust broker accounts. If there was not enough money in the broker accounts because of the shortage in the banks, then the New York Stock Exchange would collapse. Morgan told the bank presidents that they needed to raise another $25 million in the next ten to twelve minutes—this time to save the stock market and not just the banks. He had close to that amount by 2:16 P.M. The money hit the market at 2:30, and the crisis was narrowly averted. By the end of that day, most Americans believed J. P. Morgan had saved New York City, Wall Street, and probably the entire country from certain financial ruin. He did this by forcing those with the money to return their wealth to the general economy. Incidentally, all those investors benefited from the return of the country's prosperity and eventually made a profit.

There were still some hurdles to get over before the panic was completely quelled. A few weeks later, in an all-night meeting in his library, Morgan told bankers and trust company presidents to pool another $25 million into failing trust companies. By some accounts, he locked them in the room until they agreed to put up the money. Regardless, it worked, and the panic subsided. Later that year Morgan personally guaranteed a $30 million note that was needed to keep New York City from bankruptcy. It must be remembered that had the economy and banks completely collapsed, J. P. Morgan would have been nearly wiped out.

The infamous 1929 stock market crash, bank failures, and tight money supply all seemed to contribute to the Great Depression. As the depression lengthened, Roosevelt tried everything from public works to farm subsidies, but he always wanted to balance the budget. But economic thought at the time suggested that governments must increase spending and/or cut taxes in order to get out of an economic crisis. And they argued that it was not the time to worry about lowering the deficit and balancing the budget. Most of the economists believed that Roosevelt hadn't spent enough to bring the economy out of the recession until World War II. This is the same debate that unfolded in 2012. Is the solution to spend more and worry about borrowing later, or is today's solution balancing the federal budget and restoring faith in the free enterprise economy?

Between 1933 and 1936, Congress passed a series of sweeping economic programs known as the New Deal. They were passed during Franklin D. Roosevelt's first term as president, and they were in direct response to the Great Depression, which was at its peak in 1933. The New Deal focused on three things: relief, recovery, and reform. This stand catapulted the Democrats into power and helped them capture the White House for seven out of nine presidential elections (from 1933 to 1969). As is detailed in the chapter on speculative bubbles, the repeal of those reforms, under pressure from modern banks, is one of the main causes of the real estate bubble and recession in 2011.

The combination worked. The economy grew a whopping 10 percent each year between 1933 and 1936. Roosevelt supporters began to sing "Happy Days Are Here Again" as the output of goods and services returned to pre-crash levels in 1936 and corporate profits soared. FDR, and others, believed that the depression was behind them. Roosevelt also wanted to balance the budget and reduce the federal deficit. So he decided to curtail spending, particularly infrastructure spending. But he ignored a critical economic indicator: the dangerously high unemployment rate of 17 percent. In 1937, after cutting spending, the country quickly fell back into a new depression that was almost as severe as the one it was supposed to be recovering from.

It is important to note here that in 2012 there were some parallels with 1936 and some important differences. If you were to calculate the 2012 unemployment rate using the 1936 calculation, which includes the underemployed and similar groups, it would be said to be over 15 percent, or almost double the "official" rate. But unlike the high growth during the recovery after the Great Depression, the "recovery" after the Great Recession of 2008 has shown economic growth of barely 1 percent. And now many of our nation's leaders, as well as a significant number of economists, think we should cut spending and focus on lowering the deficit while balancing the budget. Perhaps our leaders should reflect on that period in the 1930s before dismissing additional stimulus spending or favoring large spending cuts at a time when the economy is so weak. The real question is not whether stimulus is needed, but whether they are doing it correctly. FDR broke the Great Depression by encouraging business growth, not restraining it with regulations and new burdens.

The other major difference today is that the United States has already spent a massive sum of money, and that puts the nation at greater risk for a depression now than it was in 1936. Perhaps not well or wisely, but hundreds of billions were spent in 2009 and 2010. If the deficit keeps increasing, America will have to find ways to cut spending, or the country will eventually go bankrupt.

In the early part of the twenty-first century, many people bought houses they couldn't afford because conventional wisdom said that housing prices could only go up; if they held on they would make money selling them later. Additionally, many speculators bought homes knowing they could resell them at a profit. Mortgages were given freely, often with little or no money down. While not a loan, the home could always be sold for more than the loan because its value was sure to increase. Then people took out second mortgages against the rising equity in their homes. Some used the second mortgages to pay off bills or fund their children's college educations. Many, however, simply lived off the increased value of their homes. They had a ready line of credit, based on soaring equity, from which to borrow for vacations, new cars, big-screen TVs, new computers, remodeling projects . . . just about anything. Many sold their smaller homes and used the equity to buy larger and more expensive houses on more land in suburbia. Banks happily financed those as well, knowing their money was safe because the value of the property would always be more than the loan amount. Life was good, for banks and underfunded buyers at least, until reality intruded.

In 2006 the housing bubble burst, and the mortgage binge was over. Many borrowers allowed their homes to be foreclosed, as they realized they would have to sell them for less than the mortgage balance—they were "underwater." Complicating this were highly speculative investments based upon the mortgages.

In some cases the margin on these hedge fund investments was so great that a few million dollars controlled a billion dollars in mortgages. Which was a good thing until the value of those mortgages plunged and the hedge funds—many run by banks using depositors' money (sure sounds a lot like 1907 doesn't it?)—found out that they had to make up the difference, but they could not. The rising foreclosure rate soon panicked the banks and hedge funds that were facing huge losses. By August 2007, the banks were afraid to lend to each other because they didn't want those bad loans as collateral, and no one could tell who was solvent and who was holding massive hedge fund debt. The bubble had burst, and what is today being called the Great Recession had begun.

Warren Buffett, one of the most successful investors of all time, once said, "Derivatives are financial weapons of mass destruction." They certainly caused mass destruction to the world economy in 2008. In the years leading up to the Great Recession (maybe it is time to admit "Depression" fits), complex derivative deals were regularly used to repackage toxic subprime mortgages. Those deals significantly contributed to the near total collapse of the U.S. economy.

A massive government bailout ensued. But credit became scarce and businesses had to adopt a defensive stance. Many cut costs through layoffs, and unemployment soared. In 2009, the government began a huge stimulus program, which did halt the decline by the third quarter. To them, the economy stopped receding in size, so this "officially" ended the recession. But like the 1937 disaster, unemployment continued to rise, and as of 2012, most economic indicators continued to be very poor for future employment growth. The risk of another recession appears frighteningly high. Many argue that, by modern standards, the Great Recession had not even really ended by 2012.

Regulations to Prevent the Next Financial Crisis

There are only so many things a government can do to affect a recession once it starts. By its nature, a recession also lowers the government's income. So many of the actions taken are to prevent or limit, rather than combat, an already existing recession. After the Panic of 1907, the Federal Reserve was created to help manage the country's money supply. And after the massive amounts of bank failures that helped trigger the Great Depression, the FDIC was created in 1933 to protect depositors' money.

In 2010 the Dodd-Frank Wall Street Reform and Consumer Protection Act was passed as a direct result of the Great Recession. The act is the largest reform of the regulatory industry since the Great Depression. It does several things, including prohibiting banks from doing too much trading of their own shares and regulating derivatives deals. It also prohibits using the taxpayers' money to bail out banks that were deemed "too big to fail" in 2008. The credit agency Moody's, in September 2011, downgraded three of the largest U.S. banks, citing an increased risk of them failing, coupled with the fact that the government will no longer bail them out. After inspecting the books of many banks under the Dodd-Frank act, federal regulators recently decided to sue seventeen major U.S. banks, alleging that they overvalued or misrepresented their securities in order to obtain federal-backed mortgage loans. Citibank has already settled for $590 million.

Federal Reserve Chairman: Savior or Traitor?

Federal Reserve Chairman Ben Bernanke seems to have a thankless job these days. Congressman and 2012 presidential candidate Ron Paul called him the "counterfeiter in chief" for printing money and pumping it into the economy. Texas governor Rick Perry, also a 2012 presidential candidate, called Bernanke's attempts at credit creation "treasonous." But Bernanke was a student of the Great Depression, and he is hell-bent on avoiding a second and possibly even worse Great Depression on his watch.

New regulations on banks and Wall Street were not the only result of the crisis. The principles of economist John Maynard Keynes are making a comeback among policy makers around the industrialized world. These are interventionist measures, such as government spending to stimulate growth. Keynes's theories were used to create policies during the later part of the Great Depression, during World War II, and in the postwar economic expansion (1945–1973). In the 1970s, Keynesian economics began to wane as stagflation took hold of the economy and noted economist Milton Friedman and others expressed doubt over interventionist government regulation through the Federal Reserve. Both Friedman and Keynes thought that expansionist monetary policy could have prevented or eased the Great Depression. But while Keynes favored active policy responses by the Federal Reserve, Friedman didn't like the idea of a central bank making and implementing those policies. He favored free-market economics, taking a more laissez-faire approach concerning taxation, privatization, and deregulation. Those were the theories also used by the Reagan administration in the 1980s to help pull the country out of recession and get inflation under control.

In response to the Great Recession, Bernanke has used a combination of Keynes's and Friedman's theories. He is using an expansionary monetary policy to ease the financial crisis and try to avert another severe downturn. Every action is being taken to force the economy to expand and grow. The Federal Reserve has lowered interest rates to help combat unemployment and promote economic growth—this being at the cost of those with fixed incomes or bank deposits. It also has been using deficit spending to stimulate the economy, adding hundreds of billions of dollars to the amount of money in circulation by just printing more bills. The Federal Reserve also has been pumping money into the economy by buying up treasury bills, a policy known as quantitative easing, because it helps to force down the interest rates given by private firms and banks, making it less expensive to borrow money.

Some economists argue that the lack of a real recovery after the Great Recession is not because of overregulation, burdensome taxation, excessive government spending, or a rising deficit—as many politicians claim—but due to inadequate credit creation by banks. They argue that the Federal Reserve should implement policies creating credit until the depository institutions begin creating a sufficient amount on their own. Milton Friedman was an advocate of this line of thought, and Bernanke has also favored these types of policies.

The reason these banks are not creating normal amounts of credit that would spur growth is because of the huge losses they suffered after the housing bubble burst. They remain concerned that they will not have adequate capital if they expand their credit creation (i.e., make loans).

The economists advocating credit creation may have a point. Today's economic/financial environment is similar to that of the early thirties. During the Great Depression, there was a high degree of uncertainty and increased government regulation of business. FDR also created an unprecedented amount of peacetime government spending. The current government spending is also unprecedented. And in the early 1930s, like the years following the Great Recession, there was inadequate credit creation by the banks. Obama's economic recovery plan consists primarily of more government spending and tax cuts. If history is any indication, both of those components will help, but they may not be enough without more credit creation. When growth in the depository credit resumed in 1934–1936, the economy roared to life and pulled out of the depression.

Taxing or Robbing from the Rich?

Warren Buffett is a modern J. P. Morgan, and also made his billions in the investment banking industry. Buffett was ranked the wealthiest person in the world in 2008 and the third wealthiest in 2012. He recently invested in the troubled, mammoth Bank of America, hoping to keep it afloat. And he is often on the media circuit, trying to reassure investors and ordinary Americans as they yank their money out of the markets because of fear and endless bad news. Just as Morgan did a century ago, Buffett often encourages investors to stay in the market and buy stocks at these bargain basement prices, hoping there is not another drop like 2008 and those stocks prove to not be bargains at all. He and his company often buy stocks and bonds during challenging fiscal times, and they want Americans to do the same and not panic.

Through the years, Buffett has urged Congress to raise taxes on the mega-rich. President Obama recently said, "Middle-class families shouldn't pay higher taxes than millionaires and billionaires. That's pretty straightforward." In his new deficit reduction plan, Obama called his critical provision on raising taxes on the rich to reduce the deficit the "Buffett Rule." The problem here is, of course, the definition of "rich." History has shown that the concentration of wealth in too few hands leads to economic and social instability. But if you define "rich" at too low a level, you are destroying the middle class and the job makers. The same words spoken by a liberal president and a conservative billionaire do not mean the same thing.

Buffett has often stated that he paid a lower percentage in taxes than his secretary does. "[Last year] what I paid was only 17.4% of my taxable income—and that's actually a lower percentage than what was paid by any of the other 20 people in our office," Buffett wrote in a *New York Times* op-ed.

How is that possible? you may ask. Well, first of all, he makes most of his money from investments, and these are taxed at a lower rate (15 percent) than most wages. Also, Social Security tax applies only to the first $106,800 in wages an employee makes each year. So his secretary probably pays that tax on most or all of her income. Buffett, however, ends up owing the tax on a very small proportion of his gargantuan income. But those earning $150,000 or $200,000 are in neither situation.

Dueling Solutions

Some strategists feel that the government should "go FDR all over again." They want a big new-jobs program financed by the government. During the New Deal era, Americans came together in a show of unity to pull the country out of the depression and support the war effort. Now, the United States has a politically polarized government, and a big spending bill will never pass Congress.

Others say "just get something done." We need big tax reform—reduce the tax rates and get rid of credits and loopholes—in order to make that happen. Political pundits say that the tax reform idea would stand a chance of passing, especially since you are arguing on the Republicans' turf.

The unions also have weighed in. They say the president must be bold—just create jobs, put America back to work. The only need is to create a million or more jobs—no more tax breaks. Incidentally, they would prefer union jobs, but when unemployment is low their work is easier because union employees have more options. With high unemployment, negotiations are hard because employers know there are men waiting to take the same job on any terms.

Still other experts believe that the only way we will recover from this crisis is to have the government, the private sector, and the labor unions all working together. Those who express the idea of working together for the common good have said that this war can't be won if we frame the argument as one of big government versus small government. They think there should be mutual action and, here is the rub, mutual sacrifice.

In poll after poll, Americans are expressing their deep disapproval of how the politicians are running the country, particularly in the area of managing the economy. They want politicians to work together, compromise, and ignore ideology to get something done. But the debate has become more complicated because now it's also a debate about the role of government. The $900 billion stimulus, passed in 2008 to pull the country out of the Great Recession, is widely thought of as not having created any new jobs.

President Obama's position on the stimulus package has changed from him first promising it would create millions of new jobs to his now much more defensible position that at least it saved jobs that otherwise would have been lost. This perception of failure has deepened the general mistrust of government. And there's a real conundrum for lawmakers and leaders: The public doesn't trust the government to handle the economy, but wants politicians to work together and do something, anything, to stop the economic hemorrhaging. But to get reelected, each party needs to convince the voters that they know best and the other side is wrong. It's a position that prevents cooperation and initialiy punishes each side for any success created by the policies of the other. Congressmen need a solution, but if the solution works, they might lose politically. This often leads to both major parties spending more time on blame, and making sure the other side's actions fail, rather than providing real improvement.

The Great Debate: Stimulate or Cut?

As far as the stimulus goes, many experts say that it did work, but it wasn't enough—that we need a much larger stimulus to get the country pulled out of the economic crisis. Others bristle at that assertion, saying the last thing we need is more government spending—big government is always a bad thing, and it needs to stay out of the economy. They worry about the long-term effect of the debt. If more debt creates runaway inflation, then say good-bye to your savings and retirement money. But if the economy continues to stagnate or recede, get used to one person in five needing a job and your home's value dropping even further. Although, if you examine the stimulus bill, arguments can be made to support both positions.

About $100 billion was put into infrastructure projects, and that money seemed to be well spent in that it saved or created some construction and related jobs, at least for the duration of the building projects. However, the amount of stimulus money doled out was not as large as most people believe. And about a third of the money was not stimulus at all but temporary tax cuts. Critics say that the tax cuts were costly and wasteful because most of the recipients were financially strapped or cautious since we were in the middle of a severe recession at that time. That means many of them either held on to that money or paid down debt; they didn't spend it, so economic activity remained flat. On the other hand, the state governments receiving stimulus money were able to hold on to school teachers, firefighters, and police officers that they would otherwise have had to lay off. The dark side of that was that the extra money postponed needed cuts in states like Illinois. However, now the stimulus money is running out, and these state and local governments say that it was only a temporary fix, and they will be forced to lay off those same teachers and officers in the near future—at a time when the economy can't really take another hit. For states, the stimulus didn't fix much; it just delayed the discomfort.

The fallacy of just throwing money around is again being understood. It was an expensive lesson. If another stimulus plan is implemented, many feel it should not be simply giving cash in the form of subsidies or extending benefits. That's not a long-term solution, and it ends up causing more problems than it solves, with many people going under when those subsidies or benefits end. The secret is to spend any future stimulus only in a way that will create jobs. It is like in the old cliché: "We have given a man a fish and he ate today. Now we need to teach the man how to fish." An understanding among even the elected officials that the solution has to be long-term—whether that means subsidies, fewer regulations, or financing research—has begun to emerge. To do this you need stability and available credit.

The other problem with some of the solutions being proposed right now is that they are relying on what worked for the past four decades or so, when credit was plentiful and consumption was encouraged. During the past forty years, U.S. consumption was around 62 percent of the GDP. That figure jumped to 70 percent in the 1980s, where it remained until the 2008 crash. Clearly, that is an unhealthy level of consumption, and we will probably never get that level back, since it was based on credit and not an increase in income. We cannot regain our economic supremacy, much less pull out of the current financial crisis, by more consumption.

Housing Solutions

Undoubtedly, 2011 was the worst year for new home sales in more than half a century. Home builders had to compete with foreclosed homes that were greatly reduced in price or with a glut of short sales (when banks allow borrowers to sell the home for less than the mortgage balance). And even with interest rates at record lows and bargain basement prices, very few were buying. To compound the problem, those who wanted to buy often couldn't qualify under the stringent qualifications. In September 2011, the National Association of Home Builders said that its index of builder sentiment fell to 14 from 15, and it remained low for the next year. The index has been below 20 for all but one month throughout the summer of 2010 to the spring of 2012. Any reading below 50 indicates negative sentiment about the housing market. The rating hasn't been at 50 since April 2006, during the peak of the housing boom. The lack of new home construction takes its toll on the economy. Statistics show that each new home that is built generates about $90,000 in taxes and creates three jobs for a year.

The first thing that needs to be done is to clear the foreclo-

sure glut. During the Great Depression, banks entered into forbearance agreements with borrowers who were late on their
mortgage payments. Basically, that is an agreement between a
borrower and lender to not foreclose on the property. The banks
worked with the borrowers, suspending payments or accepting
reduced payments, until their financial situations improved.
Today that would mean helping those millions of borrowers
who are now underwater in their loans (their house is worth
less than the amount owed on it). The house gets reappraised
at the lower market value and the banks can make a new loan
on the current value and the lower interest rates. The balance
could then be in forbearance until such time as the market goes
up or the borrower sells the property. This would be better for
everyone: the borrower can have more affordable payments
and the lender will probably receive more in the long run than
if the bank had foreclosed. Also, the borrowing requirements
need to be loosened for these types of transactions. If the borrower can afford to pay the lower mortgage payment, he will
probably stay in the home.

Some experts warn that with the housing market still mired
in a depression, the worst thing to do would be to eliminate
the mortgage interest deduction, especially when so many
middle-class borrowers rely on it. It might have a chilling effect
on an already ice-cold housing market. It has been suggested
that rather than eliminating the mortgage deduction, the banks
could double or even triple the deduction. It wouldn't cost the
banks a thing and more people would stay in their houses if
they had a big deduction to write off. It would also encourage
those renters, who currently get no deductions—even though
the mortgage interest the landlord owes is usually included in
the rent—to purchase a home.

There are also many houses in foreclosure that could be

structured as rent-to-own homes for those who don't qualify to purchase one, particularly with the larger down-payment requirements now in place. At the end of a certain leasing period, the renter has the option to buy the house at the value it was assessed at when they began renting. Then, if they choose to buy it, a portion of each rental payment can be applied as a down payment on the purchase of the house. The government would ultimately receive more in taxes because of the increased number of people purchasing homes and the resulting increase in the value of those homes as the housing market recovers.

Deficit Solutions

In September 2011, Olivier Blanchard, the IMF's chief economist, said: "The recovery has weakened considerably. Strong policies are needed to improve the outlook and reduce the risks." Blanchard said that Obama's plan to combine tax cuts with infrastructure spending will help stimulate the economy in the short term. However, it needs to be combined with a longer-term plan to reduce the deficit. The timing of the budget cuts is critical. Budget cuts "cannot be too fast or it will kill growth," Blanchard said. "It cannot be too slow or it will kill credibility."

There are still fringe groups on both sides of the political spectrum who insist that things be done their way, even if they take the rest of the country down with them. Never was that more apparent than in the recent debt ceiling debate. But most Americans were disgusted with the lack of cooperation and the destructive bickering among the leadership in Washington. The fighting, name-calling, and stonewalling came to a head when the nation was just days away from not being able to pay its bills unless the debt ceiling was raised. At the eleventh hour, lawmakers agreed to form a bipartisan twelve-member deficit reduction committee. They began meeting in September 2011. They needed to find at least $1.2 trillion in deficit reduction, to be spread out over the next decade. And they had to find those numbers by Thanksgiving 2011, or across-the-board spending cuts would have been triggered, divided equally between domestic and military programs.

Many economists and politicians think that if we don't tackle the deficit, the economy will never improve. In the near future, spiraling interest on the nation's debt will hamper the government's ability to pay for running the country, and a massive financial collapse may ensue. These experts argue that the only way to reduce the deficit is through entitlement reform, and that means scaling back Social Security, Medicare, and Medicaid. Others argue that we can't cut our way into prosperity and global competitiveness, and if we begin cutting instead of stimulating, we could plunge the country into a depression.

Economist Douglas Elmendorf, director of the Congressional Budget Office, told the deficit reduction committee in September 2011 that the aging population (with the average age of U.S. citizens going up almost three years, from 32.9 to 35.3 years, in the decade of the 1990s alone), facing soaring health care costs, rising as much as 8 percent annually since 2010, will cause the deficit to explode if policies aren't changed. Although he refused to advise the committee on how to reduce the deficit, he did warn against immediate tax increases or spending cuts. He argued that the current economy is too weak to take those fiscal hits. However, he did lay out what a solution must include: "Putting the federal budget on a sustainable path will require significant changes to spending policies, significant changes to tax policies, or both."

Well, what do we do then? There needs to be a very pragmatic approach taken to this very serious problem. How do we address the soaring deficit and get it under control—with a government that is held hostage by special interests and extremes on both ends of the political spectrum? On the far right we have a core group who say they will never agree to any tax increases under any circumstances. And on the left we have a group who will never agree to cuts of any kind for entitlement programs. Furthermore, within those two opposing parameters is the "good government versus bad government" argument. Is it good to have more government involvement and regulation, or does that interfere with whatever cures the free market will create? Or even more fundamentally, is the right economic decision to have less government and lower taxes, at the cost of less support and fewer programs, or more involvement by the government with more of the nation's money being spent by the Feds and the states? Recent history, and the experience of 1937, shows that too much government involvement, and the taxes this requires, stifles or stops economic growth, but that doing nothing in a crisis, such as Herbert Hoover chose to do, can be equally or even more economically destructive.

An Alternative to Both

It makes no sense for China to have better rail systems than us, and Singapore having better airports than us. And we just learned that China has the fastest super-computer on Earth—that used to be us.

— PRESIDENT OBAMA, NOVEMBER 3, 2010

In his book *That Used to Be Us,* Thomas Friedman has come up with five solutions to the crisis that can restore us to economic supremacy. He bases this on the lessons of the past two hundred years or so. He acknowledges that accomplishing his steps will not be easy, especially after the past decade (2000–2010), which was maybe the most economically and socially disruptive decade in the history of the United States. Between the terrorist attacks, two long wars, the tech market soaring and then bursting, and then the subprime mortgage crisis, where we teetered on the edge of a global depression, the country has been through a lot.

As Friedman was trying to come up with solutions for the daunting problems this country faces, he decided to interview some major U.S. employers, asking them what they were looking for in an employee. These employers all wanted individuals who could adapt, invent, and reinvent in their work. They wanted employees to have strong critical reasoning and thinking skills. Friedman goes on to say that the countries that will survive and thrive in this new global economy are those that are "high-imagination-enabling countries." Those nations that can grasp and use new approaches and employ the new technologies can make a difference and will form the basis of future economies.

Friedman argues that we're not going to bail ourselves out of this current financial crisis, nor will we be able to stimulate our way out of it. The only real solution, he believes, is to invent and educate our way out of the crisis. This is really not a new idea. Whenever our country was experiencing a historical turn, we educated our people above and beyond the norm in order to adapt to the huge societal changes. Whether it was the cotton gin, the telegraph machine, or the supercomputer, we trained our people in the skills needed to stay on top of emerging technologies. So the first step in Friedman's five-step plan for economic recovery is to educate the people.

The second step is to revamp the immigration rules. We are a nation of immigrants, and we must allow the most talented and innovative of them to stay in this country. Many of these foreign-born best and brightest get education visas to go to college or grad school in the United States, which is still considered to have some of the world's best universities. Give these talented immigrants an easier way to stay in this country, and allow them to create new companies and technologies once they are finished with their educations.

Third, we used to have the world's best infrastructure. It's now crumbling. By 2035, the Transportation Administration projects that without improvement, 40 percent of the nation's highways will be congested enough to severely affect the ability of companies to do business in America's largest cities. Slews of experts and congressionally mandated commissions have said that the nation will need to double or even quadruple its infrastructure spending in the next ten years just to keep up with population growth. And from a historical perspective, FDR's massive infrastructure spending helped the economy pull out of the depression in the 1930s. Others counter that it was enough to prevent a depression in 2008 but not enough to create a sustainable recovery. They want a second stimulus that should go primarily to job creation through infrastructure-type projects.

The countries such as Germany and Japan that are economically the strongest have modern, efficient infrastructure, allowing ease of commerce and employment. Repairing and replacing the U.S. infrastructure would have two major economic benefits. It would help make our economy more competitive by facilitating commerce, business travel, and commutes to jobs, schools, shopping, etc. But it also would put Americans back to work—and not just by creating the obvious construction jobs. It would also give jobs to those people whose businesses feed the construction workers, those who provide the materials and equipment for the jobs, those who transport the materials, and those who house the influx of workers who move into the areas where infrastructure jobs are plentiful. The list goes on and on. These are pro-growth investments—exactly the type that the private sector favors. These long-term projects encourage those private investors to partner up with state, local, and federal governments to fund these public works.

The fourth step in Friedman's plan is that we must have the right rules in place that encourage capital investment, while preventing recklessness. This means, for example, preventing banks from creating derivatives that are as unsound and complicated as those used in the mortgage crisis, while still allowing banks to find new ways to invest and loan money profitably. As we have seen from the calamitous subprime mortgage crisis, we had too little regulation in place; and the fiscal policies of easy credit and high-risk loans encouraged recklessness. This crisis grew so big that it threatened the entire economic world order. This also means walking the balance between preventing a company from harming the environment or community and not burdening it with regulations that prevent its success or with reporting requirements that discourage innovation or investment. It also means finding a way for the federal government to stay involved while allowing businesses to know how their actions will be met and that no unexpected taxes or laws will nullify their planning.

Finally, Friedman advocates prioritizing a comprehensive, government-funded research and development program. This spans the entire world of science and technology—both the theoretical and the practical. Knowing how particles work may not pay off in jobs next week, but the knowledge applied can be the basis of industries no one can yet even conceive of. Learning the secrets of DNA is creating both cures and jobs as the knowledge gained from research is translated into uses. The spin-off products that were developed for the space program in the 1960s and '70s created whole sectors of business, from physiology sensors that now save millions of lives each year to LED chips, satellite weather reports and surveys, and, of course, Tang. Many politicians and economists think that more funding should be poured into research and development, but they believe the government should engage the private sector in joint ventures. Some experts even suggest giving the private sector tax incentives to grow their R&D divisions.

Common Ground?

Look how successful one man, J. P. Morgan, was in convincing the private sector to cough up money or invest in securities—when the stock market was nose-diving—for the good of the country. Warren Buffett has done some of that, too. Maybe the "prosperity centers" that Clinton touted could be something both parties can agree on. There is also agreement on more funding for research and development and in overhauling the educational system to be more competitive. Neither party likes outsourcing, so perhaps putting pressure on countries where we have a huge trade imbalance, like China, might be something both sides would go for. But to eliminate outsourcing in a global economy, the governments need to make hiring Americans more appealing for positive reasons, not mandate it artificially with tariffs (that trick never works, as we have seen) or quotas. To do this, the United States needs to again encourage innovators and assist and protect the public interest, but not restrict those who will create the business infrastructure needed for the next century.

No one likes taxes, and politicians like admitting they create new taxes even less. Publicly, everyone wants tax reform, and there certainly is support for details like closing tax loopholes and ending certain tax credits in order to create a streamlined, straightforward tax. Tax cuts are also being suggested by both sides. Tax cuts take money from the government and let people and businesses spend it. That grows the economy, as happened under President Reagan when he cut taxes. But if you cut taxes, you still have to pay for the government and the services it provides. So to cut taxes you have to make difficult choices about what the government no longer will spend money on, or raise that money some other way.

While everyone is publicly for less taxes or fairer taxes, it's the type of tax cuts and how you pay for them that causes the fights. And where do the spending cuts come from? Both parties acknowledge that certain entitlement programs need to be overhauled, but some Republicans argue that it should be all entitlement cuts, and some Democrats insist it must be all military cuts. The vocal and volatile extremes in both major parties are entrenched in their ideologies. If the parties can manage to drown out the screeching coming from both the far left and the far right, they may be able to reach common ground. But history shows that not until the politics are set aside can a solution be reached.

History Says

Looking at historical solutions to the most complex and daunting financial crises of our time has some applicability today, even in the unprecedented times that we live in. The Great Depression was the worst fiscal crisis the United States has ever endured. The country was able to pull out of it with a combination of shared sacrifices and a series of stimulus measures—primarily infrastructure spending. When FDR prematurely decided that the economy had recovered from the depression and that the infrastructure spending could be curtailed, the country began slipping right back into a severe recession. It wasn't until World War II, when war spending and labor restrictions changed the entire economy, that the country was able to move out of the economic downturn and into the long period of prosperity that followed the war.

When the country began experiencing more economic problems in the 1970s and '80s, President Reagan implemented policies, known as supply-side economics, to lower taxes in order to stimulate business and spur investment. It also generated more tax revenue for the government, and the economy began to recover.

But then the country seemed to move toward more of a service economy. We weren't producing as much; we just seemed to be consuming. And this overconsumption, fueled by easy credit as opposed to increases in real income, caused first the dot-com bubble and then the housing bubble. When the housing bubble burst in 2008, it plunged the country into the worst economic crisis many of us have ever lived through.

Many people have criticized the baby boom generation, claiming that they are the "borrow and spend generation," in contrast to their parents. The generation that lived through the Great Depression and fought in World War II is sometimes referred to as the "Greatest Generation." From a fiscal point of view they were the "save and invest generation." This generation would never consider shutting down the government—even for a minute—because of political posturing, as the American people witnessed their (primarily) baby boomer politicians doing on Capitol Hill during the summer of 2011. That summer will go down in infamy as the time when the U.S. government lost its AAA credit rating and came within days of going broke over what was, in effect, political wrangling.

If there is one positive thing that can perhaps come out of the rubble left behind from this Great Recession, it is the lesson we can take away from the crisis. The baby boomers, Generation Xers, and Millennials have now lived through their own financial devastation. Those from the Greatest Generation had their values shaped by the financial trauma of the Great Depression, and those values sustained the economy for future generations. In contrast, the baby boomers seemed to have what Thomas Friedman calls "situational values": They did whatever the situation allowed. As we have now discovered, those types of values are not sustainable. To quote Walt Kelly's comic strip character Pogo: "We have met the enemy and he is us."

At this point, it states the obvious to say that even a relatively young nation like the United States has dealt with a lot of recessions in a lot of ways. But which ways have worked, and can we apply them to today?

In 1797, the nation had the problem of land speculation and importing more goods than it exported. Okay, so maybe today's recession is not that unique. The solution then was to create a central bank and find a way to cushion the people from the worst of the problems. At that time, the new law that permitted filing for bankruptcy allowed the middle class of the new nation to make fresh starts.

In 1837 the spur to recession was speculation in canals . . . canal ships and shipping being the new (high tech for almost two hundred years ago) market. Another concern was that pesky imbalance of trade. The United States still bought more goods from European countries than it sold to them. The attempted solution was to try to encourage more American jobs by introducing tariffs on imported goods. The actual result was a trade war as the European nations set up tariffs of their own. The net result was massive unemployment and a far longer and deeper recession than was needed. Expansion to the West, what we today call the Midwest, basically provided a big safety valve, and eventually prosperity returned. (Not sure how to apply that last one, unless we restart the space program and set up colonies on the moon.)

In 1857 another tech bubble burst. This one was railroads. As usual, house prices had skyrocketed as well. That led to banks failing when loans could not be repaid. The National Bank Act of 1863 was passed to restore everyone's faith in the banks, which had been doing about anything they wanted with their depositors' money. What really ended this depression was a cure worse than the disease: the Civil War.

From 1873 to 1895, the post–Civil War boom went bust. Railroads mostly were involved again. It was, at least so far, the longest recession in U.S. history, lasting for twenty-two years. (Yes, they can last that long. Take a look at Japan for the past two decades.) What happened is again comparable today to the tech bubble of 2000 and the housing bubble of 2008. The solution this time was the intervention of the richest men, refinancing, out of their personal fortunes, the failing mega-companies and the gold reserves of the biggest banks. I will leave to your imagination the probability of Citibank, Bank of America, Morgan Stanley, Microsoft, and Google risking their corporate fortunes to fight our modern recession. Feel free to note the irony that it was the founder and owner of what is now Morgan Stanley, J. P. Morgan, who acted to finally restore the nation.

Twelve years later, in 1907, it was Morgan to the rescue again. This time he organized the leaders of Wall Street to once more use their own fortunes to restore confidence and credit. Feel free to send your requests, asking that they risk their personal wealth and prestige to end the current long recession, to Bill Gates, Warren Buffett, Larry Ellison, George Soros, and Donald Trump. There are, let us say, doubts that this solution will be applied again.

The Great Depression of 1929 seems to be the model that the federal government is using today. The program then was increased spending, including directly hiring workers, through the WPA for example, to build infrastructure. A lot of bridges, dams, and roads were built. There was also serious deficit spending, and tax breaks for those who would employ new workers. It worked. Laws were passed to prevent the banks and Wall Street from repeating the same mistakes. Many of these laws, like the Smoot-Hawley Tariff Act, were rescinded in the 1990s on the assurance of the brokerage houses and banks that they would never make those mistakes again. It took them barely one decade of this unrestrained greed to destroy the economy again. Yet already we are hearing from those same banks that similar laws passed recently have just got to be gotten rid of. Let us hope Congress learned better this time. World War II quickly ended the last vestiges of the 1937 recession.

So there it is . . . the solutions of the past to the most pressing problem of today. Duties and tariffs to protect the American jobs have never worked. Sometimes the nation did legislate itself back to stability. Often those laws were designed to restore confidence and curb the abuses of the large companies that caused the problems. (There was the advantage of no lobbyists for most of this time. We have rewarded those who caused the 2006 housing crash.)

War helped end several major recessions. It changed the way business was done and forced increased government spending. The moral and real cost probably makes starting a war a very wrong cure, but it did work when it intervened. The problem with war as an economic cure is that since the Korean War, international conflicts have not been total wars with the whole population involved and sacrificing to win them. Nor have modern wars required large numbers of workers to be moved to the military or major domestic programs to be canceled. So their effect on the economy has been to generate costs, not the kinds of changes that earlier wars forced. Perhaps fortunately, modern, small wars not only don't help the economy of a nation, they divide the population and increase national debt. War is not the answer.

By the turn of the twentieth century, the courageous acts of the leading men in the economy made all the difference. And finally the United States did spend itself out of the worst depression in our history . . . so far. Note that nowhere in this survey of cures do the words "trickle-down economy" occur.

A look at history says that to recover and grow again we must stop having an economy based on consumption. We must move toward an economy that is based on investment, invention, production, and innovation. And it will require the government, the private sector, and the American people to make sacrifices and compromises. Living through job loss, the loss of a home or business, or losing your life's savings is traumatic. Such traumas change people, often for the better. They become more aware of what is really valued and the true cost of what they want. Even those who favor more government involvement become aware of its limitations and negative effects. When those who want less government in general have success and cut back on what government provides, they have to face the cost that has for those most dependent on others just to survive. What will help everyone is for companies to learn that if they step up the way J. P. Morgan did in 1907 and work for the common good, in the long run everyone from entrepreneur to retiree will benefit. So the real lesson of history is that, to solve the economic problems facing Europe and the United States, we need that shared sacrifice and a sense of unity, to put aside self-interest and work for the good of the country. Time after time in the past, when things improved, everyone benefited—both worker and owner. It is a hard lesson, repeated many times in history, and now it is our turn to learn it . . . again.

CHAPTER TWELVE

The Destruction of the Middle Class

Of the three classes, it is the middle that saves the country.

—EURIPIDES (480–406 BCE),
GREEK DRAMATIST

So are you middle class? Odds are if you are an American, unless you are very, very well off, your answer to that question is yes. From millionaires to store shelf stockers, most people in the United States, when asked, describe themselves as being middle class. The Donald Trumps of the world, who flaunt their upper-class status, are resented. Candidates with too much wealth are vilified as out of touch. It is part of our egalitarian view of society and the American free enterprise mythology to identify with the middle class, but often that alignment comes with very little understanding of what that term actually means.

According to *Merriam-Webster's Collegiate Dictionary*, the middle class is "a socioeconomic grouping composed principally of business and professional people, bureaucrats, and some farmers and skilled workers sharing common social characteristics and values." Under that definition, everyone from plumbers to store owners falls into the middle class, but not store clerks or cabdrivers. Still, if you ask almost anyone in America, they will claim to be middle class. In some ways they are correct, because in the United States, more than anywhere else in the world, it is still possible for almost anyone to pull up into the middle class. The hope of doing so also encourages this identification. However, this verbal fiction that anyone with a regular income is "middle class" has a dark side. It disguises the ongoing serious economic, and therefore social, degeneration of the middle level of American society. This is a cause for great concern because history has shown that the loss of the real middle class is a disaster that destabilizes nations.

Caught in the Middle

In the mid-twentieth century most of those who moved up to the middle class were involved in manufacturing. But today there are far fewer such jobs, and those that are left often pay less than they did sixty years ago. In 1951, 48 percent of the workforce was in manufacturing; in 2008 this percentage had dropped to 18 percent, which is a two-thirds decline. So what is happening to skilled workers and other workers in the United States? Imagine you are the CEO of a large American company that sells shirts to Walmart and Target. You are scrutinizing your labor costs to determine if you have the money to expand your plant in Pittsburgh. If you keep all your manufacturing in the United States, you have to pay a unionized garment worker $15 an hour, plus overtime and benefits. When you add those additional costs, you're looking at paying each of your workers upward of $20 an hour. Now, you can go overseas and get a Chinese worker to do the exact same thing for about eighty-six cents an hour, working twelve hours straight, no overtime pay necessary. Or maybe you would go to Cambodia, where the average garment worker makes only twenty-two cents an hour. It makes no fiscal sense whatsoever to continue to employ American workers for these blue-collar jobs that can be done just as well in a Third World country for a small fraction of the labor cost.

How can American workers compete against those paltry wages in a global labor market? Well, they can't. So Average Joe, who used to live comfortably in middle-class America, with his decent hourly wage, good benefits package, and even a generous pension after retirement, now has a minimum wage job, no benefits, and no retirement security—none. And that's if he can even get a job. He can't afford a home, or a decent car, and he lives paycheck to paycheck. Meanwhile, the business owners, shareholders, and CEOs see their profits and compensation skyrocketing because the cost of doing business in these poor countries is dirt cheap. In 1950, the ratio of the average executive's paycheck to the average worker's paycheck was about 30 to 1. However, since the year 2000, that ratio has soared, now standing at 343 to 1. And when you compare the average CEO's pay to that of their overseas manufacturing, clothing, and assembly workers, the ratio hits a staggering 500 to 1.

There is another dark side to the change. Generally, almost 80 percent of all service-job positions now pay less than manufacturing. This means that those who want to work and rise into the middle class no longer can. Those who, fifty years ago, would work themselves up into the middle class and make the big purchases that spur the economy, like cars and homes, don't have the money and can't get the credit to buy these items. This diminishing of the average worker's income also means that the government receives less income tax, and this, along with overspending and a still growing bureaucracy, makes the deficits grow. But with many workers earning less, more people need more help. Higher deficits and social spending are forcing higher taxes.

The lower class does not have any more money to pay in for taxes, and doesn't pay any. According to the IRS, about 46 percent of all taxpayers in 2011 weren't taxpayers, but were instead bene-fit receivers. They paid no federal income taxes because they did not earn enough. Nor do the major corporations pay taxes. They benefit from the many loopholes and special exceptions gained by their lobbyists in the eighteen thousand pages of the tax code. The group with the fewest special deductions is the one that pays. But as the taxes go up, more money is taken away from the middle class, and they spend less, so fewer cars or coats or even groceries are sold. With fewer sales, businesses begin failing, and the resulting unemployment means lower wages. Today, those same people who once would have been middle class become, in reality, "working class" instead. Since the income of the working class is, by definition, lower, this group has fewer resources and options; they are at the mercy of the larger employers. This can again force down wages. So the rich get richer and the middle class goes away. This certainly suits the rich, who pay the lobby-ists and contribute to political campaigns, but the disappearing middle class is already creating negative effects on the United States and European nations. History has shown us that when the income disparities are too great, conditions ripen for class warfare and social unrest. In some nations this has meant revolutions and violence. In the United States it often is manifest as third parties and social movements, which is exactly what is happening now.

The Fall of the Roman Empire's Middle Class

There is one striking example in history where the middle class of a successful empire was nearly completely eliminated as a social and economic force. This happened in one of the most long-lasting and successful of the ancient empires, the Roman Empire. Seeing what happened and the effect it had is a sobering lesson.

In Rome during the Imperial era, from 30 BCE until the fifth century CE, senators and the top patrician families were often exceedingly rich, many earning between ten and twenty million sesterces a year from their estates. That would be twenty or more million of today's U.S. dollars, annually. But like today's mega-corporations, they also paid virtually nothing in taxes. Under the Roman system Marcus Licinius Crassus, a famously wealthy statesman, was taxed only once every five years, and the amount was capped at only $7,500 in today's dollars, effectively nothing compared to his income. In Rome the rich patricians decided who paid taxes, and it is no surprise they did not make themselves pay in. Today's patricians are the corporations, and through lobbyists they often accomplish the same thing. Even the conspicuous consumption carried out by today's corporate heads, who earn tens of millions in salary and benefits, is a direct reflection of the same abuses two thousand years ago. In Rome, for the rich, nothing was too good. They competed to show off their wealth. Gold everywhere and on everything was the style statement of the day, and conspicuous consumption often ruled. Dinners of pigeon tongues and other extreme delicacies did happen, costing pounds of gold. In striking contrast, the average Roman worker in the second century was paid in brass coins, and not many of them. He rarely saw a silver coin.

The Roman Empire in its last two centuries was going broke and being forced to cut back on military spending at the same time that those with all the wealth were paying virtually no taxes. (Any resemblance to the United States today is not a coincidence; that is why we are talking about it.) The Roman government found that it had no money to fix roads, clear harbors, or even equip sailors and fleets to prevent bandits and pirates from robbing merchants and travelers. Nor did they have enough resources to keep up the quality of the legions. This new weakness of the once invincible Roman legions—more loyal to the general than to Rome—tempted barbarians of all types from the Goths to the Huns, with empire-ending results.

With all the wealth concentrated in the hands of a small group powerful enough to avoid any taxation, Rome could not afford to do the business of government. Eventually, with a lot of help from several waves of barbarian invaders, the western Roman government failed. In fact, to save on costs, and because the disenfranchised poor of Italy saw little reason to fight for Rome, non-Romans along the borders were recruited. Yes, in its last few centuries, Rome outsourced its army.

In Ancient Rome, men who had once been middle-class farmers lost their land to taxes and debt collectors as the government struggled. Soon, whole areas of Italy were in arrears. Much like the banks today in the housing crisis, Roman banks took less interest in saving the farms or homes of the middle class than in making a quick profit. So they foreclosed, some-times thousands of farms or homes in one province in a year. Like the homes being bought by speculators to rent today, the farms were resold to the rich, who consolidated them into giant estates. These estates were agribusinesses in the same sense as the giant corporate farms are today. As the rich Romans bought up huge estates, they used one of the spoils of war, captured slaves, to work the land much more cheaply than the remaining middle-class farmers could. The remaining middle-class small farmers couldn't compete when wholesale food prices dropped. They were eventually driven off their land.

The senators and other patricians then bought up even more land, passing it on through generations. Many children or grand-children of former farmers became serfs, working for the estate holders for a split of the crops on the land their family had for-merly owned. Dispossessed, they had no choice but to accept these paltry wages to labor on the estates, or move to Rome and join the masses searching for any type of work. There was no other alternative; the other choice was to watch their family starve to death. With a surplus of slaves doing many of the jobs available, the value of a laborer was negligible. The former middle class, competing and losing to slave labor, soon found themselves living in tenements and on the dole.

By the sixth century, artisans and farmworkers on the es-tates, which now covered most of the Empire, were assigned to their crafts at birth, and serfdom had become formalized. The difference between the farmworker and the slave disappeared. The great-grandson of the middle-class Roman farmer became a serf, forced to live at the whim of the landowners and always on the edge of starvation and poverty. Not coincidentally, the destruction of the class of the Roman farmers and artisans also marked the beginning of what was known as the Dark Ages.

Economies and loyalties became local while trade and education waned. There were other causes for this, but the loss of the
middle class certainly was a major factor. A healthy economy
needs an active middle class and the economic mobility it represents.

For a poor Roman, the alternative to serfdom was to flee to
a city. (Serfs were forbidden to do this by their landowners.)
Displaced Roman farmers fled to the cities in search of employment rather than face starvation. They were not happy, having
already lost their land, only to arrive in the city with no jobs
available and no way to support themselves and their families.
The reason for this was simple: slave labor had displaced much
of the workforce in every part of the Roman economy. The conquest of Greece in 146 BCE flooded Rome with well-educated,
often highly skilled slaves who could perform almost every
skilled and educated job needed. This further marginalized the
original city of Rome's middle-class artisans and scholars. Soon
there were simply the very rich and the struggling poor, a result
that changed, and eventually doomed, the Western Roman
Empire.

Today, American workers are not competing with slaves, but
they too see their jobs being offshored and taken by workers
who are paid much less. If you want to pay your workers the
least amount that you can, then using someone who works for
food and housing alone and can't quit has great appeal. So the
slaves acquired in the empire's many successful wars displaced
the Roman-born workers. Think what would happen if those
same Chinese factory workers who get paid a few dollars a day
could be transplanted and made to work for the same money in
Akron, Ohio. Nor could they complain, organize, or have any
type of union. What factory would hire a $10-an-hour Ameri-
can when they could use a $2-an-hour import, or in Rome, a

slave? Today, we have outsourcing. In ancient Rome they had in-sourcing. It was called slavery, and the effects were similar.

Formerly middle-class Romans who were displaced by cheap labor still had to provide for their families and took positions that paid far less. They dropped from the middle class. They bought less, and this hurt the economy. It began a spiral that ended not just in a recession but in economic collapse. This happened in Rome two thousand years ago. It was not a rapid occurrence. It took centuries for the Roman rural, and then urban, middle classes to diminish so far that they became irrelevant. This should serve today as a warning that the process of the decline of the middle class can be slow and barely noticeable, on a day-by-day or even month-by-month basis, but still eventually destroy the American economy. The head of the United States' largest union regularly addresses the risks the decline of the middle class has for America. Unfortunately, since the decline is slow and marked with individual failures rather than dramatic, newsworthy changes, it is hard to engender the level of concern or news coverage this deserves. It didn't in Rome, either. Hopefully we will not need another six hundred years of the Dark Ages to learn from their mistake.

> For globalization to work for America, it must work for the working people. We should measure the success of our economy by the breadth of our middle class, and the scope of opportunity offered to the poorest child to climb into that middle class.
>
> —JOHN J. SWEENEY (1934–),
> FORMER PRESIDENT OF THE AFL-CIO

So is the United States' middle class in danger of having the same fate as Rome's? During the past few decades, the United

States has moved away from the manufacturing sector, unable to compete with dirt-cheap labor and production costs overseas. Until the 1960s America was the greatest exporter of products in the world. Now we are the greatest importer. The change occurred because labor is cheaper in foreign countries, the laws are looser, and there are a lot fewer environmental controls. It is simply cheaper to have a product made overseas and shipped to the United States to sell than to make it here. Jobs that were once held by Americans making products to be sold domestically have been moved "offshore." In just the past twenty years, U.S. industry has decreased to half the size it was, constituting only 17 percent of the country's total GDP. Contrast that with Europe's industry being 26 percent of that continent's GDP. The United States has become more of a service-producing economy, and this has caused a big change in the skills employers are seeking.

In 2001 China joined the World Trade Organization. Since then, the United States has lost an average of fifty thousand manufacturing jobs per month. Bill Rodgers, former chief economist for the Labor Department, put it this way: "As we became more connected to China, that poses the question of whether or not our wages are being set in Beijing." Although globalization has moved tens of millions of people out of poverty in these Third World countries, it was at the expense of many middle-class Americans, many of whose families are now living in poverty.

Fifty years ago, many people could land a well-paying blue-collar job with just a high school diploma. In 1980 earners with a high school diploma were able to make about 71 percent of what their college-educated counterparts were making. By 2010 the percentage they could make, compared to a college graduate, had decreased to 55 percent. Now many of those blue-collar jobs have all but disappeared, and a college degree is an absolute minimum requirement for most well-paying jobs in America. But college costs have skyrocketed, and made such an education beyond the means of the children of the remaining middle class. Parents make too much money for poverty grants and scholarships, and find that the tens of thousands of dollars a year in college costs are far beyond their family's means. The higher hurdle and cost of needing a college degree has become a limiting factor in becoming one of the new "skilled" members of the middle class. Not to mention, college loans discourage young and innovative graduates from taking those chances that give rise to a Twitter or Groupon. Both the need and the cost of education are chipping away at the middle class, making it harder and often prohibitively costly for their children to become well-enough educated to live as well as, much less better than, their parents. In Ancient Rome, the result of this type of decline was the destruction of the middle class and a gradual descent to a feudal, serfdom, society.

The Great Recession: A Game Changer?

When the Roman Empire stopped expanding and gaining infusions of, well, loot, the economy began to slowly spiral downward. This was in effect a very long recession that accelerated the collapse of the middle class. While the current long recession and jobless recovery has not completely collapsed the American middle class, it certainly is assaulting it.

When discussing the years leading up to the Great Recession, University of Chicago business school professor Raghuram Rajan said the mantra during that time was: "Let them eat credit." As the income gap widened, the debt taken on by middle-class

Americans grew dramatically. Credit was cheap and easy. Average income earners were taking out second mortgages to pay the first mortgage and getting credit cards to buy groceries. As housing prices skyrocketed, people were constantly borrowing against their newfound equity. They never considered what their situation would be if that equity disappeared.

A Deutsche Bank managing director described the time period leading up to the Great Recession this way: "We were all drinking the Kool-Aid, Greenspan was tending bar, and Bernanke and the academic establishment were supplying the liquor."

Yet during the period between 2001 and 2007, 66 percent of the income growth went to the top one percent of Americans. What this means is that the cliché has expanded: not only are the rich getting richer and the poor poorer, but the middle class is getting poorer, too. Money is being concentrated in the hands of fewer and fewer individuals, just as it was in Ancient Rome.

The only thing the middle class accumulated during that time was more debt than ever before. Some economists have noted a correlation between bank failures and periods where income disparity is increasing. And this income disparity was on display during the summer of 2008, right before the U.S. banks started toppling like dominoes and the speculative bubble burst.

During the Great Recession, it initially appeared that the wealthiest in the country would take a big hit. The stock market plummeted, with the richest 1 percent of Americans sustaining 47 percent of the losses. There was outrage over CEO pay while the government was using taxpayer money to bail out the very corporations that these highly compensated individuals were running.

Americans have a short memory for their own outrage. By 2009, just a year after the bloodletting on Wall Street, bonuses for those hedge fund managers and CEOs whose companies had to be bailed out were up 17 percent when compared with 2008. Despite being mired in the worst economic crisis since the Great Depression, the number of millionaires in the United States soared 16 percent in 2009. The rich got richer even after making everyone else much poorer and causing their homes to lose value dramatically. How can this happen? In Ancient Rome, the Senate and often the emperor really represented only the rich and patrician families. They had the real influence. So the Roman government rarely did anything other than protect the wealth of the wealthy . . . and that was before lobbyists. Today, the elected officials are forced to coddle those with money because they need their contributions to get reelected. Nor are many of those in office really "of the people," since the average net worth of a U.S. Senator in 2009, after the collapse, was almost $14 million ($13,989,022.98, according to www.opensecrets.org, a comprehensive site that publishes the sources of all federal candidates' campaign contributions).

By 2010 many of the top echelon on Wall Street took home record amounts of earnings. But for the rest of America, unemployment remained high, at over 8 percent, for four years in a row, from 2009 to 2012. The housing market is in a depression and wages for those who still have a job have stagnated or even declined. This is just like Ancient Rome, when the wealthy elite indulged in every luxury while the middle class disappeared and the poor suffered.

The Haves and the Have-Mores

As we have seen, there are several factors involved in the decline in both the numbers and the wealth of the American middle class. The problem spreads across the past four decades, several administrations, and the two most recent Federal Reserve chairmen. Although some factors triggering the huge income disparities seen today started emerging in the 1970s, the erosion of middle-class America has escalated in the past twenty years. At the end of 2007, just before the recession began, the richest 1 percent had 42 percent of the country's total wealth, and the next 19 percent had another 50 percent, leaving the remaining 80 percent of the people only 8 percent of the total wealth. Contrast that with the Ozzie and Harriet era: during the 1950s, the American Dream was alive and well, with 90 percent of the nation's citizens controlling 68 percent of the economy, and the 10 percent who were the wealthiest controlling only 32 percent, with the top 1 percent less than half of that.

Job Types

By 2009, about half of all of the wealth in America was amassed by the richest 10 percent in the country. The Great Recession officially ended in 2009, but three years later the middle class in America remains on life support. With the threat of another recession looming, a disturbing trend seems to be solidifying. As corporate profits soar, primarily from the benefits of deregulation and outsourcing, American workers are finding out that in order to stay employed they must accept much lower wages than ever before. More than 40 percent of Americans are now working in low-paying service jobs, jobs that pay them a real income lower than what they earned before 2008. High-paying manufacturing jobs have all but disappeared, taking the middle class with them. In a recent survey, 61 percent of Americans say they "always or usually" live paycheck to paycheck. This number was up from 49 percent in 2008 and 43 percent in 2007.

And troubling trends have emerged in regards to retire-ment savings. It appears that there may be very little "gold" to go around during those "golden years." In 2010, 36 percent of Americans said that they don't contribute anything to retire-ment savings. A staggering 43 percent of Americans have less than $10,000 saved up for retirement when the recommended amount needed to retire comfortably over the poverty level is in the hundreds of thousands of dollars. Twenty-four percent of American workers say that they have postponed their planned retirement age in the past few years and saved nothing. When these people retire they will not be middle class, they will be struggling. This is another part of the middle-class dream slowly disappearing.

In the past twenty years, we have seen a sizable increase in productivity in the United States, but the workforce has shrunk and wages have stagnated or even declined. The huge increases in productivity have primarily benefited the top ninety-ninth percentile, much like that of the estates in fifth-century Rome. The productivity increase has resulted partially from advances in technology that has made many jobs obsolete. But there is also something akin to the Roman peasant exploitation going on in some industries. In order to keep their jobs, many Ameri-can workers must now take huge pay and benefit cuts and work longer, harder, and faster than ever before to keep the pink slips at bay. Even so, many people have lost their homes, and with them, the American home-ownership dream. This even has the side effect of driving rents up because of increased demand, making it harder to save or recover from any setback.

Like Imperial Century Rome, the U.S. government is feeding more and more families. In 2012, three years after the "official" end date of the current recession, more than forty million U.S. citizens were receiving food stamps. This was a 40 percent increase from 2008.

Is There Hope?

Solutions to the problem of the declining middle class are complicated and difficult to implement. Activists often argue for the reemergence of a strong labor movement to protect workers from exploitation. Wage growth needs to be decoupled from productivity. Union experts also say we should encourage a more union-friendly environment, since declining memberships greatly contribute to income inequality. Others say this will be possible only when the unions are reformed and are once more controlled by their members. Yet others disagree and point out that the driving up of wages and lowering of productivity hurts business and ultimately makes things much worse. They point out how union rules helped to bankrupt both GM and Chrysler.

Some experts are convinced that the only way for the middle class to survive and grow again is for the government to intervene to help dying industries compete globally and stop the outsourcing of well-paying jobs. Economic isolationism and tariffs have their own built-in disaster. (See the sections on causes of the Great Depression.) But other economists say that what is needed is for the government to create more programs to retrain the workers who were in dying industries, giving them new skills in more sought-after industries. There is a shortage of skilled workers in areas requiring technical skills and math even during this period of high unemployment.

Conventional wisdom says that getting a higher education is the key to getting a higher-paying job. But Princeton professor and Nobel laureate Paul Krugman argues that simply graduating more students from college is not going to restore the middle class. During the past few decades it has become clear that obtaining a college degree is no longer a guarantee of securing a good job. We need to recognize that one size doesn't fit all when it comes to education. So a key element in preserving the middle class is to change the educational system to something that affordably prepares their children for well-paying positions. We also need to consider widespread retraining programs for all those displaced blue-collar workers. And for future generations, we need to educate them for jobs that focus on innovation and creativity, traits the American worker was known for in the past. That may or may not include a college degree.

Historical Perspective

There are several explanations offered for the troubling destruction of the American middle class. Many experts argue that the shrinking of the middle class is correlated with the decline of the labor unions. Others suggest it was faulty economic policies like deregulation of the rich. Today this means the banks and investment industries, and in Rome it meant the factories and estates. All agree this is bad, and as you can see from the effect it had on Rome, it can be disastrous.

As it was in Rome, the destruction of the middle class is both a symptom and a cause of economic collapse. The process is slow (it took Rome four centuries), and it is hard to see any day-to-day difference, but it is continuing, and even accelerating, today. Perhaps the first step is to remind the decision makers to take the long view, and yes . . . maybe learn from history.

The cause of the modern decline of the middle class is real

and measurable. The simple, sad fact is that the middle-class families of today earn less than they did in 1999. Americans are having a difficult time reaching and staying in an economic class that being a part of was commonplace just a generation ago. Children no longer grow up expecting a better life than their parents, and that dismal outlook is too often becoming accurate. For many of today's American families, the dream of home ownership has evaporated, saving for their children's rising college costs has become virtually impossible, and a secure retirement seems completely out of reach. It is no longer rags to riches, but riches to rags. Based on the other times this has happened, the attitude of the general population toward their government changes, and the nation's identity and confidence suffer.

In spite of an epic global recession in 2008–2009, America's rich are richer than ever: the top 1 percent now own more than one-third of the nation's wealth—more than at any other time in U.S. history. If the pattern of history holds true, that ratio is a national poison, economically and socially. As history has shown us, a strong middle class provides a more stable society. We must find a way back to the economic middle ground. The example of Rome serves as a warning, but this is because of its stark failures. Because the process is gradual and has little effect on those most influential with the government, preventing this decline—which can, over time, destroy the United States—is not being given any real priority. We need to pay attention before the trend is too far along to reverse and history can someday say a second superpower was crippled and then fell because it destroyed its own middle class.

CHAPTER THIRTEEN

Britain, Former Superpower

Britain will be honoured by historians more for the way she disposed of an empire than for the way in which she acquired it.

— LORD HARLECH (1918–1985)

Much as the United States was after the fall of the Soviet Union, for more than three centuries, Great Britain was the only real worldwide superpower. Other nations could be superior in Europe, but only Britain ruled a worldwide empire and controlled the wealth that this provided. The original North American seaboard colonies were British, with British governors, and were for a long time quite loyal to the king of England. Culturally, the Americans in the original colonies saw themselves as transplanted Englishmen. The original broadsides (pamphlets) written by the those who became the revolutionaries and founding fathers of the new United States did not originally call for independence. They demanded that they be given the same rights as Englishmen who lived in Britain. If these rights had been granted in the 1760s, there is a good chance there never would have been an American Revolution.

Britain truly became a world power in 1588. Spain was the dominant player at the time, thanks in large part to the extraordinary wealth it had gained from its empire. Spain's King Philip II was frustrated with England. As a devout Catholic, he viewed Queen Elizabeth I as a heretic. Between 1584 and 1606, there was in effect an undeclared war at sea going on between Spain and England. Spanish merchant ships had been constantly assailed by English privateers, which were essentially pirates commissioned by the English crown who paid England a cut of their loot. In response to the privateers and religious differences, Spain assembled a massive fleet, the armada, with the intent of invading Britain. Yet the formidable galleons of the Spanish armada did not fare well against the smaller, more maneuverable English ships. With the help of some fortuitous storms and Philip's appointment of a general who had no sea experience to command the armada, the English fleet defeated the larger Spanish force. With this ill-fated voyage, the Spanish Empire began to decline as Britain began its ascension to world dominance.

England continued to prosper, thanks to a blossoming maritime trade network and the world's finest navy. It competed with France for imperial footholds in India and the Americas. This competition eventually manifested in the Seven Years War, those years being 1756 to 1763. In the Americas, this is often called the "French and Indian War," to differentiate the American theater from the European one, as that war actually started in 1754 and so would have to be named the Nine Years War. Brit-

ain and its ally Prussia claimed victory over Spain and France.
In the ensuing peace agreement, Britain claimed most of North
America, including Canada and Florida. The treaty also emas-
culated France's military presence in India by severely limiting how many troops France could have and where they could
go (not far from the few bases they already had). Within a few
decades the French were gone, and the French East India Company dissolved itself in 1794. This paved the way for two centuries of British rule on the subcontinent.

The moment of Britain's ascension in many ways mirrors
that of the United States. Each vanquished the world's then-
most-powerful nation en route to becoming a respectable global
power. Britain competed frequently with France and Russia
during the nineteenth century, whereas the second half of the
twentieth century revolved around America's icy relations with
the Soviet Union. Yet both the British Empire and the United
States had, or have, unrivaled influence.

Ironically, few things ensured the vitality of the British Empire
better than the American Revolution. After the war, Britain retained many of the benefits it had gleaned as colonial master.
The United States became Britain's best trading partner, as well
as the destination of countless British emigrants. Though these
relations hiccupped during the War of 1812, the two countries
have enjoyed a special friendship ever since. Moreover, Britain
learned from its mistakes. In 1837, when faced with insurrection
in Canada, Britain commissioned a career Whig politician, John
George Lambton, the first Earl of Durham, to investigate possible policy responses. In an 1839 report that was mostly penned
by his secretary, Charles Buller, Lambton recommended various
administrative reforms. In particular, he suggested that Britain
cede greater autonomy to its settler colonies. This report would
become the template for governing colonies like New Zealand.

Britain's relationships with these colonies flourished and remain harmonious today. What is often overlooked by many Americans is that over a dozen former colonies still technically consider the British Crown their sovereign.

Britain's empire flourished primarily because of its extensive trade network. Britain stripped many of its colonies of their natural resources. A good example of this was Cecil Rhodes, the South African mine owner and politician, who lied about his intentions and started a war against the local tribes. His real intention was just to secure lucrative mining rights. He won. Rhodes went on to become a loyal leader during the British takeover of Boer (Dutch descendants') lands in South Africa, as a result of the Boer War (1899–1902). After the British victory, he became premier of the Cape Colony.

If deemed necessary, Britain was not above forcibly promoting "free" trade. Europe wanted Chinese goods and the British wanted to sell them, but had little the Chinese wanted in return. To create some way to balance out their expenditures in China, the British introduced opium into Chinese society and supplied it. Yes, to support their Chinese trade, the British became what today would be considered drug lords. Within a decade, opium was visibly hurting Chinese society and their emperor saw the threat. When China began restricting imports of opium in 1839, Britain seized several Chinese ports and forced embarrassing concessions from China's Qing government. Eventually Western tactics and technology gave Britain virtual control of most of the key cities in China, as well as of the last Qing emperors. This proved a successful tactic until World War I, when Britain would pursue a strategy of installing puppet rulers in China, Egypt, and elsewhere.

Britain, like Rome, truly reveled in its mastery of the world. It was joyfully noted that the sun never set on the British Empire.

This meant that they ruled so many lands all around the world that it was always daytime in one of them. While some British criticized imperial policy, most believed Britain was endowed with the sacred task of "civilizing" the benighted regions of the world. It became obsessed with exposing its colonies to the English culture, religion, and institutions. Famed English poet Rudyard Kipling summed up the British view perfectly in his poem "The White Man's Burden." The poem is directed at the United States, imploring it to join Britain in civilizing the "inferior" races. It was written in 1899 and begins:

Take up the White Man's burden—
Send forth the best ye breed—
Go bind your sons to exile
To serve your captives' need;
To wait in heavy harness,
On fluttered folk and wild—
Your new-caught, sullen peoples,
Half-devil and half-child.

The third stanza lists the justifications for the British creating their empire. This was an attitude that Kipling and most British firmly took on faith.

Take up the White Man's burden—
The savage wars of peace—
Fill full the mouth of Famine
And bid the sickness cease;
And when your goal is nearest
The end for others sought,
Watch sloth and heathen Folly
Bring all your hopes to naught.

An amazing read for someone in today's politically correct society, but indicative of the world view that justified an empire where the sun never set.

The United States has also possessed such a messianic view of itself. In the nineteenth century, the United States believed in Manifest Destiny, a view that the country was destined by fate, God, or just because they were Americans to expand across North America, subjugating "inferior" peoples if necessary. This justified the Mexican War and the taking of nearly half of Mexico's land, now the American Southwest.

The most glaring reason for the dissolution of the British Empire was the effect of two world wars. Britain mobilized its empire during each war, and many soldiers from India and Africa served in British units. Britain was devastated by the wars. Generations of young men disappeared, slain by disease or in combat. During World War II, much of Britain's public infrastructure was destroyed by relentless German air raids. Meat was still being rationed in Britain in 1952 and often the only meat available was Spam, a canned pork product. Spam became so much a part of English life, even into the 1960s, that the comedy troupe Monty Python did one of their most famous routines based on the product being the only dish available in a restaurant. After more than a decade of deprivation and the loss of so many lives, the British public had no appetite for the extensive military and financial effort that would have been needed to retain their colonies and no longer had the financial wherewithal to remain the dominant economic power.

The cost of the Second World War was also a major factor. Britain ended that war owing a massive debt to other nations, mostly the United States. In 1945 alone, Britain borrowed $5.5 billion from the United States and Canada (that would be $68 billion in 2012 dollars). They did not pay off the last of this war debt until 2006. Between paying back that debt and restoring their national infrastructure, even with the aid provided by the Marshall Plan, the British government had little to spare. Britain's day as the leader of Europe and the financial power-house of the world passed. The British Empire declined. The peoples it ruled became restive and were eventually freed. The attitude shown in Kipling's "The White Man's Burden" became less popular and even stigmatized as the world preached self-determination as the politically correct attitude. Nor was having colonies as beneficial as it once had been.

At one time, the greatest benefit colonies provided was that you could force them to buy only from your own businesses. But free trade treaties after World War II changed that and no one could maintain a closed market. British business no longer benefited from the monopolies that colonies provided. Nor did those businesses want to pay taxes to support the massive over-seas army that would have been necessary to maintain control of India and parts of Africa. To them the British Empire no longer made good economic sense. India became independent in 1947 and the last real British colony was freed in 1979, effec-tively ending four centuries of Empire.

We should learn from how debt played a great part in the decline of Great Britain as a world power. Most of that debt was acquired to support their military. In both world wars, the very existence of Great Britain was in jeopardy. The nation, with a sixth the population of the United States, had no choice but to go into debt to the tune of almost half a trillion of today's dol-lars just to survive. It paid a high price for doing so. Today, the larger United States is not under threat of invasion, but is going trillions of dollars into debt each year. There is no reason to expect this debt burden to not have an effect on America like the less massive debts did on Britain.

Some of the other challenges that led to Britain's decline are also present for the United States today. America is feeling the economic and social strain caused by wars in Afghanistan and Iraq just as Britain was when trying to maintain control of its increasingly restive colonies and dominant world position. There are many economic parallels, such as the fact that the United States vies politically with China and Russia for dominance in a battle that is no less cut-throat and competitive than the Great Game of the nineteenth century.

The massive American debt to the Chinese is analogous in some ways to Britain's post-WWII debt to the United States. In other ways it is a much more dangerous proposition, as Britain's creditor, America, was a firm ally. This is something that certainly cannot be said for China. The American "empire" and its influence are based more on economic power than on military strength.

Where Britain had colonies, America has markets and megacorporations. That is part of what makes the export of jobs as great a threat to the American future as any Chinese or Russian military invasion. This is also why Admiral Mike Mullen, the eighteenth chairman of the Joint Chiefs of Staff, the highest ranking officer in the United States military, called the rapidly increasing debt the American government owes to China and Japan "the single biggest threat to our national security." He went on to explain this in an interview appearing in *Forbes* magazine on May 10, 2012, saying, "Obviously it's complex, but the way I looked at it, if we didn't get control of our debt, there would be continued loss of confidence in America." A loss of confidence, isolationism, and a desire to not confront foreign threats forcefully were symptoms that led to the decline of Britain. These also could be a catalog of emerging problems and attitudes in America today. Still, even if facing challenging economic times, the United States remains economically and militarily the most powerful nation on the planet. This is not to say that we need not look at what caused the decline of the British Empire and avoid the same mistakes and traps. A look at the parallels reveals little indication that we're learning from their experiences.

Like the British 170 years ago, the United States finds itself intervening and spending money and lives on situations based on immediate moral or political concerns that have no long-term, real benefit to the nation, such as Serbia, Iraq, and Libya. Just as the British public lost interest in maintaining and controlling their restive colonies and protecting them against the other powers, Americans too are showing foreign-affairs fatigue. After years of war, the American public is beginning to express isolationist yearnings reminiscent to those of Britain's in 1937. In America this manifests itself in activities ranging from antiwar and Get US Out of the United Nations protests to lobbying against giving foreign aid and the desire for ever higher tariffs to keep our foreign goods.

War Weary

In 1938 most British were more than reluctant, after the massive casualties in World War I, to risk another war, and this led to what was a generally very popular policy of appeasement. They sold out an ally, Czechoslovakia. This policy of peace at any cost, supported by the French, strengthened and encouraged the Nazis. It made World War II inevitable. The lesson here is that being weak and "reasonable" because you fear challenging aggressors can cost you dearly later. Incidentally, a survey taken just weeks before Pearl Harbor showed that the majority of Americans still wanted to stay out of World War II.

Another difference lies in military strength. The United States' military dominates in all areas: land, sea, and sky. Britain was truly unrivaled only in naval strength. While Britain's ground troops had little difficulty putting down indigenous resistance, they were not especially remarkable compared to the armies of Britain's European rivals. The discrepancy enjoyed by the U.S. Armed Forces compared to its next rival is greater than it was for Britain or indeed Rome.

British Lessons

The British Empire faced many of the problems now facing the United States. Some they solved; some tore apart their empire. Some, like financing World War II, were insoluble necessities and could only be tempered.

The British reaction to their greatest speculation bubble, the South Seas Company, and the dozens of questionable stock companies that followed was to ban the sale of stock for several years. By the time the ban was lifted, they had created market regulations that would prevent such extreme speculation. For hundreds of years, those being regulated have complained, like the U.S. banks in the 1990s, that such restrictions are not needed. Yet every time they are removed, another bubble and its collapse ensue.

Because of its extensive trade network, England suffered from numerous plagues. Its ships sailed from every part of the world and occasionally brought with them a cargo of disease. The British learned early to destroy the bodies and even homes of those infected. They also have used science well to help prevent outbreaks or control them. For example, until the middle of the eighteenth century, many illnesses were blamed on "foul airs," as germs and virus were unknown. Cholera, a waterborne disease, struck London in 1853 and 1854, killing ten thousand Englishmen. Such pandemics recurred with frustrating regularity every time London had a warm summer. A doctor named John Snow mapped the outbreaks and was able to connect them to polluted water and wells. By 1859 this evidence, and several hot summers, enabled Joseph Bazalgette, chief engineer of London's Metropolitan Board, to obtain the funds needed to create the multilayered sewer system still in use in London today. This was a radical concept for its day, and shows the value of taking new approaches to preventing old diseases. The cycle was broken, and the threat of cholera greatly lessened.

The British reaction to terrorists varied, but always involved investigation and infiltration. Britain also took a strong approach. When that approach alienated the local population, the British invariably failed. The IRA was not formed to battle with the English settlers in Northern Ireland, but to counter the British army sent there to maintain order. Britain's use of its army in Palestine against the Zionists and radical Islamists also failed and subjected it to serious casualties. Like the French, they have found that a large military presence was not enough to contain popular discontent—a lesson learned again by the United States in Iraq, and still being learned in Afghanistan.

The British failure to eliminate Gaelic in Ireland, even after three hundred years of repression, shows just how difficult forcing such a change can be. The success of English as a common language in India has a message, too. After its independence, many on the subcontinent wanted to eliminate the use of the language of their former colonial masters. All attempts failed. This showed how a language that serves a purpose, such as being a common tongue in a multilingual nation, has great resilience and can survive even major efforts to expunge it. Languages do what the people need, not what a government wants.

From Britain's experiences, the United States can learn how to handle change and can see how detrimental taking actions that are not for the long-term benefit of the nation can be. One lesson is that Britain, from World War I to 1979, paid a high economic and social price for holding on to its colonies. There was also a high cost for having appeased the Nazis, and this should serve as a warning for the United States on what not to do with Russia or China. Financially, the American government is finding that there are other costs to going into massive debt. Using borrowed dollars to support other nations like Pakistan that are not true allies and to intervene in foreign wars where no American interests lie is hazardous in both the long and the short term. Such debt helped change Britain from a world leader into just another Western nation. Debt, as the former head of the American Joint Chiefs of Staff warns, creates its own risks by constraining what the financially burdened nation can do.

All is not darkness and gloom. Perhaps the most encouraging lesson is this: even though Britain lost its superpower status in the twentieth century, it has remained stable and strong and has survived two challenging wars against Germany. It may no longer be the world's economic hyperpower, but it has enjoyed peace and prosperity in the years since ceding that role to the United States. If America avoids the mistakes that cost Britain so dearly, and learns from what that country did right, it will bode well for a long and prosperous future.

CHAPTER FOURTEEN

America and the Roman Empire

Great empires are not maintained by timidity.
—TACITUS (56–117 CE), ROMAN
SENATOR AND HISTORIAN

If you have a family with wildly divergent political opinions, kick off the next reunion with this question: Is the United States a modern version of the Roman Empire? The neoconservative uncle will likely respond that the United States doesn't act imperially enough, whereas the ultra-liberal aunt might decry Iraq and Afghanistan as examples of imperial warmongering. Those caught between these two extremes will likely deny, with varying degrees of conviction, that the United States is imperial at all. The debate will rage until the children become consumed with boredom and ask, "Rome? Who cares?"

The answer is that every American should care. The similarities between the United States and the Roman Empire are undeniable: each had humble beginnings, a republican tradition, and a swift ascension to world hegemony. Beyond that, it becomes a matter of debate. While many critics of American foreign policy describe the United States in imperial terms, apologists counter that it remains a democracy without territorial ambition. Their attitude would come as a surprise to historians in the Philippines, Spain, and Mexico. Remember, the United States has a colony, albeit a willing one, in Puerto Rico, which freely voted to apply for admission into U.S. statehood in 2012. It would not surprise the people of Iraq, many of whom are more worried about what is now happening since the United States withdrew than they were concerned that the American troops were there.

Here are just some of the most obvious parallels between the Roman Empire and the United States:

Both nations were colonies, offshoots of another major power. The story in Rome is that it was founded by those who fled Troy when it fell. The United States was, of course, a former colony of Britain.

Both nations were founded and initially ruled by an oligarchy—Rome by the Senate and not the people. Rome was never a democracy. In fact such elements as the College of Electors are a direct remnant of the American Founding Fathers using Rome as a model. There was, in both, a fear of "mobocracy." In fact, most U.S. senators were, at first, appointed by the states and not elected.

Both the United States and Rome began as small states and expanded aggressively. This expansion was often at the cost of their neighbors or the former residents. Ask the American Indians, the Spanish, the Hawaiians, or the Mexicans about how the

United States expanded. Rome, of course, conquered or intimidated the entire Mediterranean Basin and beyond.

Rome saw it as both a necessity and a duty to bring Roman
control and the *Pax Romana* to the entire world. Americans had
a term for their right to control all of North America and more:
Manifest Destiny. Both succeeded.

Both empires (okay, Americans do not use that term, but
there are American territories, so it is technically correct)
became the policemen for their known world.

Latin, and today English, have spread to be commonly used
in large parts of the world. Both Roman and American culture
were and are exported in large amounts to other nations.

As with Rome, the United States in the early twenty-first century has, unquestionably, the most powerful and effective military, using the latest technology and techniques. Both also saw
the armies that they could field stretched to the limit.

From the Maccabees to the British tribes, facing the Roman
legions in a straight-up battle was suicide. Resistance to Rome
often involved, at least initially, terrorism, secrecy, and rebellion. America also can dominate any battlefield it chooses, and
so its opponents use those same tactics today.

In Rome, the partisan politics were between the noble, eques-
trian class, known today as the patricians, that traditionally
provided the senators and governors, and the plebes or common
people, who discovered that their numbers did mean power.

Both Rome and America had violent social upheavals where
the lower and middle classes learned to assert themselves. The
United States has experienced class warfare several times, particularly during the late nineteenth century with the advent of
the union movement, and at the peak of the Great Depression.
Republican Rome, as just mentioned, had similar events. The
clash between the two economic classes was called the Social

Wars for good reason. This battle between the two parts of one nation occasionally even erupted into a level of violence that makes any protest held in Washington, D.C., or even the riots in London, Athens, and Spain look mild by comparison. The worst of this class warfare in Rome occasionally resulted in actual warfare. In the second century BCE, the Gracchi brothers organized the plebes into mobs and took control of much of the city in an effort to make the political system more open to the lower classes and those who were not born of a noble family. They also championed reforming land ownership, which threatened the large landowners, again the patricians. The result was ten years of off-and-on rioting and mob battles in the streets of Rome, interspersed with the occasional assassination. This resulted in hundreds of dead and wounded and the occasional major fire.

The Roman civil war between Caesar and Pompey was the first time Roman legions fought other legions. It was really part of the class warfare, with Caesar having the backing of the plebes and Pompey being the standard bearer of the patrician class and Senate. Caesar won, but thousands of Romans died fighting other Romans over which class would control the government. Ironically, neither did, since Caesar soon became emperor and, from then on, neither class had much real control. In Byzantine Rome the two largest chariot racing factions, the Blues and the Greens, became politicized and often fought pitched battles in the streets of Constantinople, using swords and clubs and involving thousands of racing fans. Today, this would be like MoveOn.org and the Tea Party hiring private armies to fight it out in Times Square. Inconceivable? It has happened more than once.

Another cause of the Social Wars and later social unrest in Rome was the concentration of wealth. Ownership of land changed from the yeoman farmer to large estates. (This is discussed in more detail in the chapter on the destruction of the middle class.) This drove the former farmers into the cities, where as much as a quarter of the population of Rome was dependent on the emperor for food and housing. Cue the Great Society and several generations of welfare recipients, please.

A great civil war convulsed both nations, the one following Caesar's assassination changing and scarring Rome forever, and the American Civil War. The War Between the States left lasting emotional and social scars that took a century to heal, and some dispute whether they ever healed at all.

Foreign wars made Rome rich, but these had been offensive wars whose success was rewarded with loot and slaves. Once the Empire's expansion stopped, the cost of maintaining defensive wars in Germany and the Eastern Mediterranean nearly bankrupted Rome and was a contributor to the end of the Empire. Trillions of deficit dollars for wars in Iraq, Afghanistan, and elsewhere are certainly worsening the economic situation facing the United States. These too are like the Roman defensive wars, as Americans are proud to explain, where we do not in the end expect to retain the land or wealth of the nations we are spending so much to fight in.

If Russia is Carthage to the United States' Rome, then the Cold War can be thought of as the modern Punic War. The Punic Wars lasted over a century. They really comprised economic, hot, and cold wars between the two empires based in the cities of Rome and Carthage as they emerged as world powers. The battles were mostly fought over and on the territory of lesser powers and allies. The competition erupted into fighting three times, with Rome victorious each time. Only the final stages brought the conflict to Italy, as in Hannibal and his famous elephants. Carthage eventually lost and Rome certainly settled with Carthage in a much more permanent way than the United

States handled the collapse of the Soviet Union. The North African city remains in ruins and is virtually uninhabited even to this day.

Rome was challenged by culturally different groups, the barbarians and Parthia, and America in the last century has faced first Nazis, then Communism, and now radical Islam. But despite all the similarities there are also some important differences between the Roman Empire and the United States.

To argue about whether the United States is a modern Roman Empire might in fact be primarily semantic rather than substantive. It is more important to understand what the similarities portend for the future of America. The United States shares many similarities with the Roman Empire; it even has much in common with the later British Empire. The most significant reason people squirm at the comparison is that the Roman Empire, like all empires, eventually collapsed. This is an important perspective. No nation can last unchanged forever. Empires—no matter how great or wealthy—eventually decline. The same happened with the Mongol Empire, after almost two centuries of almost worldwide domination, and to the British Empire, which lasted as a real empire from around 1600 until the independence of Britain's last colonies in 1979. Time was shorter for the once greatly feared Soviet Empire, lasting only from the 1905 Bolshevik Revolution until the collapse of Communism in August of 1991.

Today, the sun sets on the British Empire every day; the Mongols haven't terrorized anyone in seven hundred years; after being home to almost a dozen empires in early history, Persia is only a historical designation; and Rome fell twice. To admit that the United States is like Rome requires people to accept that America's superpower status is ephemeral.

Bread and Circuses

The phrase "bread and circuses" does not mean food and entertainment, though they were involved. What it really means is the dependency of a good portion of the population on the government for their day-to-day necessities. There is a parallel in how current developments in the United States may mirror the later days of the Roman Empire. "Bread and circuses" is often used as a term of disdain for those who accept government largess and become dependent upon it. But back then it was considered the right of the people, and riots occurred when the bread came late.

As also mentioned in the chapter on the decline of the middle class, Rome began as a nation of small farmers who rallied to defend their city. But as the Empire grew, there was a change. Success in war brought in both wealth and slaves. But slaves are of no use unless you have land for them to work. Many of the small farmers found they were competing with massive estates, just as today's family farmer competes with giant agribusiness complexes. Between that and taxes, many farmers found themselves losing money or struggling. The rich families also controlled the government, including the Roman Senate. They began to buy, or force, out the small farmers and create massive estates. Their land and homes gone, tens of thousands of displaced rural Romans swarmed into Rome and the other cities. Rome itself grew until it had more than a million residents. The capable Roman engineers were able to supply water and sewers and even create buildings six and seven stories high to house these masses, but no one could figure out how to find jobs for most of them.

The result was that by the end of the first century, a quar-

ter of all the men in Rome were unable to find work. This created a problem. There had been riots in Rome in the past, some
leading to the fall of emperors and doing great destruction. No
Roman emperor wanted an angry, hungry mob, numbering in
the tens of thousands, storming his palace. So, the city provided
free bread in the poorer neighborhoods. To then gain the support of the unemployed and others, the politicians provided entertainment. There was no television, so the best way to deliver
mass entertainment was in large stadiums: the circuses. Fed
and entertained, the masses remained content. Within a generation, tens of thousands of Romans had known no other life and
accepted, even demanded, bread and circuses as their right.
The cost of these did not bring development or new businesses;
the large expenditures just bought internal peace. When the
emperors could no longer afford the expense, discontent would
lead to riots and political upheaval. The simple parallel is that
both then and now the governments have created a welfare-
dependent subculture. The good news is that, since the Reagan
administration, the American government has become aware
of this concern and taken the first actions to limit this dependency and break the multigenerational cycle. Still the problem
remains, and in other ways has even grown dramatically.

In 2011, almost half of all U.S. residents paid no federal
income taxes for the services they received, and more than 67.5
million Americans received some sort of direct payment from
the government—that is one in five, with the number increasing
by more than 8 percent in 2011 and the first half of 2012 alone.
This includes food stamps, Medicaid, Medicare, rent subsidies,
child support, and a number of individually humane and worth-
while programs. But that means the modern United States is
approaching the same percentage of people who are dependent
on the government to survive as the city of Ancient Rome had at

the time of what we now think of as being the days of bread and circuses. Ten centuries on, will these be the days they refer to, with equal disdain, as the era of TV and Big Macs?

The Roman Way

Since there are a lot parallels between the Roman Empire and the United States, it can be instructive to take a look at how Rome solved, or fell to, some of the problems we have discussed in earlier chapters. The United States dates from 1776, less than 240 years ago. Rome was founded in 753 BCE. The Roman Empire really began to take shape in Italy in the fourth century BCE. The last Roman emperor and Constantinople fell in 1453. That is a span of 2,200 years. So in some form or another, Rome as a nation and then an empire existed continuously over two thousand years. If the United States as a nation can match that record, it will continue on into the fourth millennium.

As the United States has found in Afghanistan, Iraq, and Vietnam, foreign wars are costly. They are expensive, strain society, affect military preparedness, and warp our diplomacy. This was also the case with Rome. The Romans had one advantage: where the United States, at least since World War II, makes a careful effort to not dominate or exploit nations, like Iraq, this was not the case with the Roman Empire. Rome had no problem plundering or forcing beneficial agreements to help them pay for and justify the war. Augustus Caesar, Julius's heir, studied the cost of foreign wars and basically stopped Roman military conquest. What he also did was keep the Roman legions at full strength and in place. Barring a few civil wars, this led to more than a century of peace and prosperity. There is also a darker side to this decision. It meant Rome never completed the conquest and Romanization of Germany. Perhaps this was the right decision. The Western Roman Empire continued for another four hundred years and the Eastern Roman Empire survived for another thousand. The darker side of this is that four centuries later, some of those same German barbarian tribes were occupying Rome and the Roman provinces. If there is a Roman lesson on foreign intervention, it is to take the long view. Four centuries is twice as long as there has been a United States, but what we do now will affect what happens in a hundred or two hundred years.

That is a rather vague conclusion, but one that is much easier to draw when you consider that the parallel to Roman experiences is the cost of losing your military superiority. When the Western Roman Empire weakened and its citizens lost interest in joining their army, the quality and number of legions dropped. Soon the still-rich empire was being protected by barbarian legionnaires of lesser loyalty. It became an irresistibly rich target for wave after wave of invaders. So if the military history of Rome gives one obvious lesson, it is that the United States and Europe need to follow Augustus's plan and stay militarily strong, even if not actively using that army to fight a war. The cost of a weak army has, through all of history, been high . . . whether Rome, fifth-century England being defenseless when the legions left, or China falling to the Mongols. It is hard to see this when managing a deficit budget, but being unwilling to defend yourself makes a nation vulnerable, limits its diplomacy, and hastens its decline, if not its conquest.

As mentioned in the chapter on terrorism, Rome set the model for dealing with internal terrorists. It repressed not only terrorists but all those supporting them. This is not to say that this tactic always worked. The same type of repression, backed by soldiers in the streets, that kept the Hebrew daggermen in check also eventually led to a revolt that cost Rome one entire legion and years of sieges and unrest. The cost to the Jews, who not surprisingly lost the revolt, was much higher and included the destruction of their rebuilt main temple in Jerusalem. Rome had an efficient intelligence force and used it to discover and thwart terrorists. Being willing to take any measures needed, doing what it takes to find out what is needed, and backing the efforts with the world's most effective army made the Roman strategy work.

It took a painful wake-up call on 9/11, but America seems to have learned this lesson. It uses the same pattern of intensive intelligence gathering, firm counteractions against the terrorist groups, and a willingness to use its army to fight terrorism. This was the expressed purpose for the wars in both Iraq and Afghanistan. The virtual dismantling of al-Qaeda and the lack of a major terrorist success in the United States since the 9/11 attacks seems to indicate that this response remains effective.

Rome was an empire based on ease of travel and transport. It centered on the Mediterranean for a good reason: the sea provided an easy and inexpensive way to move people and goods. This was a key factor in the prosperity and the stability of the Roman Empire. However, the excellent roads were also a factor that contributed to the spread of plagues. When travel is easy, infected individuals and creatures can spread disease quickly and widely. One diseased individual or flea-carrying rat could and did infect an entire city. If this was a major concern two thousand years ago, when a ship would take days to sail between Alexandria and Rome, it points out just how exposed everyone in the world is now. The flight time between Delhi and Chicago is fifteen hours, and literally millions of people fly internationally every month.

One of the most effective ways to fight the spread of a plague is to isolate the infected areas. Rome did this as a policy, closing the ports of infected cities and forcing diseased individuals to remain separated from the general population. But the fact that plagues spread throughout the Roman Empire also demonstrates that this policy alone is not totally effective. What the Roman experience really points out is that we cannot expect to contain a plague in the modern world. If the bird flu ever jumps to humans in China, just as the bubonic plague in Roman times often spread through out the empire when travel was much slower, it will soon be a threat in Peoria, Illinois.

At first glance it would seem impossible for the Roman emperors to inflate their currency. The Roman currency was made of gold, silver, and copper, so how could it lose value? This was true only when the value was the weight of the precious metal. But at the peak of the empire the Roman money was actually being used at a premium. Why? Because it was dependably consistent and kept its value. During the first few centuries after Julius Caesar, a Roman coin could buy from one and a half to almost three times its actual weight in raw gold or silver. This meant that when Rome stamped new coins, the empire instantly made a profit above the value of the metal it used.

Still, there is a way for any government to change a good thing. When the emperor Nero ran out of money for his massive building projects, he decided on an inventive way to save on the costs. He made the Roman money smaller, reducing the denarius, for example, from 4.5 to 3.8 grams of silver. Everyone noticed the coins had gotten smaller and soon there were different values for the old denarii and the new, smaller ones. Nero took the first step toward inventing inflation. Because his smaller coins could buy less, Nero found another way to temporarily beat his own system: the Roman emperor began to debase the metal in the coins. Instead of the coins being pure silver, he had other metals added. The new denarius coins were the same size and about the same weight, but eventually almost half that weight was made up by cheaper metals, not gold or silver. This meant he could make twice as many with the same amount of silver.

If you have ever seen in a movie or play where the character bites on a gold coin, this is why. Gold is soft, but it hardens when mixed with other metals. If you bite a pure gold coin, your teeth sink in, but one mixed with lead is much tougher. The biting determined how much gold was actually in a coin. It is likely that money handlers during the Roman Empire became experts at determining this. Unfortunately, everyone rather quickly figured out the new coins were worth less, and serious inflation, a new thing for the Roman Empire, occurred. Other nations began to distrust the Roman coins and even the old ones lost some of their premium value.

The solution came from the emperor Vespasian, who forced the mints to again use pure metals. This did not completely set prices back to their old, pre-inflation levels, but it did restore Rome's trading partners' confidence in the currency. Other emperors, facing hard times, again debased the coins. This led to different emperors' coins being worth different amounts and complicated banking and trade; each time inflation resulted, and the eventual collapse of the Western Roman economy can be partially attributed to this practice.

So what is the lesson today? If you are creating too much money, money becomes worth less. We do not need to look to Rome to see this. A one-dollar bill in 1980 bought as much as three one-dollar bills will today. What Vespasian Rome's experience has shown is that fiscal discipline can restore the balance, but not reverse the inflation that has already occurred. The relative collapse of the Western Roman economy stands as a stark warning against continuing inflation as a monetary policy. Whether it is printing, debasing, or borrowing, too much money created for short-term needs can have a high long-term cost.

The Romans never really dealt with unemployment effectively. The influx of slave labor led to high unemployment. As many as a quarter of all the men living in Rome in the second century were effectively unemployed. The results were significant, as discussed earlier, from bread and circuses and creating a permanent dependent class to the strain on the economy affecting everything from defense to keeping up the aqueducts.

History's older solutions to high unemployment are not options the modern nations want to emulate. These were war and plagues. The barbarian invasions and local famines "helped" cut down the surplus population. It was not until the Black Death almost halved the population in the fourteenth century that the problem of more workers than work was resolved. Since killing off half the population is unlikely to be popular, Rome can serve more as a warning than as a model for any solution. The surplus of workers and feeding them remained a problem for much of Europe and encouraged the continuation of the virtual slavery of serfdom and the Dark Age.

In the first centuries of the Roman Republic (before Julius Caesar) the middle class of Rome consisted of farmers and merchants and even small manufacturers employing others to make weapons, pottery, and tools. The family farmers provided the core of the early Roman economy. They also were the largest group serving in the legions.

The most famous of Rome's citizen-soldiers was Lucius Quinctius Cincinnatus. This farmer was working his field when word came that Rome was under attack. He was an experienced military leader and while, because of his age, he was not required to go when summoned, he obeyed the Senate and hurried to Rome to become "dictator." Back then, a dictator was a temporary leader granted full power over the city during a military crisis. Cincinnatus defeated the invading Aequi tribe and drove them from Italy in the matter of just a few weeks. Then, even though he could have legally kept absolute power for another five months, Cincinnatus resigned and returned home to his farm.

The very success of the legions and the growth of the empire also doomed this true middle class of Roman society. As the empire grew larger, the demand for legionnaires became greater. Men were called away from their farms for longer periods to fight wars farther away from Italy. By the time of Julius Caesar this meant many were gone at war so long that their farms failed and were taken over. They then returned to find that the empire they helped to build had taken their means of making a living. The veterans and their families found themselves in the slums of Rome, part of the lower-class, often-unemployed masses.

Who took the farms? The rich patricians, the upper class that also controlled the Roman Senate. One of these men was Marcus Licinius Crassus. He was the richest man in perhaps all of Roman history who was not a king or emperor. He was so rich and influential that when Julius Caesar cut a deal with Pompey the Great to control Rome, they also included him in their triumvirate (council of three rulers). Much of his wealth came from taking over the land from small farmers and creating vast estates.

The legion's success in war had another result as well: the destruction of Rome's middle class. Defeated enemy soldiers and the residents of resisting cities were often enslaved. This eventually flooded Rome and Italy with slaves. It was these slaves who provided the cheap labor that made the estates of the rich patricians, including Crassus, so profitable. (Yes, the leader of the slave revolt, Spartacus, was one of these captured and enslaved soldiers.) They also meant that there was no work for the formerly middle-class farmers who flocked to the cities. But in the cities many of the jobs were now done by slaves as well. If you did not have a special skill, odds are a slave could do the same work as you and a lot cheaper. The middle class in the cities was restricted generally to artisans, and even the hardest-working laborer could rarely rise in class.

The success of a few centuries changed the face of Rome and undermined the middle class that had made it a world power. The rich got much richer and most everyone else got poorer. The effect of this was the decline of the empire. This did not happen overnight, but the slide continued with few hesitations. It is worth remembering that we are speaking of a superpower and empire, and that this gradual decline took four centuries. Without a significant middle class the general population of the empire had little stake in its success or preservation. The rich controlled the Senate, and generally the rich families fought to have their own become emperor. When combined with the large dependent class discussed earlier under "Bread and Circuses," the politics of even later Republican Rome were fierce and often violent. The middle class is needed for social stability. If there is hope for a better life, then even the lower classes can strive and expect it. But with no real social mobility, the picture is much darker. The lack of a middle class in Rome especially had a dramatic and negative effect on Roman life.

Finally, one of the major contributing factors to the decline of Rome was the economy failing. An important factor in this was the destruction of the middle class. Middle-class farmers and merchants had paid taxes, and as soldiers, often served without payment. The loss of the middle class diminished the number of those who would pay taxes on their land, and the loss of a consumer middle class meant that there was less demand for most goods and so fewer tariffs on imports. When you add to this the cost of maintaining the social welfare programs and similar necessities, the emperors never had enough money. The results were a diminished military, social discontent, and such economic gimmick practices as those mentioned earlier.

This is a cautionary tale. The Romans never brought back the middle class. The rich stayed rich and the poor stayed poor. The legions grew weaker and filled with foreigners who worked for less. Then the barbarians came, followed by the Dark Ages.

There is a lot to learn from Britain, Rome, and all of history. Not making the same mistakes as they did is a good start. Are we learning? Not always. Reread the chapters on the destruction of the middle class or inflation if you think so. Can things get better? Certainly. We have learned much about dealing with terrorism and disease. The real lesson is that some things done in the past do work. Fiscal restraint, preserving the small businessman and farmer, maintaining a strong defense with a volunteer army of citizens, are possible and effective. But perhaps the most important lesson we can learn from history is that short-term solutions and quick profits come at a great price in the long run. If the United States or a European Union wants to last until the year 4000, we need to learn from the past and think in the long term.

About the Author

Bill Fawcett is the author and editor of more than a dozen books, including *You Did What?*, *It Seemed Like a Good Idea . . .* , *How to Lose a Battle,* and *You Said What?* He is also the author and editor of three historical mystery series and two oral histories of the U.S. Navy SEALs. He lives in Illinois.

BOOKS BY
BILL FAWCETT

DOOMED TO REPEAT
The Lessons of History We've Failed to Learn
ISBN 978-0-06-206906-1 (paperback)

An engrossing and fact-filled collection
that sheds light on the historical lessons
we've failed to learn and the failures this has
doomed us to repeat over and over again.

HOW TO
LOSE THE CIVIL WAR
**Military Mistakes of the War
Between the States**
ISBN 978-0-06-180727-5 (paperback)

Chronicles the thrilling history of the
conflict between the Union and the
Confederacy, with its high stakes, colorful
characters, and the many disastrous decisions
made by both sides.

HOW TO LOSE WWII
Bad Mistakes of the Good War
ISBN 978-0-06-180731-2 (paperback)

Going back to the subject of Fawcett's
bestselling collection, *How to Lose a Battle*,
How to Lose WWII is an engrossing and
fact-filled collection that sheds light on the
biggest, and dumbest, screw ups
of the Great War.

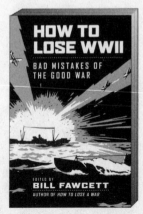

HOW TO LOSE A WAR
More Foolish Plans and Great Military Blunders
ISBN 978-0-06-135844-9 (paperback)

From the ancient Crusades to the modern age of chemical warfare, history is littered with horribly bad military ideas, and each military defeat is fascinating to dissect.

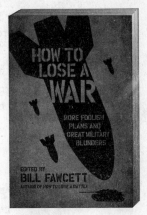

HOW TO LOSE A BATTLE
Foolish Plans and Great Military Blunders
ISBN 978-0-06-076024-3 (paperback)

Whether a result of lack of planning, miscalculation, a leader's ego, or spy infiltration, this compendium chronicles the worst military defeats and looks at what caused each battlefield blunder.

IT LOOKED GOOD ON PAPER
Bizarre Inventions, Design Disasters & Engineering Follies
ISBN 978-0-06-135843-2 (paperback)

This book is a collection of flawed plans, half-baked ideas, and downright ridiculous machines that, with the best and most optimistic intentions, men have constructed throughout history.

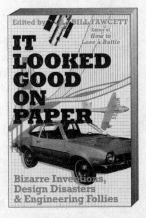

YOU DID WHAT?
Mad Plans and Great Historical Disasters
ISBN 978-0-06-053250-5 (paperback)

History has never been more fun than it is in this fact-filled compendium of historical catastrophes and embarrassingly bad ideas.

YOU SAID WHAT?
Lies and Propaganda Throughout History
ISBN 978-0-06-113050-2 (paperback)

Fawcett chronicles the vast history of frauds, deceptions, propaganda, and trickery from governments, corporations, and historians.

OVAL OFFICE ODDITIES
An Irreverent Collection of Presidential Facts, Follies, and Foibles
ISBN 978-0-06-134617-0 (paperback)

Features hundreds of strange and wonderful facts about past American presidents, first ladies, and veeps.

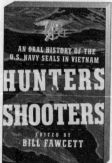

HUNTERS & SHOOTERS
An Oral History of the U.S. Navy SEALs in Vietnam
ISBN 978-0-06-137566-8 (paperback)

Fifteen former SEALs share their vivid, first-person remembrances of action in Vietnam.